RELIGION AND SOCIETY IN SCOTLAND SINCE 1707

RELIGION AND SOCIETY IN SCOTLAND SINCE 1707

Callum G. Brown

EDINBURGH UNIVERSITY PRESS

In memory of Jayne D. Stephenson 1963–1994

© Callum G. Brown, 1997
Edinburgh University Press
22 George Square, Edinburgh

Typeset in Linotype Ehrhardt
by Koinonia Ltd, Bury, and
printed and bound in Great Britain by
Cromwell Press, Broughton Gifford, Melksham, Wiltshire

A CIP record of this book is available
from the British Library

ISBN 0 7486 0886 9

CONTENTS

LIST OF TABLES
AND FIGURES

PREFACE

At the end of the second millennium, Scotland is secularising with extraordinary speed. The nose-dive in church membership, churchgoing, religious marriage and baptism which started in the early 1960s continues, whilst what one commentator called the 'close-mouthed eighteenth-century presbyterianism' of those, my teenage years, has been lifted like a shroud from rapidly-liberalising Scottish society. Yet, since the first edition of this book appeared in 1987, interest in religious history has risen appreciably, especially in two fields. First, international scholars of religion and society have rejected the heart of secularisation theory which held that religion declined with the industrial revolution. Second, the rise of Scottish nationalism has led to a search for Scottish identity in the country's religious past.

This book is based on my *The Social History of Religion in Scotland since 1733* (Methuen, 1987), but it has been substantially re-written, updated and re-organised to take account of new agendas and recent research. New chapters and topics have been added, more evidence and source referencing has been included, and the latest statistical, oral-history and autobiographical material has been incorporated as much as possible. The imprint of the original editor, Professor Hugh McLeod, is still there, I hope, and I reiterate thanks to him and those others who assisted me – including Century Hutchison Publishing Group Ltd for permission to reproduce 'Pisk, Pisky' from *A Breath of Border Air* by Lavinia Derwent. For this edition, I thank Dr Peter Hillis for permission to reproduce statistical material in Table 6, and Dr Gavin White and Dr David Bebbington for pointing out previous errors. All remaining errors and shortcomings are entirely my responsibility.

Special gratitude goes to those who partnered me through the two editions. The revised book would not have appeared but for the fortitude and forbearance of Lynn Abrams, who read the manuscript and gave me much advice for Chapter 8. It would have been the poorer but for the inspiration and hard work of Jayne Stephenson who conducted much research for me and amongst whose notes I continue to find new nuggets. This is dedicated in love to her memory.

ABBREVIATIONS

BPP	*British Parliamentary Papers*
GCA	Glasgow City Archives
NSA	*New Statistical Account*
OSA	*Old Statistical Account*
RSCHS	*Records of the Scottish Church History Society*
SAS	Stirling Archive Services
SHR	*Scottish Historical Review*
SOHCA	Scottish Oral History Centre Archive (Department of History, University of Strathclyde)
SRO	Scottish Records Office (Edinburgh)

CHAPTER 1

PIETY AND PROGRESS

DISCORDANT DISCOURSES

Religion has shaped much of modern Scotland, yet it is now barely perceptible in the lives of most Scots. In the 1950s, the Scottish Sabbath still marked out the nation's religious character: the close-mouthed day of shut pubs and hotel drinks for 'bona fide' travellers, no games, no sports and tied-up swings in public parks; instead, the endless round of Sunday school, church and mission service, rounded off with cold meals and – for the strictest of presbyterian families – an unplugged television. The 1950s was very much a 'religious decade' for Scotland, with Christian Commandoes and a 'Tell Scotland' mission. Billy Graham preached in 1955 to a hundred thousand in Hampden Park, and the communicants lists of the Church of Scotland hit their all-time peak. Scotland remained in the grip of a puritan culture moulded by its presbyterian heritage. The greatest challenge lay not in secularism but in other religions, and especially Roman Catholicism which continued to grow in active support until the mid 1970s and which achieved a kind of emergence into Scotland's public culture through the visit of Pope John Paul II in 1982.

Yet, Scottish religion changed, and changed rapidly. Within seven years of the all-time peak of presbyterian communicants in 1956, the numbers had reached the lowest for the century, and in the next three years – 1963 to 1965 – public participation in religion plummeted: the proportion of marriages religiously solemnised fell, baptism declined, and the Church of Scotland's recruitment rate of its baptised children into full communicants collapsed from 82 per cent to 60 per cent, stabilising in the early 1980s at a haemorrhaging rate of a mere 28 per cent. By the 1990s just over half of marriages took place in church (and a third of cohabiting couples did not even marry), only half of all infants were baptised, under a third of the population adhered to any church, less than a tenth of children attended Sunday school or equivalent, and little more than a tenth of the Scottish people attended a place of worship in any week.

Just as the religious demographics changed between 1963 and 1990, so did the culture. The puritanical regime of old Scots religion died with little fuss, fluttering to the ground lighter than a house of cards. Puritanism had so dominated eighteenth- and nineteenth-century Scotland that few of the country's religious rules had ever been made into laws. Sunday shopping, for instance, had always been legal: no-one till the 1970s had dared open a shop. Only modern games and recreation had been regulated on Sundays as they developed after the 1870s, and restrictions on these collapsed in the 1980s. The drinks laws were liberalised in 1976, cinemas, sport and outdoor leisure blossomed from the later 1970s, and DIY superstores and then food stores opened as the new Sunday cathedrals. As late as 1978 a newspaper columnist had mused exasperatedly:

> It is difficult for tolerant, liberal-minded chaps like myself to grasp the reason why the majority of Scots, the non-church-goers, should have, with the connivance of the state, a close-mouthed, eighteenth-century Presbyterianism so heavily imposed upon them.[1]

Within ten years, twelve at the most, the oppressive public culture against which he railed was gone. By the time Glasgow was 'European City of Culture' in 1990, and the pubs stayed open until three o'clock in the morning all year long, nobody really doubted that religious Scotland was dead.

Though the religious culture of Scotland may have withered in the last four decades of the twentieth century, the theme of religious decline has in fact been a constant concern of the churches since the eighteenth century. The cause has usually been seen as economic and social change, and especially the irreligious popular culture which arises from it. In 1785 one of Scotland's first factories, the Adelphi cotton-spinning works at Deanston in Perthshire, brought high wages to the countryside. A local remarked:

> the consequence was very distressing. So many people collected in one house refined each other in all manner of wickedness. The duties of the family were neglected; the Sabbath was profaned; the instruction of youth was forgotten; and a looseness and corruption of manners spread, like a fatal contagion, every where around.[2]

Nearly two centuries later, in 1952, the minister of the parish of Forgan in north Fife reported:

> Forty years ago, everyone went to church; now no one goes because it is the thing to do; social convention that compelled the unwilling to come to church on Sunday now pushes them to the cinema on week nights. So preachers address congregations in which the aged and aging outnumber the young, but not as much as the women outnumber men; congregations, meagre in the morning, in the evening thin away to vanishing point, and disappear altogether as the day lengthens.[3]

Piety as the victim of progress is a notion with a long history in Scotland. The decline of churchgoing, as the minister of another Fife parish put it in 1952, was 'due not so much to indifference, far less to hostility, as to scarcely appreciated changes in habit of living'.[4] Whilst political secularism and organised anti-clericalism lay at the root of secularising trends in France and Germany, it was lifestyle rather than ideology that seemed to instigate religious decline in Scotland.

That lifestyle has never taken a unified form. Scottish culture, perhaps more than in most countries, has been characterised as a struggle between religion and irreligion, a struggle that has been important to identities of the Scots and to notions of progress in Scottish society. Stereotypes of the Scot – in postmodernist parlance 'discourses' – have owed much to the puritan and the hedonistic entangled in combat. Outsiders have railed at the Scots as the peculiar products of the Calvinist heritage of a poor and semi-barbarous country only partially enveloped by the civilising tendencies of modern society; as Samuel Johnson remarked to Boswell on their Scottish tour of 1773, 'Sir, we are here as Christians in Turkey.'[5] The heritage demanded so much of the individual in terms of religious behaviour and moral 'respectability' that the people were divided into the good, the bad and the hypocrites. The Scots seem dour, determined that the purpose of the Reformation was, in the words of a recent Scottish poet, to 'eliminate Purgatory by getting it over while we're still alive'.[6] They have long been noted for thriftiness, a kirk minister having instigated the savings-bank movement in the 1810s and the Scots until the 1980s having preferred interest-earning deposit accounts rather than cheque accounts at banks. Teetotalism held the centre of the moral highground of public and political culture in Scotland from the 1850s to the 1930s; in 1922 a candidate of the Scottish Prohibition Party defeated Winston Churchill in a parliamentary election in Dundee. The staunch Sabbatarianism of the Highlands and Hebrides, vice-like in its grip on public behaviour from 1800 to the 1960s, lingers still in Lewis and Harris and other islands of the north-west, underscoring the power of dissenting presbyterian clergy there whom one historian described as 'Hebridean ayatollahs'.[7] There has been a noted predilection for hell-fire preaching and strict moral codes enforced by stern church courts. The Calvinist emphasis on the doctrine of predestination, whereby the individual cannot know nor influence his or her salvation, has been used to explain features of the Scots as diverse as their glumness, their aggression to succeed in worldly affairs, and their Rabelaisian qualities. The ironies were acutely observed in the early nineteenth century by the poet James Hogg, the Ettrick Shepherd, when he wrote of the Scots: 'Nothing in the world delights a truly religious people so much as consigning them to eternal damnation.'[8]

The discourse on the puritan Scot has sat alongside, though often estranged from, the discourse on the dissolute Scot – characteristically a Glaswegian. The Industrial Revolution produced an urban culture consisting of tenement slums, heavy drinking and 'rough' pastimes. From the late 1830s onwards it was an axiom of social reform that the worst confluence of physical and moral degradation was to be found in Scottish cities. J. C. Symons, an assistant Royal Commissioner on handloom-weaving, stated in 1839: 'It is my firm belief that penury, dirt, misery, drunkenness, disease and crime culminate in Glasgow to a pitch unparalleled in Great Britain.'[9] For many in Scotland and in Britain as a whole, Glasgow, the Gorbals and more recently Easterhouse were bywords for everything in urban and industrial society which was antipathetic to Christian belief and morality. The Scot at work in factory, shipyard or mine was matched by the Scot at leisure. The pub, the 'off-license' (like its product, the 'cairry-oot', a Scottish invention of 1853), the dance-hall and the football ground were venues for drink, loose morals, 'hard men' and the violence of the razor gang and the 'Glasgow kiss' (a head butt). The sectarianism of Catholic versus Protestant, increasingly centred after 1900 on Celtic-Rangers football rivalry, has given a distinctive rough edge to sports culture in Scotland. The street bookie, his runners and lookouts formed the locus for street culture until 1961, and Scots gambled in a frenzy of ways; Scotland invented postal betting (to serve English punters between 1853 and 1874 when off-course betting remained legal north of the border) and gave its name in the 'Scotch coupon' to the football pools. And the Scot on holiday was, and for some remains, an unmatched sight – a drunken spendthrift on hedonistic entertainment on 'Fair' or trades fortnights to Blackpool and Benidorm.

In this way Scots, as a recent poet has observed, 'are supposed to be dour, canny, pawky, coarse, fly, stingy, pedantic, moralistic and drunken all at once'.[10] And the repeated clash between 'rough' and 'respectable' has given religion a pivotal position in Scottish culture between the late eighteenth century and the present. Economic progress was openly fostered on a puritanical religious agenda which encouraged the workforce to hard-work, self-reliance, thrift and sobriety. 'It is a righteous and irreversible law of Divine providence,' Robert Buchanan, a leading Free Church minister, told Glasgow merchants in 1850, 'that the *moral* rules the *economic* condition of society. We must begin at the right end.'[11] The churches' evangelisation of the Victorian city thrived on the business money donated in response to fund-raising speeches such as this. Entrepreneurial economics and conversionist evangelicalism became harmonised as the kirk continued to fight for a 'godly commonwealth' of Reformation dreams that could foster the labour force to serve industrial capitalism. The industrial village, town and city was the great challenge for organised religion, and to contemporaries seemed the ultimate test of progress. For Scotland's most famous clergyman of modern times, Thomas Chalmers, the face of the nineteenth-century city was infected with 'frequent and ever-enlarging spots of a foul leprosy, till at length we have spaces in many a town ... comprehensive of whole streets, nay, of whole parishes, in a general state of paganism.' Chalmers pioneered the churches' social-scientific study of what he described as 'the deep and dense irreligion which, like the apathy of a mortification or paralysis, has stolen imperceptibly on the great bulk of our plebeian families.'[12] It was the rise of the modern city that seemed to challenge piety.

Campbeltown is a small town on the Mull of Kintyre, a long peninsula which is attached to the Gaelic-speaking West Highlands. It is some thirty sailing miles from Northern Ireland, and lies on a latitude twenty miles south of Scotland's Lowland metropolis of Glasgow. Its position almost equidistant between three regions and cultures, at the centre of the migration of people, economic trends and churches, makes it a useful microcosm of organised religion in Scotland. In 1980 Campbeltown contained three congregations of the Church of Scotland and one each of the Roman Catholic Church, the Free Church, the United Free Church, the Scottish Episcopal Church, the Open Brethren, the Salvation Army and the Jehovah's Witnesses. At other times it has also had congregations of the Methodists, the Baptists, the Congregationalists, and the Good Templars. The names of these denominations bear witness to past migrations, social schisms, moral campaigns and ethnic mixing. Scotland's topography created significant regional differences in church life, with some denominations thriving in certain areas or in little pockets surrounded by hostile religious traditions. From the fertile arable farmland of the Lothians in the east through to the vast expanses of mountains and moors in the inaccessible territory of the northern Highlands in the north, and in around 700 islands off the western and northern coasts, great variation developed in the religious complexion of communities as the country emerged into the modern commercial age. Economic change had a big impact on religion and society. Campbeltown may have been small and situated just within the Highland region, but it experienced the sharpest of changes from the late eighteenth century onwards. Commercially organised fishing developed there as it did in villages all around Scotland, but at the same time the parish economy acquired commerce and manufacturing characteristic of the new industrial order of the Lowland cities: small trades, commerce, shipping, whisky distilling, textile manufacture and coalmining. Campbeltown like Scotland as a whole went from being an economic backwater to being part of a vibrant mixed economy.

A vast new range of occupations was created, leading to great variation in standard of living, popular culture and religion. With the dismemberment of old communal sources of identities, and the erosion of the landed elites' paternalistic bonds with the common people, different social groups and even occupations sought new identities in specific churches or in none. Whilst many landowners adhered to the Episcopal Church and others to the Established Church, crofters gave allegiance to a puritan presbyterianism which swept them into the Free Church in 1843. Irish migrants, whether working as seasonal harvesters or as permanent factory-workers and labourers, were predominantly Catholic. Herring fishers, noted in the 1790s for dissoluteness and drunkenness, developed a strong evangelicalism between the 1850s and 1920s which swept significant numbers into the Open and Close (or Exclusive) Brethren, the Congregationalist Church and the Methodist Church. Tradesmen such as masons, wrights and butchers, and some groups of textile workers adhered strongly to dissenting presbyterianism, and notably to the Relief and Secession Churches; with time tradesmen developed into an important section of the Victorian middle classes, and those two churches united in 1847 to form the strongly bourgeois United Presbyterian Church. Although such correlations of occupation and church were by no means uniform throughout Scotland, the creation of new denominations and sects often came to reflect the new social divisions created by economic and social change after 1780.

There was another consequence. Large numbers found no home in any church. Clergymen became conscious of the 'unchurched' in a way they rarely had in pre-industrial society, and developed a powerful discourse on the 'home heathens' – the supposedly irreligious and immoral working classes. The Rev. Dr John Smith, Church of Scotland minister of Campbeltown in the early 1790s, said:

> One circumstance in the general character of the lower class of people, both in town and country, according to the complaint and experience of their clergy, consists in the little attention paid to every thing beyond their worldly interests, and a woeful ignorance in matters of religion; ... and ... a more than usual neglect in attending public worship ...[13]

The alienation of the 'lower class of people' is a recurrent theme in the social history of religion in industrial society. The growth of factories, of divided social classes and of large and anonymous cities seemed to generate social problems and social divisions which adversely affected proletarian churchgoing. The discourse on the 'rough' popular culture of the working classes persisted for a century and a half with ministers finding fault with every new change to lifestyle. It was only in the 1950s that it became clear to clergy that what had once been associated with the working classes was now general. Non-churchgoing was no longer associated with poverty, intemperance and 'rough culture'. 'Rough' and 'respectable' were becoming less and less defined in religious ways, and with it religion became less important to class identities. As a consequence, the values which had underpinned churchgoing were displaced by a socially widespread disinclination to waste valuable work and leisure time on the Sabbath.

With religious decline came ecumenicalism. The two may not necessarily be linked, though there is much evidence from Scotland and elsewhere that emptying churches and financial problems instigated church union. But the removal of older identities based on occupation and social class, however outdated they might be, removed one of the bulwarks to church adherence in Scotland. When presbyterian churches united in 1900 and 1929, and congregations merged to sell off spare church buildings, all the evidence suggests that there were significant membership losses. There was disruption of individuals' sense of belonging, even down to the certainty of knowing which pew to sit in. A woman from Stirling recalled the impact of the closure of her own congregation in the early 1930s:

> I put my lines in the Viewfield Church eventually. So I went to the Viewfield church a good bit, but I don't know – sometimes you thought you were taking somebody's seat. You used to have your own seat in the church – your name was at the end of it. But they don't do that now. You can go to any seat. The first seat I went to when I went up to Viewfield church – here it was somebody's; it was filled up. The same the next. So here I noticed this one at the very back. There was nobody in it. So I just thought I'd get myself in there. So I was there a long time. And Mrs A and her husband used to speak. But I don't know what it was – because you werenae brought up the church or no. The ones that I knew were very nice, but I always felt sort of, och. I still keep myself a member, and I go to communion. I go up and down once or twice. I always keep up my church. But I mostly go up to the Baptist chapel.[14]

So membership could be kept with one denomination whilst worship was made at another. If those who were 'churched' had such feelings of unease in the modern congregation, the temptations to the more stridently apathetic were immeasurably greater.

If ecumenicalism could weaken religious identity, the twentieth century brought other challenges to the churches. Industrial decline, suburbanisation, the liberalisation of culture, the explosion in modern recreation and the break-up of the 'traditional' family – amongst other things – tended to disrupt the role of the urban congregation. There were great difficulties for the churches in keeping pace; the very instability of modern society seemed to threaten the tradition of communal worship and the relative tranquillity of the agrarian life upon which piety and faith were founded. The importance of social class, for instance, seems to have waned considerably in both Scottish and British social life since 1900. Communities have been torn asunder by slum clearance, the construction of peripheral housing estates and the continuing depopulation of rural peoples. When the structures of society – the houses, streets, towns, factories, and the land itself – have been so subject to change institutions like the church were bound to be affected.

What Thomas Chalmers called in the 1830s 'the ecclesiastical economy' – the whole system by which organised religion operated – had to change constantly to survive. Piety, the spiritual affection and religious sensibilities of the individual, had also to survive, even if divorced from church connection. Was this possible? Could piety and faith be repeatedly recast in new moulds? Or was religion inevitably doomed by social and economic modernisation to become the victim of secularisation?

RELIGIOUS CHANGE AND SECULARISATION

It should already be evident that Scottish clergymen have long been critical of the piety of the people. In the late eighteenth century, ministers of the Church of Scotland were worried that the new industrial workers were in revolt by forsaking the parish church for dissenting meeting houses. The minister of the new mining town of Lochgelly in Fife was worried one year after the French Revolution of 1789 that dissenters outnumbered adherents of his own Established Church by two to one, and, though relieved that they obeyed civil government, he warned: 'They could, however, be easily stirred up to sedition in matters of religion.'[15] By the 1820s, Thomas Chalmers acknowledged that dissenters were not the problem but were part of the solution: 'The country, in fact, lies under the deepest obligation to the dissenting clergy ... who have done so much to retard the process of moral deterioration ...'[16] Fear of dissent had turned into fear of what Chalmers called 'masses of practical heathenism', into the alienation of the working classes and the poor from the ministrations of any religion and church. Horace Mann, the compiler of the government's Religious Census of 1851, wrote in his report to parliament that the large town was the centre of irreligion. 'What Dr. Chalmers calls "the influence of locality" is powerless here: the area is too extensive and the multitude too vast.' Mann declared an 'emergency' at 'the alarming number of non-attendants' at Sunday worship revealed by the census, declaring that whilst 'The middle classes have augmented rather than diminished that devotional sentiment and strictness of attention to religious services by which, for several centuries, they have so eminently been distinguished,' in contrast 'in cities and large towns it is observable how absolutely insignificant a portion of the congregations is composed of artizans'. Echoing many statements of Chalmers, Mann likened them to 'the people of a heathen country'.[17]

Protestant churchmen in much of the English-speaking world came to accept this analysis, and so too did historians and sociologists in the twentieth century. The key features of historical analysis were until very recently that religion declined as cities grew, that middle classes were 'religious' and that the working classes were generally alienated from the churches. These three points became the central features of the sociological *theory of secularisation* to which church and social historians, sociologists of religion and the churches themselves, clung until the 1980s. In the 1950s, the pioneering E. R. Wickham wrote; 'From the emergence of the industrial towns in the eighteenth century, the working class, the labouring poor, the common people, as a class, substantially, as adults, have been outside the churches.'[18] In 1963, K. S. Inglis agreed, quoting an Anglican bishop who said in 1896: 'It is not that the Church of God has lost the great towns; it has never had them.'[19] Church historians were joined by social historians of religion in this view. In 1976 Alan Gilbert concluded that secularisation proceeded in nineteenth-century England and Wales because: 'Community sense collapsed in the industrial city ... Thus while the associational dimension of religious commitment can be effectively sustained only where a church or chapel congregation is linked with some viable community, the history of English religion from the late eighteenth century onwards has offered little evidence that religious associations can themselves provide the basis for fashioning communities out of an amorphous urban population ...'[20]

The country that produced Thomas Chalmers did not neglect his analysis. Scottish historians and sociologists between the 1960s and the 1980s tended to portray the city dweller of the late eighteenth and nineteenth century as the harbinger of late twentieth-century religious indifference. The most recent comprehensive ecclesiastical histories of modern Scotland, written in the 1970s by A. L. Drummond and J. Bulloch, blamed the Free Church of 1843 for destroying the institutional strength of religion built up in Scottish civil life since the sixteenth century, and concluded that the break-up of the machinery of the parish state in the 1840s led to the religious alienation of the new working classes: 'The social structure of the industrial areas was a pyramid and its broad base was pagan.'[21] The discourse on the 'pagan' and 'heathen' working classes that had been constructed and broadcast so widely by Chalmers in the 1820s was sustained into modern church historiography. One textbook on Victorian Scotland proclaimed that 'the bulk of the urbanized masses remained unchurched',[22] whilst another opined that 'the decay of Christian fellowship was manifest in the increasing alienation of the "lower orders" from every kind of religious faith and practice.'[23] Even when the modern historian has managed to dispense with the vocabulary of the religious discourse inherited from Chalmers, there has been a continuing failure to dispense with the discourse itself – even by Marxist historians.[24] The preoccupation with the themes of religious decline and working-class irreligion have remained, leaving the clergyman's agenda of *c.* 1800 still dominating the writing of Scotland's modern religious history.

But the approach has recently changed. The historiography of religion in urban and industrial societies – including Scotland – was transformed in the later 1980s and 1990s by a widespread repudiation of the theory of secularisation. The historians' agenda is no longer obsessed with the 'pessimistic' history of religious decline in urban society and with the irreligion of the working classes. Instead, an 'optimistic' interpretation has been constructed upon new forms of evidence – statistical, oral, autobiographical – and new forms of historical interpretation (including poststructuralism) are providing a shift in focus from secularisation to religious change. The statistical evidence of church membership and religious worship shows that religious adherence did not decline during the industrial revolution nor urbanisation, but, if anything grew – certainly down to the 1880s and possibly later in Britain.[25] The role of religion in the cultural activities of the people, in local government and in social policy is being shown to have been extremely important.[26] In addition, there has been the beginnings of investigation into the quality and intensity of the religiosity of the common people which has dramatically altered the way in which historians perceive the role of religion in society.[27] The net effect of this revisionist 'optimistic' research has been to re-timetable when religious decline set in – from the late eighteenth and early nineteenth centuries to the late nineteenth and twentieth centuries.

If you set out to find the one country in the world in which social and economic change should have posed the greatest challenge to religion, then you would likely end up with Scotland. The pace of agricultural improvement, industrialisation and urbanisation surpassed any country in the world between 1700 and 1850, turning her in those 150 years from a predominantly subsistence farming economy into a leading industrial zone, and turning Scots from the most rural people in Europe into the second-most urbanised. The intensity of social change was, as a consequence, probably also more acute than anywhere else; Scottish cities were widely acknowledged to have the worst housing conditions in Britain, the Highlands (along with Ireland) the most oppressed rural plebeians in northern Europe, and in the 1910s and 1920s a working class with a reputation for radicalism. If the problems were extreme, so were the ultimate solutions. Between 1919 and 1980, Scotland achieved the highest level of state-owned housing outside of the communist bloc (surpassing even some of the levels there), and the peasant-crofters of the Highlands and Islands were protected after 1886 by a degree of interference in the rights of landed property rarely matched in capitalist societies. Both the problems created by economic change and their solutions were the most daunting prospects for religion in any modernising society. This book is about how religion coped with those challenges.

NOTES

1. Jack Maclean, *The Scotsman*, 9 September 1978.
2. *OSA*, vol. 20, pp. 535–6.
3. A. Smith, *The Third Statistical Account of Scotland, vol 2, The County of Fife* (Edinburgh and London, 1952), p. 802.
4. Ibid., p. 676.
5. R. W. Chapman (ed.), *Johnson's Journey to the Western Isles of Scotland ...* (London, 1970), p. 205.
6. Alasdair Maclean, *Night Falls on Ardnamurchan: The Twilight of a Crofting Family* (London, 1984), p. 198.
7. A. I. MacInnes, 'Evangelical protestantism in the nineteenth-century Highlands', in G. Walker and T. Gallagher (eds), *Sermons and Battle Hymns: Protestant Popular Culture in Modern Scotland* (Edinburgh, 1990), p. 43.
8. J. Hogg, *The Private Memoirs and Confessions of a Justified Sinner* (London, orig. 1824, 1970 ed.), p. 201.
9. Quoted in A. K. Chalmers, *Public Health Administration in Glasgow* (Glasgow, 1905), p. 8.
10. Alastair Reid, quoted in *The Observer* 24 November 1996.
11. Rev. Dr R. Buchanan, *The Schoolmaster in the Wynds; or, how to educate the masses* (Glasgow and Edinburgh, 1850), p. 32.
12. T. Chalmers, *The Right Ecclesiastical Economy of a Large Town* (Edinburgh, 1835), p. 21.
13. *OSA*, vol. 10, p. 560.
14. Oral testimony of SOHCA/006/Mrs C.1, pp. 10–11.
15. J. Sinclair (ed.), *The Statistical Account of Scotland*, vol. 1 (Edinburgh, 1791), p. 457.
16. T. Chalmers, *The Christian and Civic Economy of Large Towns* (Glasgow, 1821), p. 111.
17. Census of Great Britain, Religious Worship, England and Wales, *BPP* lxxxix (1852–3), p. cxxviii.
18. E. R. Wickham, *Church and People in an Industrial City* (London, 1969 ed.), p. 14.

19. K. S. Inglis, *Churches and the Working Classes in Victorian England* (London, 1963), p. 14.
20. A. D. Gilbert, *Religion and Society in Industrial England: Church, Chapel and Social Change 1740–1914* (London, 1976), pp. 113–4.
21. A. L. Drummond and J. Bulloch, *The Church in Victorian Scotland 1843-1874* (Edinburgh,1975), pp. 40–1. The third volume of their trilogy sustains the discourse: 'During the industrial revolution the poor and destitute had been lost to them [the churches] and become pagan.' A. L. Drummond and J. Bulloch, *The Church in Late Victorian Scotland 1974–1900* (Edinburgh, 1978), p. 144.
22. S. and O. Checkland, *Industry and Ethos: Scotland 1832–1914* (London, 1984), p. 123.
23. A. C. Cheyne, *The Transforming of the Kirk: Victorian Scotland's Religious Revolution* (Edinburgh, 1983), p. 110.
24. See for instance T. C. Smout, *A Century of the Scottish People 1830-1950* (London, 1986), pp. 181–208, and the Marxist approach of A. A. MacLaren, 'Presbyterianism and the working class in a mid-nineteenth century city', *SHR* 46 (1967), and his *Religion and Social Class: The Disruption Years in Aberdeen* (London and Boston, 1974).
25. See for instance C. G. Brown, 'Did urbanisation secularise Britain?', *Urban History Yearbook* 1988; the chapters by Brown and Finke in S. Bruce (ed.), *Religion and Modernization: Sociologists and Historians Debate the Secularization Thesis* (Oxford, 1992); and M. Smith, *Religion in Industrial Society: Oldham and Saddleworth 1740–1865* (Oxford, 1994).
26. S. J. D. Green, *Religion in the Age of Decline: Organisation and Experience in Industrial Yorkshire 1870–1920* (Cambridge, 1996); J. Morris, *Religion and Urban Change: Croydon, 1840–1914* (Woodbridge, 1992).
27. H. McLeod, 'New perspectives on Victorian working-class religion: the oral evidence', *Oral History Journal* vol. 14 (1986); S. Williams, 'Urban popular religion and the rites of passage', in H. McLeod (ed.), *European Religion in the Age of Great Cities 1830–1930* (London and New York, 1995); S. Williams, 'The language of belief: an alternative agenda for the study of Victorian working-class religion', *Journal of Victorian Culture* vol. 1 (1996).

CHAPTER 2

THE CHURCH STRUCTURE IN SCOTLAND 1707–1997

THE LEGACY OF THE EARLY-MODERN PERIOD

The creation of industrial societies has characteristically led to dramatic change in the structure of religious denominations. This was partly the product of population movement between country and town, region and region, and country and country, creating new mixing of ethnicity, culture and religion. Scotland experienced this along with England, Western Europe and North America in the eighteenth and nineteenth centuries, and it accounts in the main for the growth of non-presbyterian churches (especially in the Scottish Lowlands and particularly industrial districts). But urbanisation and industrialisation also destabilised church monopoly amongst the indigenous people. When the pre-industrial bonds of paternalism and deference between social ranks started to loosen, religion diversified into a multiplicity of denominations and sects with marked distinctions of social class, community type and region. This chapter approaches the complex structure of Scotland's churches – what Robert Louis Stevenson described in the 1870s as her 'large family of sisters where the chalk lines are thickly drawn' between 'people who think almost exactly the same thoughts about religion'[1] – in this context of social change.

The Scottish Reformation of 1560 was a relatively peaceful entrée to the more violent excesses of the seventeenth century which only abated with the accession of William and Mary in 1689. Whilst Roman Catholicism was securely overthrown everywhere bar a few isolated communities in the north and north-west, the century and a quarter following the Reformation witnessed a protracted struggle between presbyterians and episcopalians for control of the Established Church. Presbyterians like John Knox were the main instigators of the reformed kirk, and just as he pronounced in 1558 that '[t]he papistical religion is a mortal pestilence',[2] so they became resolute from the seventeenth century that rule by bishops under episcopacy was merely 'popery' in another guise. Episcopacy was seen as the religion of royalty and aristocracy and but a short step from Catholicism, and everything associated with it attracted presbyterian hostility: the episcopal prayer book, liturgy, and celebration of saints' days (including Christmas which presbyterians prohibited). Using the 'covenant' or bond, presbyterianism became with time a focus and a means of social protest in which an extreme puritanism laid stress on observance of moral law. The Church became in periods and places of presbyterian rule the unrelenting inquisitor and persecutor of a wide range of civil and religious offences. This puritanism was accepted slowly in Lowland Scotland, finding its earliest support from the burgess class in the larger towns like Edinburgh, who found in presbyterianism an ideology which promoted their social standing, their business principles and the virtue of hard work. During the seventeenth century, and especially the 'Second Reformation' of 1638–50 which later zealots looked upon as the zenith of godliness in Scotland, kirk discipline and the unrelenting preaching of the Word established wider acquiescence, unity and enthusiasm in Lowland counties. Whilst the Highlands, Hebrides and north-east remained fairly solidly episcopal, in the south-western and central counties the bulk of the peasantry became pres-byterians and covenanters. They resisted episcopal gentry and monarch alike in the 1670s and 1680s by armed guerrilla warfare, keeping their faith alive by meeting in hillside conventicles and praying societies. It was amongst this group that the basis of modern presbyterian dissent was laid.

The 'hillmen' or 'society men' regarded the presbyterian church that was restored in 1690 as corrupt and unworthy. With a handful of sym-pathetic clergy, they stood back from the state church without actually leaving it entirely. They described themselves in a manifesto of 1692 as 'the poor, wasted, misrepresented remnant of the suffering, anti-popish, anti-prelatic, anti-erastian, anti-sectarian, true Presbyterian Church of Scotland'.[3] Their struggles with episcopal landowners, particularly in the south-west, made their outlook one which combined religious and social protest. On one occasion their movement emerged as active resistance to economic change. In 1724 peasants in Kirkudbrightshire opposed the enclosure of open fields by landowners. For four months, the 'Galloway Levellers' overturned dykes marking out new fields where once common fields had existed. In a manifesto affixed to the door of Borgue Church they proclaimed that it was 'directly opposite to the law of God and man that the poor should be destitute of bread upon God's earth' and that God 'hath denounced fearful judgements against all oppressors'.[4] The Levellers were led by an unidentified hill preacher and the covenanting tradition was central to their ideology and self-justification. It was but a momentary violent resistance, for the weight of the state, the landowners and the Church of Scotland was against them, and it was snuffed out.

Yet, it marked a shift in the covenanting ideology of the peasantry from one centred on resistance to religious persecution in the seventeenth century to one more broadly focused by the second quarter of the eighteenth century on unease with change in rural society. Throughout the early-modern period there can be detected in the struggles of the kirk a significant popular participation. Although Scottish society was perhaps more homogeneous than English society, presbyterianism came in part to represent a plebeian culture where the right to 'sit under' a minister of popular choice was defended as scriptural and legal right. In the 'society men', in occasional instances of religious revival, and in hostility to the intrusion of episcopal and 'popish' practices, there was an episodic and inchoate resistance to the loss of what was regarded as popular culture. A kirk session in Dumfriesshire complained in 1721 of a sect of covenanters 'that have separated from us', the McMillanites, not submitting to church discipline, and in another parish in the same county a minister complained of being sworn at by members of another sect, the Hebronites.[5] In 1736 the first dissenting presbyterian church, the Secession Church, started to absorb the vast bulk of the covenanters of the south-western and central counties by admitting the Hebronites, resolving to 'make some step towards the relief of the Lord's oppressed heritage'; the Secession then went further by making covenanting, a normally annual 'bonding' of the congregation with the Lord, a qualification of membership during the middle decades of the eighteenth century.[6] In this way the covenanters were the precursors of modern presbyterian dissent, canalising latent social divisions and antagonisms into the religious sphere.

The emergence of Scottish religious dissent was very much a product of the eighteenth century. Nonconformism of the sort known in sixteenth and seventeenth century England was alien to Scotland where the Established Church remained contestable territory for all groups but the Catholics. The result was an important tradition of internal and informal dissent in Scotland in which groups could drift in and out of close harmony with the prevailing party in the church. Not only did this tradition survive into the nineteenth century, it permitted the continuation of the concept of a 'recoverable' Established Church which could be reclaimed from perceived corruption at an opportune moment by the maintenance of 'true' presbyterianism in dissenting churches and sects. The focus of intellectual disagreement was the qualified nature of establishment in the Church of Scotland. Unlike the state churches of England, Ireland and Wales, the monarch was not the head of the presbyterian church but was accorded observer status at the meetings of the supreme court, the general assembly. Consequently the Lutheran notion of 'twa kingdoms' – that of the monarch and that of Christ (i.e. the church) – was adopted. Presbyterian churchmen were sensible of the need for a civil magistrate to govern society and defend the church, but independence from his intrusions was jealously guarded. The nature and extent of the church-state relationship, thus imperfectly defined, remained an issue for disputation. In the context of the economic changes of the eighteenth and nineteenth centuries, social aspirations became identified with presbyterian freedoms and inspired denominational schism. In this way the seventeenth-century presbyterian struggle with Catholic and episcopal monarchy had the capacity to be translated into a vocabulary of general resistance to social authority. As Knox said: 'Princes and bishops are alike criminal'.[7]

On the threshold of the agricultural and industrial revolutions, Scotland was not homogeneous in religion. In the central and southern Lowlands there were significant differences in the cultural interpretation of presbyterianism, between the urban professional and business groups and the rural peasantry. In the Lowlands north of the River Tay episcopacy was strong and resisted presbyterian invasion. In the isolated Highlands and Hebrides, presbyterianism was weak and even episcopacy and Catholicism were enveloped within a popular religious culture of superstition. Such differences had not given rise to true dissent, perhaps in part because of the inefficiency of persecution. It was the economic and social changes of the eighteenth and nineteenth centuries which were to introduce a belated but very rapid and extensive process of pluralisation in religion.

THE PRESBYTERIAN CHURCHES

The Established Church of Scotland was the origin of all the dissenting presbyterian churches. Its form of government and doctrine was laid down in its principal subordinate standard, the Westminster Confession of Faith of 1643, to which practically all of the dissenters adhered. Thus there was little which separated the presbyterian churches in doctrinal terms. Dissent arose because of perceived laxity in Established Church adherence to the expected standards and because of differences over the extent of the church-state relationship. Initially the dissenters were not opposed to the principle of a state church, only to the prevailing party which governed it. But from the end of the eighteenth century there was a gradual and inexorable shift to a 'voluntaryist' position – or belief in the separation of church and state. Thus, the established status of the Church of Scotland was being constantly challenged by continuous defection and by the growing political influence of dissent.

The Church of Scotland, as the example to which most of the presbyterian churches adhered, has been organised as a democratic or ostensibly democratic hierarchy. The congregation of each parish elect (in theory) lay elders and a minister to act as the kirk session; in practice elders often became self-perpetuating whilst ministers could be chosen by lay patrons between 1712 and 1874. The kirk session is the congregational court in matters relating to discipline and religious provision, supplemented in some congregations by a deacons' court which may have oversight of financial matters. Kirk sessions of a district send some elders and all ministers to sit on the presbytery which supervises the clergy and is first court of appeal. In turn, presbyteries used to send representatives to provincial synods (the least important Established Church courts, which were abolished in 1992), and presbyteries (and until 1925 royal burghs) send representatives to the national general assembly which meets annually (usually in Edinburgh in May) in full session and in smaller 'commission' form at other times. All the courts above the kirk session are composed as nearly as possible of equal numbers of ministers and elders, known more prosaically as 'teaching elders' and 'ruling elders' respectively, and no distinction is drawn between them in terms of rights to speak or vote. Similarly, those appointed as chairmen, usually called 'moderators' or sometimes 'preses', hold no special powers or authority. So opposed is the presbyterian tradition to the concept of bishops that except for the parish minister, who is automatically the moderator of the kirk session, moderators are customarily elected for short periods such as one year. In such ways, the system was on the surface expected to be receptive to protest and responsive to the popular will.

Amongst the many constraints upon this democracy, the most controversial and profound was the system of patronage whereby an hereditary owner of the right of presentation selected and installed his choice of minister in the parish church. Patronage was associated in the seventeenth century with episcopacy and was abolished in 1690 when elders and heritors were given the right to make the 'call' to a minister for a vacant pulpit. But the British parliament reintroduced patronage in 1712 as part of the larger package of inducements to the Scottish landed classes to forsake the Jacobite cause. The general assembly opposed its return but was mollified by the power of presbyteries to overrule a presentation. Until 1730 the Church sided with popular feeling and there were few disputed presentations. But a few did end in violence, presaging the more widespread controversies of the later eighteenth and early nineteenth century. At Bathgate in West Lothian in 1717 there was 'the unseemly spectacle' of a minister selected by the patron 'being guarded to church upon a Sabbath by files of dragoons, amid the noise of drums, and the flashing of swords'.[8] Such occasions became more numerous after 1729 when the courts of the church started to back patrons, resulting in the defection of four ministers in 1733 to form the Secession Church. From this point, the claims went beyond a return of rights to elders and heritors, to a restitution of what was claimed to be the presbyterian 'custom' of parishioners as a whole making and signing a 'call' to a new minister.

An important division was emerging in Scottish presbyterianism. On a theological level, there was a trend amongst some ministers, mostly in rural parishes, to adopt a more relaxed attitude to the standards of presbyterian discipline, preaching and morality. By the 1750s this group emerged as the Moderate Party in the Church of Scotland – a party which absorbed rationalism from the Enlightenment, and which despised 'enthusiasm' and excess in religion. On a political level the Moderates became associated with government, being seen as an agency of the state and of the Whig government in particular. On a social level, the Moderates were the party of the landowners who came to favour the refinement in taste, 'lukewarmness' in religion and anglicisation required to become members of the larger British ruling class. In this context, patronage became a device to ensure the political correctness of the clergy and of the general assembly. Though probably in the minority amongst the clergy, the Moderates had powerful support and were well organised, and they controlled the Established Church through its general assembly until 1833. Consequently, the ideals, outlook and manner of an increasingly English-orientated Scottish landed class dominated in the Church's supreme court.

The opposing Popular or Evangelical Party was larger but less influential and more divided because of its varied social composition and confused ideology. The agricultural revolution of the eighteenth century was creating a large section of rural and small-town society which was becoming alienated from the landed classes. By the 1790s the rise of factory labour and the urban middle classes created two further groups who shared little in common with each other or with the peasantry. But all three of these groups were alienated from aristocratic Moderatism and turned to evangelicalism for their religious identity. Patronage was anathema to all of them, giving them single-issue unity, but beyond that the movement was not denominationally united. Large numbers of the rural lower orders left the Established Church in the 1760s and 1770s as a result of often violent patronage disputes which rent parishes asunder. They formed congregations of the Secession Church or, less often, the

Relief Church which came into being in 1761. By 1766 there were claims in the general assembly of 120 dissenting churches with 100,000 adherents, and though religious tensions eased in the last two decades of the century, presbyterian dissent remained strong in agricultural counties of the Scottish Lowlands. In growing commercial and industrial towns and cities the Church of Scotland faced loss of adherents too, firstly in 1740–80 to small sects of a congregationalist bent and after 1780 to the Relief and Secession churches.

The loss to the Established Church is difficult to calculate and varied enormously on a local basis. By the 1790s more than 70 per cent of the adult population of Jedburgh in the Borders had joined dissent, whilst a more representative figure for industrialising districts might be drawn from the suburbs of Glasgow (the Barony) where the proportion was one-third. In Lowland parishes the dissenters were comparatively thin on the ground in the south-west but were by 1800 accounting for about a quarter of the population elsewhere. With considerable growth of cities and industrial parishes, the national proportion of dissent had risen appreciably by the 1830s. Even in Edinburgh, the least industrial of the larger cities, the Established Church could attract only 41 per cent of the churchgoers in the middle of that decade. Contemporary calculations by those sympathetic to the Established Church tended to weight statistics against dissent. One 1826 compilation arbitrarily doubled the number of Established Church adherents – 'for anomalies' – but still showed that a fifth of the population adhered to other non-established churches; a reworking of the data would suggest a more realistic figure of 38 per cent, of whom three-quarters belonged to presbyterian dissent. Consequently by the 1820s, around 29 per cent of the total Scottish population, and about 32 per cent of the population of the Lowlands, were recent defectors from the state church.[9] This was an enormous loss, but worse was to follow.

The position of evangelicalism was not confined to the churches already mentioned. An equal or even greater proportion of evangelicals remained in the Established Church in the late eighteenth and early nineteenth centuries, maintaining a stress on faith as an element in salvation and urging the Moderate-dominated general assembly to pursue conversion through foreign missions and church extension and missionary activity at home. Established Church evangelicals were predominantly urban, attracting middle-class and popular support, but their influence was severely checked by identification with the dissenters during the difficult times of the French Wars of 1793–1814. During those years, both Moderate clergy and the government spied upon Established and dissenting evangelicals as 'democrats' and 'revolutionaries'. One Moderate informant of the government wrote in the late 1790s that 'the whole of this missionary business grows from a democratical root', and commented that even evangelical Sunday schools were 'calculated to produce discontent, to foster an aversion to the present order of things'.[10] Though few evangelicals were French sympathisers, their cause was severely retarded until after the end of the Napoleonic Wars. But their numbers in the Established Church were growing as a result of urban expansion, and they toppled the Moderate Party from control of the general assembly in 1834 – in part because of increased evangelical representation from the newly reformed burgh councils which were entitled to send assembly commissioners. Between 1834 and 1843 there was, between Moderates and Evangelicals in the Established Church, an intense and bitter contest known as the Ten Years' Conflict, in which the dominant Evangelicals vainly sought government legislation and support for their position on patronage and evangelisation. An evangelical Veto Act of the 1834 assembly permitted congregations to veto a patron's choice of 'intruded' pastor, but the civil courts rejected the alternative 'call' as having no legal foundation. Parliament's repeated refusal to pass modifying enactments, and the government's rejection in 1842 of an evangelical *Claim of Right* to spiritual independence from the state, made schism inevitable. On 18 May 1843 the Evangelical Party dramatically walked out of the general assembly in what was known as the Disruption, taking with them 38 per cent of the clergy and between 40 and 50 per cent of adherents, and constituted the Free Church of Scotland.

The Established Church, already weak from the growth of older dissenting churches, was severely reduced in strength and status. The Established Church was deprived by the Disruption of its most active lay and clerical members, retarding evangelisation schemes such as Sunday schools and the temperance movement until at least the 1870s. As the *Free Church Magazine* gloated in early 1844:

> It is a notorious fact, and one openly confessed and lamented by friends of the Establishment, that the best ministers have left it ... It is a notorious fact, that the really good elders, the men of spiritual character ... have ... gone out of the Establishment. It is a notorious fact, that almost the whole of the Sabbath school teachers throughout the land, who belonged to the Established Church before, left it at the disruption, and carried with them the great body of the young whom they had under their instruction. It is a notorious fact, that the people who have gone out are the most faithful in their attendance on public ordinances, most liberally contribute to missionary and other objects, and are the most distinguished for their knowledge and love of Scripture truth ...[11]

The scale of the schism was demonstrated by the 1851 Religious Census; the state church could attract only 32.2 per cent of Sunday church attendances compared to 31.7 per cent for the Free Church and 59 per cent for presbyterian and evangelical dissent as a whole. In the space of just over a hundred years the Church of Scotland had shifted from a position of near monopoly in religion to that of one denomination amongst several.

By the last quarter of the nineteenth century the Established Church could lay claim to the adherence of less than 15 per cent of the total population. Moderatism was effectively discredited within the Church where remaining evangelicals slowly grew in power, and the enormous political strength of the dissenters who, like English nonconformists, aligned with the Liberal Party, pushed the Church ever closer to disestablishment. Patronage still caused over sixty cases of disputed settlement between 1843 and 1869 and contributed to its abolition in 1874. Desire for the reunion of Scottish presbyterianism compelled the severing of the state connection, and this was achieved slowly by parliamentary enactments between 1904 and 1926 dealing with doctrinal attachment to the Westminster Confession (which defined the church-state relationship) and the divesting of private ownership of church property. In October 1929 the vast bulk of presbyterian dissenters rejoined what was to be dubbed henceforth the 'National Church of Scotland'.

Since 1929 the Church of Scotland has accounted for more than nine-tenths of Scottish Protestants. In that sense it is a church with a broad social composition and a wide geographical distribution, though one in which formerly dissenting congregations have maintained distinctive traditions. However, for the whole period since 1780 the Church of Scotland has represented a less cohesive and more heterogeneous denomination than other churches. It is in the dissenting churches that we can perceive more clearly some of the important social characteristics of Scottish religion.

The United Presbyterian Church (1847–1900) and its antecedents. The Secession and Relief Churches which originated in 1733 and 1761 respectively and which united in 1847 to form the United Presbyterian Church are the most potentially interesting churches for sociological enquiry. Unfortunately these are also the least studied of Scottish churches, largely because ecclesiastical historians have viewed them unsympathetically from a twentieth-century ecumenical standpoint as schismatics, fanatics and inward-looking sectarians who 'thought little of the unity of the Church' and whose prime concern was 'a determination to have their own way'. There has been equal condemnation from more liberal commentators – from Thomas Carlyle who described their clergy in 1866 as 'hoary old men', to twentieth-century historians who have described them as 'the cave-dwellers of Puritanism' and hair-splitters.[12]

These churches, and especially the Seceders, have had a bad press which distracts attention from the scale and social significance of presbyterian dissent before the 1843 Disruption.

The four clergymen who founded the Secession Church in December 1733 were stunned by their popularity evident in a stream of petitions from praying or 'correspondence' societies craving 'sermon and super-intendence'. The initial Seceders were mostly located in the counties of Fife, Stirling and Perth, but there was a powerful influx of old covenanting societies in central and south-western counties. The first Secession congregation south of the river Forth met in 1739 on a hillside in West Lothian when a minister joined a pre-existing praying society which drew its attenders from a twenty-mile radius. The minister preached from Ezekiel 37 v. 26: 'Moreover I will make a covenant of peace with them; it shall be an everlasting covenant with them; and I will place them, and multiply them, and will set my sanctuary in the midst of them for evermore.'[13] Between 1750 and 1780 the Seceders were recruited from existing covenanting societies, though also from patronage disputes in the Church of Scotland.

In this way, the apparently dormant tradition of covenanting resistance was revitalised after 1750 in the puritanism, fiery oratory, fierce discipline and internal rancour of the Seceders. They were a group tinged with millenarianism, calling frequent days of 'fast and humiliation' in reflection of 'the manifest and abounding Sins [of] the Day and Generation' ranging from 'Uncleanness of all Sorts' to 'evilspeaking, backbiting, envyings, grudgings' and 'Scandalous Sins and Miscarriages, that are breaking out among us of this congregation'.[14] The Secession was the most divisive of the endemically schismatic dissenting churches of the late eighteenth century. The Seceders split in 1747 on the issue of the Burgess Oath introduced to Glasgow, Edinburgh and Perth in 1745 at the time of the Jacobite Rebellion to prevent Catholics from obtaining public office. The largest section known as the Antiburghers refused to submit to the oath since it implied recognition of the Established Church, and those who were willing to take it became known as the Burghers. Since refusal to take the Oath entailed a hefty fine, it is not surprising that Burghers were the more numerous of the two sections in towns and cities. Although the Church of Scotland noted as early as 1766 the prevalence of dissent 'in the greatest and most populous towns' the Secession Church's main growth in the 1760s and 1770s was chiefly in Lowland rural parishes, thus explaining the strength of the Antiburghers. But the surge of rural support seems to have stagnated dramatically in the 1780s when parish clergy all over the Lowlands reported a decay in Seceders' 'blind furious zeal', 'forbidding asperity' and 'moroseness and acrimony'. An Established clergyman in Renfrewshire commented in 1790 that the 'Secession has not been very fashionable of late',[15] and the Antiburghers noted it themselves. Their Stirling Presbytery appointed days of humiliation in 1789 to lament the passing of many leaders 'while few seem to be raised in their stead endowed with equal zeal'. A year later the same court mourned 'that in our several congregations the work of Christ is so low': 'instead of walking with God as a people married to the Lord, we have broken his bonds'.[16] As a result the number of disputed settlements in rural parishes fell considerably after 1780, and the Secession Church entered upon a new phase of its development.

In the last decade of the eighteenth century, the Seceders' strength started to shift towards urban districts in which artisan and lower-middle-class groups came to identify with evangelical dissent. Within the Secession Church this shift was marked by the emergence of 'New Licht' theology which split the Burghers and Antiburghers into four separate denominations between 1799 and 1806. The 'New Licht' (Light) eased Calvinist doctrine, stressing the offer of salvation, and at the same time moved considerably along the road towards advocating disestablishment of the state church. Whilst the minority 'Auld Lichts' were 'looking backward while the world was advancing'[17] the majority adopted a religious culture appropriate to their position in the expanding economy of Lowland Scotland: a culture focused on individualism, 'respectability' and entrepreneurial opportunity. With the removal of the Burgess Oath in 1819, the two branches of the New Licht united the following year to form the United Secession Church and ten years later they abandoned support for state religion and became voluntaryists. Having started in the 1730s as a 'suffering remnant' in rural society, the Seceders had become within a hundred years a large religious group led by the aspiring and socially mobile in urban and industrial districts.

Like the Secession, the Relief Church had its origins in Fife but spread throughout the Lowlands and even into corners of the Highlands. Offering 'relief of oppressed Christian congregations' under the patronage system, the Relief was more liberal than the Seceders with a fairly free communion and a relaxed attitude to discipline and central church control. Its congregationalist leanings made it popular with a wide social spectrum in urban society, attracting rising entrepreneurs as well as textile workers and tradesmen. From the outset it lacked the rustic social stigma attached to the Secession, and its lax internal discipline and better relations with the Established Church allowed it to develop as a form of informal dissent. Many dissatisfied Church of Scotland congregations joined the Relief as a temporary protest over the disputed presentation of a minister. The Relief Church was respectable where, in the late eighteenth century, the Secession was not; in Jedburgh, the formation in 1757 of what was to become a Relief congregation was a civic occasion attended by the magistrates in their regalia, and 40 per cent of the inhabitants including reputedly the entire town council joined it. In many towns such as Glasgow, Campbeltown, Hamilton and Clackmannan, the Relief Church achieved high status and popularity, and its appeal stretched to the American revolutionaries who found in its voluntaryism a religious counterpoint to political liberty. For some commentators, the 'Relievers' were the 'Scots Methodists'.[18]

The changing social composition and ideology of the Secession Church in the early nineteenth century drew it closer to the Relief, and the two united in 1847 to form the United Presbyterian (U.P.) Church: a powerful, strongly middle-class and by then predominantly urban denomination with some 518 congregations nationally. It achieved considerable political influence in Edinburgh and Glasgow, with many town councillors and several MPs. In the 1851 Religious Census the U.P. Church was the largest single denomination in Glasgow, claiming 23 per cent of attendances, and in the country as a whole they claimed slightly under one-fifth of churchgoers. Though suffering slightly lower growth rates than most other churches, the membership of the U.P. Church continued to expand until 1899. Its doctrines were liberalised rapidly with a formal breach from Calvinism in 1879, but in a wider sense the distinctive testimony and ideology of the old dissenters was being eroded by the appearance of the rival Free Church with which they came to share an acute crisis in the late Victorian period, culminating in ecumenical union in 1900.

The Free Church (1843–1900) and the United Free Church (1900–29). The Disruption of 18 May 1843 was the most spectacular ecclesiastical event in modern Scotland. It created a large and influential denomination almost literally overnight amidst scenes of great excitement and public attention. All over Scotland, ministers left their manses and elders and congregations left their parish churches to meet the following Sunday in farmyards, graveyards, public halls, barns, gravel pits, caves, beaches, on hillsides and on board anchored ships. The event was to become symbolic of a great sacrifice of money and security, and as the ultimate statement of social and religious self-determination. But the formation of the Free Church did not reflect a single split in society. In different regions and different types of community it was the product of varied social tensions and segregation.

The ideology and power of the Free Church were held by its middle-class urban adherents, many of whom were of a new and upwardly mobile generation of businessmen, agents and bank staff. There is evidence that this new bourgeoisie had been acting as a coherent group by establishing new religious fashion a decade or more earlier. In Glasgow the erection in the 1830s of Church of Scotland extension churches had attracted large numbers of them from city congregations of the older parish churches, whilst in the Borders and south-west the sons and daughters of Seceder parents were reportedly returning to the evangelical-controlled Established Church.[19] Elsewhere, the Free Church attracted widespread support from areas where dissent had been weak hitherto. In Aberdeenshire the Disruption coincided with a wave of agricultural improvements and the Free Church became identified with the 'sufferers [who] are principally her members'.[20] And in the Highlands and Hebrides the progress of improvement and the Clearances had already generated an alienated and highly evangelical crofting community, and the peasants there entered the Free Church *en masse*.

The varied elements in the Free Church can be seen in the geographical pattern of secession amongst the clergy; this is customarily taken as a measure of lay secession for which no accurate statistics exist.[21] A total of 454 (or 37.9 per cent) out of 1,195 ministers left the Established Church, the largest proportions coming from urban districts and parts of the Highlands and Hebrides. In the city of Aberdeen all fifteen ministers 'went out', whilst in Glasgow and its suburbs the proportion was 25 out of 40, or 63 per cent. The further into the countryside, the lower was the secession. In the whole Presbytery of Glasgow which included rural parishes the figure dropped to 53 per cent, and in adjacent Dumbarton Presbytery it was a mere 22 per cent. In Edinburgh Presbytery 62 per cent seceded, but the overall figure for the Edinburgh province (Lothian and Tweeddale Synod) was 43 per cent. In the Borders where the Secession Church was strong and in the south-west where it was not, the Free Church walkouts were equally low – 25 and 20 per cent respectively. In the heartland of the Seceders in Fife, Perthshire and Stirlingshire the Free Church claimed a vigorous 47 per cent of ministers. In the north-eastern counties the 33 per cent secession was strongest outside of Aberdeen in the Inverness area, Moray and Nairn and in coastal fishing communities. The ministerial secession in the Highlands and Islands varied from 76 per cent in Easter Ross to 35 per cent in the Hebrides and West Highlands, but this is an unreliable guide to what was a fairly uniform defection to the Free Church by the peasant laity. Nationally, few parts were untouched by the Disruption with even the northern island groups of Orkney and Shetland experiencing a walkout of 32 per cent of the clergy.

The strength and geographical breadth of the Free Church gave it cause to claim the status of 'the true old Church of Scotland'. But despite its social diversity, it was from the start a church dominated by the ethos and style of the bourgeoisie. This was reflected in the great concern that the Disruption would incur loss of status and income – 'ministers in one day signing away more than £100,000 a-year'.[22] Solidarity was maintained and fears allayed by careful planning from at least October 1842 when money was pledged and conclaves of supporters organised. The Sustenation Fund, the central source of Free Church ministers' stipends, was planned in advance of the Disruption, and after it the Church was managed on very strict business lines. The dependence on 'Christian liberality' sustained concern for its financial state, and 'Free Church progress' was judged year by year on the volume of donations to central funds. In ten months it raised £418,719 (equivalent to more than £20 million today), more than half being used for building churches – often by securing loans, thus accessing even more funds.[23] Churches and manses rapidly appeared all over the country. Those members with money or the ability to secure loans came to dominate in kirk sessions of the new church, giving rise to a comment in an Established Church propaganda pamphlet in 1844: 'Money! money! with the "F.C." is everything'.[24]

The Disruption was a powerful and popular event of the grassroots amongst the evangelical movement in the Church of Scotland. The Rev. Dr Thomas Chalmers has long been regarded by ecclesiastical historians as the key inspirer and organiser, but it is clear that he was forced reluctantly to back the policies on which the evangelicals 'went out' and that he was too much a high Tory to understand or applaud the popular democracy unleashed. From the outset the Free Church was drawn into close harmony with the dissenters. They were given the use of Secession and Relief churches in the months after the Disruption, became closely involved with the United Presbyterian Church in home and foreign mission work, and like other dissenters tended to support Liberalism. The 'Frees' were *de facto* dissenters and voluntaryists, and with the United Presbyterian Church reflected the social virility of the urban middle classes and their ideology of self-help and individualism.

However, the fact that the union of the Free and U.P. Churches did not take place until 1900 is significant. From the 1880s a crisis developed in British evangelicalism – a crisis which will be examined in Chapter 6 – and it pushed the two denominations towards amalgamation in the face of mounting difficulties; over 90 per cent of United Presbyterian kirk sessions and 95 per cent of Free Church presbyteries agreed to union. Although the new United Free Church became the largest church in

Scotland in 1900, its rate of growth during the first quarter of the twentieth century lagged far behind that of most other churches. Throughout its entire but brief history, the United Free Church was negotiating a reunion with the Established Church that was accomplished in 1929. It was hailed at the time as a glorious event for the Scottish Church, but the spirit of ecumenicalism that has come to play such a prominent part in the twentieth-century reformed kirk had roots in fundamental difficulties afflicting late Victorian evangelicalism.

The minor presbyterian churches were products of the endemic divisiveness in Scottish presbyterianism. They form a confusion of splits and amalgamations rarely recorded in full in ecclesiastical histories and mostly ignored by social historians. Our understanding is thus fairly limited but some significant patterns are apparent. They fall into three major groups: those which emanated from the seventeenth-century covenanting tradition, most of which passed through the Secession Church and avoided its final *embourgeoisement* in the United Presbyterian Church; various indigenous Independent churches, which though not presbyterian in government, were closely harmonised with presbyterian evangelicalism; and churches, mostly of the Highlands and Hebrides, which emerged from the nineteenth-century Free Church as a result of its inherent social and ideological tensions. Characterising most of these, and especially the first and the last, is intense puritanism and introversion which makes them bastions of old-style Scottish presbyterianism.

The oldest of them, and the extreme Calvinist conscience of all Scottish presbyterianism, is the Reformed Presbyterian Church which comprised the descendants of the covenanters from the south-western and central counties. In 1714–43 the 'society men' had only one minister, and according to their own strict presbyterianism could not constitute a presbytery and appoint clergy as it would have signified 'bishop-like' qualities in their one pastor. Not surprisingly the bulk of them joined the Secession Church in the late 1730s to avoid extinction, and the remainder were saved from that fate in 1743 when a Secession minister joined them to permit the formation of the Reformed Presbytery. Of all the dissenters the 10,000 or so Reformed Presbyterians went to the greatest lengths to distance themselves from secular affairs and the state. Though not 'voluntaries', they opposed erastianism and viewed successive British governments as unworthy. After several of their members were enfranchised by the Reform Act of 1832, the Church forbade voting in civil elections. They were also forbidden from starting legal actions, enlisting in the armed forces, and joining outside organisations – even missionary societies of which the Church actually approved. This was the cause of frequent schisms as sections of the membership became urbanised, upwardly mobile and affectionate of modern attitudes. Nearly half the congregations left in 1753 when they adopted the doctrine of universal atonement; aspiring middle-class adherents were estranged for becoming tax collectors, burgesses and excise officers (positions involving recognition of the state); and four congregations were lost in the 1830s over civil voting and swearing oaths of allegiance to Queen Victoria. After 1850 adherents found it difficult to swallow the social isolation and impotence implied by such tenets, and the bulk of the Church united with the Free Church in 1876. A minority stayed out, still surviving with an ageing membership of 300 in Scotland in 1980 but with stronger branches in Northern Ireland and overseas.

The minor branches of the Secession Church shared the covenanting tradition of the Reformed Presbyterians and suffered virtually identical problems. A succession of tiny remnants, mostly adhering to 'Auld Licht' theology but others stuck fast to various stages of Secession development, emerged in 1790–1829 and struggled constantly against the desire of members to adapt to modern life. From the 1810s they split apart in different directions with the bulk joining the Established, the Free, the United Presbyterian or Reformed Presbyterian Churches during 1839–52. Whilst one 'new licht' group, the Evangelical Union, left the Secession in 1843 and eventually joined the Congregationalists in 1896, a more puritan remnant called the Original Secession Church (former Antiburghers) survived with 3,000 communicants in 1871 and just under 2,000 in 1953. Their tradition of a suffering remnant was difficult to sustain. In East Campbell Street Burgher Church in Glasgow, for instance, the remarkable growth in wealth of its adherents in the early nineteenth century had to be compensated by refusing to install heating.

The Independent tradition emerged from Scottish presbyterianism between 1730 and 1770 amongst groups in society who were generally receptive to the economic opportunities of commercial and industrial life. Groups called the Glasites, the Old Scots Independents, the Scotch Baptists and the Bereans were relatively strong in both town and country parishes along the River Tay and on the Fife and Kincardine coasts, but were also to be found as far west as Glasgow and Paisley. Their members were overwhelmingly rising manufacturers, such as the Sandemans of Perth and David Dale of New Lanark, and weavers. In Dundee in 1790, the Glasites were the second-largest denomination after the Church of Scotland, having grown from a mere 71 members to 1732 to over a thousand – reputedly due to 'an indispensable law of the society, enjoining early marriages.'[25] The same spirit of economic opportunity and independence also promoted the emergence of Scottish Independency led by James and Robert Haldane. Excited by Painite ideas and by popular evangelism, they initiated a wave of evangelical enterprises in 1796–1800 which established Sunday schools, day schools and tabernacles in many parts of both the Lowlands and the Highlands, Hebrides and Northern Isles. They were denounced by the government and by the Established Church as subversive, their supporters referred to by the general assembly in 1799 as 'persons notoriously disaffected to the Civil Constitution of the country'.[26] But with strong support from visiting English evangelicals like Charles Simeon, their denomination recruited strongly from within the presbyterian tradition, though it split in 1808 into Congregationalist and Baptist Churches. Both bodies had mixed social compositions of urban middle classes, especially in Glasgow and Dundee, and peasant and fishing communities in the north-east, Orkney and some west-coast ports and islands. They maintained links with presbyterian dissent with whom there was a shared evangelical agenda, and the Congregationalists actually united in 1896 with an offshoot of the Secession Church called the Evangelical Union. But in the main neither the Baptists nor the Congregationalists achieved high growth rates, tending to remain socially diverse and geographically scattered.

The Lowland Free Church was highly aware of the peculiarities of the Gaelic-speaking crofters in the nineteenth century. But the liberalisation of the Church's doctrine in the 1890s, which led it to abandon Calvinist tenets, caused a secession of some north-western congregations who constituted the Free Presbyterian Church. This was followed in 1900 by the refusal of many Gaelic congregations to join the United Free Church. The Free and Free Presbyterian Churches – known affectionately, though perhaps a little disparagingly, as the 'Wee Frees' and the 'Wee Wee Frees' respectively – have continued throughout the twentieth century to enjoy the adherence of from half to two-thirds of the Protestant crofting population in the Hebrides and West Highlands, upholding seventeenth-century presbyterian standards (which ironically never affected that area then) within a distinctive Gaelic medium for worship. The Free Church is less strict than the Free Presbyterians and the two have an uneasy and sometimes hostile relationship, but together they have sustained the cultural distinctiveness of a part of Scotland that has never felt the full economic benefits of modern industrial society. Since the mid 1980s, however, each has been threatened with two developments. The first is the decline of Gaelic-speaking in the western Highlands where, between 1987 and 1996, services held in Gaelic have been almost wiped out. The second development has been the emergence of schismatic tensions within both churches as younger clergy and laity – products of the liberalisation, even *embourgeoisement*, of Highland society – have challenged the older crofting *mentalité*. The F.P. Church's 1988 disciplining of Lord Mackay of Clashfern, the Lord Chancellor, for attending a Catholic requiem mass led in the following year to the breakaway of about half its adherents, predominantly the younger and more evangelical section, to form the Associated Presbyterian Churches. Meanwhile, a Sheriff dismissed charges of sexual assault against a Professor of the Free Church in 1996. These charges were apparently brought as a result of an alleged conspiracy orchestrated by clergy and laity of the conservative wing to secure his removal because of his liberal views on doctrine and worship. With the formation on Lewis in May 1997 of a conservative-wing 'Defence Association', the possibility of schism in the Free Church remains a possibility. The decline of linguistic identity, and even of poverty, in the crofting counties may be undermining the previous resilience of those churches which have stood firm in the faith.

THE NON-PRESBYTERIAN CHURCHES

The Roman Catholic Church was by 1980 the largest denomination in Scotland in terms of churchgoers. This is a fact which has failed to sink into the presbyterian consciousness, and the Church is still widely regarded as an alien intrusion. But the faith that was nearly obliterated in Scotland at the Reformation and that experienced a very gradual removal of restrictive laws in 1793, 1829 and 1926 now accounts for some 43 per cent of all churchgoers and around 15 per cent of the adult population.

In 1755 Catholics in Scotland were enumerated by Alexander Webster at 16,490, or just over one per cent of the population. The vast majority of these lived in a narrow band across the north of Scotland stretching from the islands of Barra and South Uist in the west through inner Hebridean islands such as Rhum, Eigg and Canna, the peninsulas of Knoydart, Morar, Moidart and Kintail, up the Great Glen to 'the Enzie' in Banffshire and parts of Aberdeenshire. A number of Catholic nobles enabled Catholicism to survive on their estates in the north-east, but the Catholics of the Western Highlands and Hebrides were almost uniformly peasants who after 1770 came to share with their Protestant peers else-where in that region a popular culture shaped by oppressive landlords, clearances and evictions. From 1770 Catholic migrations to Newfoundland and, from 1792, to the Lowlands were under way. Though out–migration has continued ever since, the Catholics of the Highlands have survived in communities distinctive in religion and culture both from their Protestant near-neighbours and from Lowland Catholics.

Irish immigrants of whom roughly two–thirds were Catholic first became a major feature in the south-west of Scotland where substantial numbers became, quite unusually, agricultural workers and even tenant farmers. Between 1810 and 1850 as many as 25,000 harvesters came annually to Scotland through west-coast ports, but for the most part Irish immigrants entered industrial-related employment ranging from 'navvying' on canal, railway and, in the twentieth century, hydroelectric construction, to cotton spinning and weaving, and coal and iron mining. The vast majority settled initially in Lanarkshire, Renfrewshire and Ayrshire, transforming the religious composition of the area. In 1778 there were reputedly only twenty Catholics in Glasgow meeting semi-secretly for worship in a private house. The numbers rose to around sixty in 1791 and to 2,300 in 1808, and the first resident priests since the Reformation arrived in the city from the north. With the introduction of cheap steam-boat travel from Ireland, numbers of Catholics in the city rose to 10,000 in 1820 and 27,000 in 1831, representing some 13 per cent of the population. The percentage of Irish-born people in Scotland reached 4.8 per cent in 1841, peaked at 7.2 per cent in 1851 after the potato blight, and then fell slowly to 3.3 per cent in 1921. However, the Catholic population grew by natural increase. It rose from around 1 per cent of total population in 1755 to 8.5 per cent in 1891 and 15.7 per cent in 1970.

The Irish Catholic immigrants of the nineteenth century were more uniformly poor than other groups, most entering the lower end of the working classes, and poverty was a factor restraining church attendance in the nineteenth century. During the twentieth century social mobility amongst Catholics in Scotland has increased markedly over that of the Victorian period, but it is still true to say that the Catholic Church's adherents are more proletarian in composition than those of the Church of Scotland. In the context of a hostile presbyterian reception, the incoming Irish turned to the chapel and its activities for cultural and ethnic identity. But the Catholic Church encountered great difficulties. Despite the removal of restrictive laws against priests, the holding of mass and the ownership of property by Catholics, Protestant sentiment prevented the restoration of an official church hierarchy until 1878. The Church in Scotland was short of resources with which to build chapels and its priests were probably the lowest paid in the country; in the 1830s, Glasgow priests' salaries were £40 compared to at least £100 for Secession ministers and as much as £425 for parish ministers of the Established Church. Partly because of its poverty and partly because its doctrines stressed the availability of pastors rather than buildings, the Church concentrated its efforts on providing clergy until the middle of the nineteenth century, leaving the main part of its church-building schemes until after 1850.

The 'labour-intensive' nature of the Catholic Church's operations created its own problems. The indigenous Scottish Church had its traditional headquarters in the Aberdeen area and drew its priests from surrounding parts, but this 'Scottish' section was overwhelmed by the Irish influx of the nineteenth century. The Scottish Church was reluctant to recruit Irish priests and few attained promoted posts before the late nineteenth century. This caused periodic and sometimes severe ruction between Scottish priests and Irish laity, and between Scottish and Irish priests. Tensions were reduced after 1869 by the judicious appointment of a pointedly 'neutral' English Archbishop to the Glasgow archdiocese. However, the intrusion of Irish republican politics to Scottish Catholic affairs was, and to some extent remains a headache for the Church authorities; in the 1880s priests were disciplined for standing at municipal and school board elections as candidates supporting Irish Home Rule. This has put the Church under pressure from the presbyterian-dominated civil establishment to keep its house in order, but the Church's efforts in this direction did not prevent waves of approved anti-Catholic agitation from the Church of Scotland and other churches. One such outbreak in the 1920s and 1930s led the Catholic novelist Compton Mackenzie to comment: 'This fury of sectarian hate still rages more fiercely in Scotland than anywhere else on earth.' Official Catholic policy in Scotland in the 1980s was still to meet Protestant bigotry 'by the Church keeping a low profile'.[27]

As in most European countries, the decline in churchgoing in Scotland during the present century has been less steep amongst Catholics than amongst Protestants. General reasons can be adduced for this, such as the relative lack of compromise in Catholic doctrine in the face of growing secularism in popular philosophy and morality. This is very marked in Scotland where the Catholic Church and its adherents have tended to be more conservative on moral issues like abortion and birth control than either Scottish Protestants or English and Welsh Catholics. But the Catholic Church has also been more alert to building new churches in growing towns and housing schemes. However, in the 1980s and 1990s serious problems have emerged: dramatic shortages of candidates for the priesthood, declining religious observance amongst the young, widespread ignoring of church teachings on birth control, and widely-reported sexual scandals amongst priests. The signs are that a dramatic change in the fortunes of the Catholic Church is now underway in Scotland.

The Scottish Episcopal Church has in some respects had a similar modern history to that of the Catholic Church. Both started the period as

churches of the Highlands, Hebrides and the north-east, and the
Episcopal Church was regarded in the presbyterian Lowlands as a sur-
rogate for 'popery'. Indeed it continued to drift more towards
Catholicism and away from presbyterianism, deleting the word
'Protestant' from its Code of Canons in 1838, and courting Eastern
Orthodoxy in its liturgy and doctrines. In the twentieth century large
numbers of English episcopalian immigrants find even the presbyterian
Church of Scotland more to their taste. In the eighteenth century the
Episcopal Church was also politically identified with Catholicism.
Episcopalians formed the mainstay of the Jacobite armies of the Catholic
Stuart pretenders and, like the Catholic Church, were the object of penal
laws which were repealed in the early 1790s. Thereafter, episcopalians
were accepted back into the fold of respectable British politics –
symbolically in 1827 when six bishops were received by George IV at
Holyroodhouse in Edinburgh. Like Catholicism episcopacy was
reabsorbed into Lowland and urban Scotland during the industrial
revolution, but in the process it became a denomination more split by
social and ethnic divisions than any other in Scotland.

These splits became evident early in the eighteenth century when the
penal laws instituted against the Church and its adherents for supporting
the Jacobite cause divided it into those clergy and congregations willing
to swear loyalty to the Hanovarian monarchs and those unwilling:
respectively the juring or 'English' chapels and the non-juring or
'Scottish' chapels. The latter were technically illegal but as Samuel
Johnson pointed out, they were meeting freely by the 1770s in the
strongly episcopalian areas of the north-east 'by tacit connivance'.[28] In
the south, by contrast, the Church emerged in the eighteenth and
nineteenth centuries with a varied social composition but one dominated
by an anglicising upper middle class who eventually brought the whole
Church into full communion with the Church of England. The first
juring congregation in Glasgow was formed in 1750–1 with a membership of prominent manufacturers and merchants, two of whom attained
high office on the town council. In the fashionable Clyde coast town of
Helensburgh, residence for many of the wealthier Glasgow business
families, the Episcopal Church included the titled gentry. The Church's
cultured liturgy and decorous furnishings exuded a refinement and
wealth which appealed to sections of the Scottish middle and upper
classes. A very large proportion of the high nobility (86 per cent
according to an estimate of 1843)[29] and perhaps as much as two-thirds of
the landowning classes generally were episcopal. In many parishes all the
heritors of the Established Church were actually members or supporters
of the Scottish Episcopal Church or of its equivalent the Church of

England. Moreover, large numbers of the children of the *nouveaux riches,* educated at English public schools, seceded from the Church of Scotland in the mid-nineteenth century to swell episcopal ranks.

The Church's identification with the landed and middle classes made its relations with other social groups more difficult. There was a sweeping loss of peasant adherents in the Highlands, the north-east, Perthshire, Angus and Kincardineshire as presbyterianism grew in strength in the north of the country after 1750. In the Lowland industrialising districts recruitment of immigrant working-class episcopalians was very low. In Greenock in the 1840s the Anglican hatters from Lancaster, earthenware workers from the Potteries, glass-blowers from Newcastle, chain-makers from Liverpool and Lutheran sugar-boilers from Germany were all reportedly excluded from membership of the upper-middle-class Episcopal chapel. More seriously in numerical terms, the episco-palians from Ireland seem to have been almost uniformly neglected by the Church. The City Chamberlain of Glasgow calculated in 1831 that there were 8,551 of them in the city and its suburbs, and twelve years later an Episcopal clergyman estimated that there were some 10,000 in the same area devoid of religious provision. A Glasgow clergyman said of Episcopalians in the city in 1839 that 'a large proportion are miserably poor, without the means, and what is worse, without the inclination, of supplying themselves with spiritual instruction'.[30] In some places the Church was more active in recruiting from the industrial working classes: for instance, amongst iron and steel workers in Coatbridge in the 1840s. But in the larger cities of Glasgow, Edinburgh and Dundee there seems to have been a general resistance to admitting Irish clergy, culture and people to the Church until late in the nineteenth century.

One major reason for this situation must be introduced. In Scotland, episcopalianism has always been seen as resting on the Catholic side of the Protestant-Catholic divide. In England, Anglicanism has had a more ambiguous position, whilst in Ireland the episcopal Church of Ireland has traditionally placed itself on the Protestant side. Indeed, Irish episcopalians were strongly Orangeist and undoubtedly contributed to the introduction of Orange lodges to nineteenth-century Scotland. Although documentary evidence for this might be scarce, it seems clear that Irish episcopalians with a strongly Protestant tradition could not possibly have come to terms with the pro-Catholic tendencies of the Scottish Episcopal Church.

The Church's relatively poor membership patterns in the twentieth century emphasised the debilitating effects of social division. Whilst it has been alert to opening churches in post-1945 new towns, it has suffered dramatically in the larger cities. In Dundee its membership stayed constant between the two world wars but then fell nearly 40 per cent by 1949 and by half ten years later. But the Church has maintained greater strength in parts of the Highlands like Argyll, and in the north-east and rural districts generally. However, the Church has lost significantly through episcopal landowners living in England and sitting in the 'laird's loft' in the parish church when in Scotland 'for the season'; as an episcopal clergyman noted in the 1840s, landowners supported the Established churches on both sides of the Border 'simply for the sake of example and propriety'.[31] This practice highlighted the socio-religious divide. A children's rhyme in an early-twentieth-century Borders parish noted the alien practices brought to the presbyterian kirk by seasonal episcopal occupants in the loft:

> Pisky! pisky, A -men!
> Doon on your knees an' up again!
> Presby, Presby, dinna bend!
> Always sit on your hinnerend.[32]

The Scottish Episcopal Church has never lost this identification with rural landowners and with a culture connected closely with that of the English upper classes. Its failure – arguably a deliberate failure – to broaden its social and ethnic appeal prevented it from sharing with most other churches in industrial Scotland the high growth rates of the eighteenth and nineteenth centuries.

The Methodist Church in Scotland suffered, like the Episcopalians, from major ethnic divisions resulting from Irish and English immigrants of the nineteenth century 'bringing national habits, feelings and usages into conflict at the Quarterly and Leaders' Meetings'.[33] Migration from England (such as malleable iron-workers from Staffordshire who moved to Airdrie, Coatbridge and Hamilton in the early nineteenth century) contributed to Methodist growth, but Methodism in Scotland depended more on native Scots. Success, however, was highly localised. The prospects seemed promising in the 1740s and 1750s with George Whitefield and John Wesley attracting large audiences of presbyterians during Scottish tours. Methodist societies were set up in textile and fishing villages, including Shetland where Methodism was particularly strong, but it was the larger cities where the bulk of Methodists were located; Glasgow and Airdrie accounted for 43 per cent of all Scottish members in 1819, and from the 1840s to the 1950s Glasgow continued to account for 20 to 30 per cent.

But from the 1760s Scottish Methodism failed to grow at the pace of other churches or of the population as a whole. During 1767–84 annual growth of members averaged less than 0.2 per cent per annum compared to 5 per cent in England, nearly 6 per cent in Wales and nearly 8 per cent in Ireland. A surge in the decades around 1800 gave way to widespread contraction between 1810 and 1840 when congregations collapsed in weaving and fishing communities all over Lowland Scotland. The immediate cause of the collapse of the Methodist circuit in Dumfriesshire in 1836 was the scandal of the preacher selling a cure for VD, but a more general reason was defection to the dissenting presbyterian churches: to the Seceders and the Free Church. An Aberdeen preacher noted an 'extraordinary decrease of male members, especially amongst the intelligent and useful class' during 1835–50.[34] Wealthier members tended to defect first, leaving working-class adherents who could not pay preachers or meet the chapel debt. Despite increased mission work in the late Victorian and Edwardian periods, Scottish Methodist membership never rose above 15,000. In Glasgow by 1954 there were seventeen chapels but only 1,468 attenders, representing only one per cent of all churchgoers.

Accounting for this general and seemingly unique failure of Methodism amongst an English-speaking Protestant manufacturing population has been a matter of some debate since the eighteenth century. On one level Methodist preachers coming north from England noted the Scots' desire for fully-ordained clergy rather than mere lay preachers; Wesley granted this concession in 1785, resulting in a doubling of membership in four years, but it was reversed after his death in 1791 with an immediate contraction of members. Scots, and especially the middle classes, felt that lay positions in the Church did not match the status given by the eldership in the presbyterian churches, and they certainly seemed to favour the dissenting presbyterian churches after 1830. More contentiously, Allan MacLaren has argued that the Arminianism of Methodism did not appeal to Scots' Calvinism, and that in reflection of this Methodists in Scotland vainly preached Calvinism and the doctrine of the elect.[35] But David Wilson, a Methodist preacher in Aberdeen, argued convincingly in 1850 that Methodists did not preach a limited atonement but merely failed 'to proclaim to perishing sinners a *full, free, present and assured salvation*' that was already becoming available in the presbyterian churches. The central issue, as he pointed out, was that the Free and United Presbyterian Churches no longer taught a limited atonement but were preaching exactly the same as the Methodist Church and were stealing its distinctive preaching and its adherents.[36] Thus, accounting for the failure of Methodism in Scotland focuses on the character and doctrinal alignment of presbyterianism, and this will be examined in Chapter 8.

The minor non-presbyterian churches. Scotland like any industrial society has acquired a variety of small churches. The Quakers date back to the seventeenth century, but their numbers have remained small and largely confined to the large cities and the north-east. Individual presbyterian ministers sometimes led congregations into small denominations such as the Unitarians. The later nineteenth century brought an influx of East European Jews, many skilled in the tailoring, furniture and fur trades, who congregated in working-class districts like the Gorbals in Glasgow. Estimates of their numbers vary, but the largest community in Glasgow may have been 1,000-strong in 1879, around 5,000 in 1900 and perhaps 20,000 in the 1950s.

A variety of other churches appeared after 1850, mostly imported religions from England and, increasingly, the United States: the Mormons, Jehovah's Witnesses, the Church of the Nazarene and the Salvation Army amongst many others. Perhaps most notable for their geographical spread and their strength are the Open and Exclusive (or Close) Brethren. In 1884 the Open Brethren had 116 meetings in Scotland, 156 by 1907, and 350 in 1960 with around 25,000 people (with the Exclusives numbering perhaps a further 3,000). They became very strong in the inter-war period amongst fishing families in Orkney and the north-east, in mining communities in the central Scottish coalfield, and in other industrial districts in the Lowlands. They are also socially spread, the Open tending to be strongest amongst professional and business people in the cities and the Exclusives amongst the poorer fishing families of the Moray Firth coast. The Brethren recruited from dissenting presbyterians and Methodists, and were in the same mould as the Congregationalists and Baptists who were also strong in the fishing communities. The Brethren assumed a strong anti-Catholic stance, some sharing the view with the Free and Free Presbyterian Churches that the Treaty of Rome and the European Community were 'popish' devices.

In many ways, several of the minor presbyterian and non-presbyterian churches since the 1880s have been 'religions of the disinherited'.[37] They adopted rhetoric and puritanism redolent of the covenanters and rural Seceders of the mid-eighteenth century, feeling themselves estranged from the benefits brought by economic change and social advancement. Amongst crofters, smallboat fishermen and miners, it was common to find congregations of the Brethren, the Free and Free Presbyterian Churches, the Salvation Army, the Church of Christ, the Evangelical Union, the Congregationalists and the Baptists adopting semi-millennialism and aggressive insularity. In large cities and towns, however, congregations of these churches have often been more wealthy, and especially since the 1940s. Middle-class congregations have come to dominate many of the mostly lowland sects which, though remaining small, have often experienced vigorous growth.

PLURALISATION, ECUMENISM AND RELIGIOUS CHANGE

It used to be an axiom of sociology that religious pluralisation of the kind that Scotland experienced between 1733 and 1850 was an element of the secularisation process. The multiplication of churches destroyed the universal religious worldview which alone could – it used to be argued – sustain the significance of religion to a society. If people started to believe different things and worship in different churches, the 'plausibility of a single moral universe in which all manner and conditions of persons have a place in some grand design is subverted.'[38] Fewer scholars now subscribe to this view. Historians doubt it because of the evidence of religious enthusiasm generated by pluralisation of churches, and the power of the culture of a diffusive religion still to provide a single moral universe of religious values and behaviour patterns in a fragmented church structure; and some sociologists have come to doubt it because of the evidence that at any given date the more religiously pluralist communities (i.e. the ones with more denominations) tend to have greater levels of churchgoing.[39]

If relating pluralisation to church decline is problematic, there is greater cause for linking ecumenical union with decline. Those small churches which refused to join in church unions invariably joined larger churches, though usually after many decades of separate existence. Steve Bruce has argued that those churches that remain 'firm in the faith', even when small in scale, tend to have greater success in sustaining their membership than larger churches which compromise with liberalising and secularising social values.[40] But the recent crises in the Free and the Free Presbyterian Churches would seem to testify to a similarity to the decline of the Cameronians, the original Seceders and the Evangelical Union in the nineteenth century. Amongst larger churches, the unions of 1900 and 1929 – which brought more than 90 per cent of Scottish presbyterians together again in one church – were clearly linked with crises of decline: decline in attendances, finances and faith. Ecumenical pressures have dominated the crisis-ridden second half of the twentieth century, and more church unions remain possible. These crises will be examined in later chapters, but it is important first to assess the available quantitative evidence of where and when church growth and decline occurred.

NOTES

1. R. L. Stevenson, *Edinburgh: Picturesque Notes* (London, 1879), pp. 16–17.
2. R. A. Mason (ed.), *John Knox: On Rebellion* (Oxford, 1994), p. 57.
3. The Sanquhar Declaration quoted in M. Hutchinson, *The Reformed Presbyterian Church in Scotland: Its Origins and History, 1680–1876* (Paisley, 1893), p. 116.
4. Quoted in J. Leopold, 'The Levellers' Revolt in Galloway in 1724', *Journal of the Scottish Labour History Society*, vol. 14 (1980), pp. 18–19.
5. H. Kirkpatrick, 'Holywood Kirk Session Minutes 1698–1812', *Transactions of the Dumfriesshire and Galloway Natural History and Antiquarian Society*, 3rd series, vol. lv (1980), p. 118; W. McMillan, 'Sanquar Church during the eighteenth century', ibid., vol. xxii (1938–9), p. 69.
6. J. McKerrow, *History of the Secession Church* (Glasgow, 1841), pp. 100–1.
7. R. A. Mason, op. cit., p. 125.
8. J. McKerrow, op. cit., p. 34.
9. Calculations based on data from *Edinburgh Christian Instructor* quoted in J. Sinclair, *Analysis of the Statistical Account of Scotland*, vol. ii (London, 1826), Appendix p. 14. See also vol. i (Edinburgh, 1825), p. 81.
10. Rev. William Porteous of Glasgow to Lord Advocate, 24 January 1797 and 21 February 1798, Edinburgh University Library, Laing MSS, LaII500.
11. *Free Church Magazine*, January 1844, pp. 12–3.
12. A. L. Drummond and J. Bulloch, *The Scottish Church 1688–1843* (Edinburgh, 1973), p. 51; Carlyle quoted in J. Barr, *The United Free Church of Scotland* (London, 1934), p. 81; W. L. Mathieson, *The Awakening of Scotland: A History from 1747 to 1797* (Glasgow, 1910), p. 233; W. Ferguson, *Scotland 1689 to the Present* (Edinburgh and London, 1968), p. 126.
13. J. Primrose, *The Mother Anti-Burgher Church of Glasgow* (Glasgow, 1896), p. 15.
14. Leslie (Fife) Associate (Burgher) Congregation, kirk session, MS minutes 2 December 1744, SRO CH3/319/1; Stirling General Associate (Antiburgher) Presbytery, MS minutes 9 January 1781, SAS CH3/286/ 1.
15. *OSA*, vol. 2, p. 150.
16. Stirling General Associate Presbytery, MS minutes 29 December 1789, 2 December 1790, SAS CH3/286/2.
17. A. Thomson, *Historical Sketch of the Origin of the Secession Church* (Edinburgh and London, 1848), p. 151.
18. Quoted in G. Struthers, *The History of the Rise, Progress and Principles of the Relief Church* (Glasgow, 1843), p. 254.
19. *NSA*, vol. iii, p. 143; vol. iv, pp. 100, 204.
20. *Free Church Magazine*, 1848, quoted in I. Carter, *Farmlife in Northeast Scotland 1840–1914* (Edinburgh, 1979), pp. 163–4.
21. The statistics that follow were calculated from data compiled on 10 October 1843 by J. McCosh, *The Wheat and the Chaff Gathered into Bundles* (Perth, 1843).
22. T. Brown, *Annals of the Disruption 1843* (Edinburgh, 1884), pp. 91, 97.
23. *Free Church Magazine*, November 1844, p. 351
24. Quoted in A. A. MacLaren, *Religion and Social Class* (London and Boston, 1974), p. 104.
25. *OSA*, vol. 8, p. 232.
26. *Principal Acts of the General Assembly of the Church of Scotland, 1794–1812*, pp. 38–45.
27. C. Mackenzie, *Catholicism and Scotland* (London, 1936), p. 151; A. Ross, 'The Church in Scotland' in J. Cumming and P. Burns (eds), *The Church Now: An Inquiry into the Present State of the Catholic Church in Britain and Ireland* (Dublin, 1980), p. 34.

28. R. Chapman (ed.), *Johnson's Journey to the Western Islands of Scotland* ... (London, 1970), p. 15.
29. Figure calculated from data in J. P. Lawson, *History of the Scottish Episcopal Church* (Edinburgh, 1843), p. 432.
30. Rev. Robert Montgomery, quoted in ibid., p. 431.
31. Ibid., p. 433.
32. L. Derwent, *A Breath of Border Air* (London, 1977), p. 125, and idem, *Lady of the Manse* (London, 1985), p. 116.
33. D. Wilson, *Methodism in Scotland* (Aberdeen, 1850), p. 19.
34. Ibid., p. 14.
35. A. A. MacLaren, op. cit., 41; idem (ed.), *Social Class in Scotland* (Edinburgh, 1976), p. 43.
36. D. Wilson, op. cit., pp. 5–6, 22–6.
37. P. Thompson et al., *Living the Fishing* (London, 1983), p. 258.
38. Steve Bruce, 'Secularization: the orthodox model', in S. Bruce (ed.), *Religion and Modernization: Sociologists and Historians Debate the Secularization Thesis* (Oxford, 1992), p. 12.
39. R. Finke and R. Stark, 'Religious economies and sacred canopies: religious mobilization in American cities, 1906', *American Sociological Review*, vol. 53 (1988).
40. S. Bruce, *Firm in the Faith* (Aldershot, 1984), pp. 37–40.

CHAPTER 3

PATTERNS OF RELIGIOUS ADHERENCE

THE MEASUREMENT OF RELIGION

Statistics of church adherence are an important tool for the historian in assessing the social significance of religion. They can assist in a variety of ways to illuminate the relative popularity of different denominations and the changing patterns of religious activity and inactivity. However, they pose problems.

In the first place there was very little collection of national statistics of church adherence in Scotland before the mid-nineteenth century; only the Methodists for instance produced membership data annually between the 1760s and the 1860s. The concept of a church membership which could be counted and distinguished from non-members was essentially the product of modern industrial society. In the largely agrarian society of the early-modern period, where the Established Church was expected to be the monopolistic provider of ecclesiastical facilities, there was little interest in the numbers attending church or taking communion since it was assumed that all but the small numbers of heretics and schismatics were under the superintendence of the one and universal kirk. As a result statistical estimates before the 1790s in Scotland were invariably of 'papists' whom the suspicious presbyterians and the government were intent on monitoring. As far as the historian is concerned, pre-1800 statistics of Scottish religion are principally guides to political conformity rather than religious 'choice' in a modern sense.

From the late eighteenth century there was a growing interest in enumerating the people's religious preferences. The statistics collected were at first estimates, haphazard in their geographical coverage, and only gradually systematised between the 1830s and 1860s. An important motive for the churches' interest was denominational competition, especially on the part of the presbyterian dissenters during their heyday in the 1850s and 1860s. But increasingly in the mid- and late-Victorian periods there was an alarm at the extent of non-churchgoing and the size of 'the lapsed masses'. By the 1890s the religious condition of the people was an integral part of 'the condition of England' debate which enveloped Scotland also, and in the context of examining the nation's moral and physical well-being statistics of religion were taken to be 'unimpeachable witnesses to vigour, progress and interest'.[1] The historian must be cautious about sharing this alarm and reading into the figures the disappearance of a golden and usually bucolic age for religious observance.

The problems do not stop there. Even when information was collected on numbers of church members and churchgoers there were frequent lapses in the reliability of enumeration, in completeness, and in continuity in defining categories. In counting church members, for instance, churches differed according to whether they used numbers of active members or eligible communicants. The Catholic Church, with no category of 'membership', has produced estimates of Catholic population (sometimes using a statistical base such as numbers of baptisms but sometimes relying on informed guesswork), whilst the Episcopal Church has produced data on communicants and baptised persons. The category of eligible communicants used by many of the presbyterian churches varied considerably between denominations and over time according to the strictness of the criteria for keeping names on communicants' rolls. In counting churchgoers there has always been the insurmountable problem of distinguishing attenders from attendances because of the practice of going to church more than once on a Sunday. Some counts of attenders included children whether they went to church or separate Sunday schools. Furthermore, some churches like the Glasites and the Brethren have been hostile to or uninterested in collecting statistics of any kind. Indeed, our knowledge of the numbers adhering to smaller dissenting churches is weak for all periods since the eighteenth century and has undoubtedly led to an underestimation of their strength.

Additionally there is a fundamental problem over the accurate and impartial measurement of religious adherence in Scotland. Government inquiries into religion were not conducted with the rigour and exactitude that were applied in other parts of Britain or in other countries. The two main investigations, the Royal Commission on Religious Instruction in 1837–9 and the Census of Religious Worship taken on 30 March 1851, left the collection of statistics to churchmen – with the result that the first was haphazard in its coverage and the second was incomplete. The 1851 religious census of Great Britain is a key source of information about churchgoing, the extent of church accommodation, and the relative size of denominations. But the Scottish section of the census is markedly more inaccurate than its English and Welsh counterparts. In relation to attendances there were no returns from 32 per cent of

Established churches, 12 per cent of Free churches and 10 per cent of United Presbyterian churches. This creates an underestimation of churchgoing in the population as well as an imbalanced impression of denominational adherence. The absence of a proper state census of religion in Scotland forces us to use church-collected membership figures wherever possible, since ironically they are more complete and reliable in what they show. However, the data from 1837–9 and 1851 remain at the forefront of churchgoing analysis as there is little alternative information.

These are just some of the problems in preparing statistics of religion for tabulation. But once they are assembled and all the qualifications made about reliability and comparability, it is important to be clear about what such data can demonstrate. Figures for membership and churchgoing reveal very little about belief – about its intensity or its content. Attendance at church does not mean someone is a devout Christian and non-attendance does not necessarily imply atheism or agnosticism. But in so far as our concern is for the social significance of religion, we must accept church membership and attendance as important measures in themselves.

DENOMINATIONAL AFFILIATION

One of the things that statistics of religion can show is the growth and decline of different denominations: their individual patterns of support and how they changed over time, and the geographical areas where each church found its greatest popularity. In most cases, however, it is not possible to extend such workings before about 1850 because of the lack of data. In the eighteenth century, for example, the high degree of informality to dissent led to some groups who were alienated from the Established Church still being classified as within its pale. In the northern half of Scotland episcopalians did not entirely abandon the state church for their own denomination, and in the Lowlands it was common practice for members of the Relief, Secession and independent churches to worship in parish churches. Although these denominations imposed heavy penalties upon members who 'heard sermon promiscuously', it is clear that large numbers of ordinary churchgoers were slow to accept the principle of membership of one denomination. Disciplinary cases continued well into the nineteenth century, testifying to the continuation of the practice. The parish minister at Stonehouse in Ayrshire commented in 1790: 'It is not easy to ascertain the precise number of dissenters from the Established Church, principally, because many scarcely know to what particular sect they belong.'[2]

Whilst the practice of 'sermon tasting' never disappeared but, indeed, remained a highly fashionable practice for the ardent churchgoer, the better provision of churches in rural and industrialising parishes by the middle of the nineteenth century permitted the inculcation of a stricter notion of exclusive membership. Data from the Royal Commission on Religious Instruction in the 1830s and from the 1851 Religious Census, given in Table 1, give an idea of the relative strength of the Scottish churches. What is immediately apparent from the figures for Scotland's two largest cities is the weakness of the Established Church even before the Disruption of 1843. In both Glasgow and Edinburgh presbyterian dissenters were equal in number to attenders at the state church in the mid-1830s, while the influence of Irish immigrants was already dramatically changing the religious complexion of Glasgow where Catholics accounted for 13 per cent of churchgoers.

Though the figures for these two cities exaggerate the extent of dissent in the country as a whole, they highlight the downturn in the growth of the Secession and Relief Churches from the 1830s onwards. In

Table 1 Churchgoers by denomination, 1835/6 and 1851 (% all churchgoers)

	Edinburgh		Glasgow		Scotland
	1835/6	*1851*	*1835/6*	*1851*	*1851*
Established Church of Scotland	44	16	41	20	32
Presbyterian dissent:					
Free Church		33		22	32
Secession Church ⎫ United	21		14		
⎬ Presbyterian		27		23	19
Relief Church ⎭ Church	9		13		
Congregationalists	3	5	5	5	4
Baptists	4	3	2	3	1
Reformed Presbyterian Church	1	1	2	2	1
Others	4	1	4	3	1
Non-presbyterian:					
Roman Catholic Church	5	5	13	16	5
Scottish Episcopal Church	5	5	2	3	3
Methodist Church (all branches)	3	2	3	2	1
Others	1	2	1	2	1
	100	100	100	100	100

Sources: Figures based on data in Royal Commission on Religious Instruction, *BPP* (1837) xxx, 12–13, and (1837–8) xxxii, 13; Census of Great Britain, Religious Worship and Education, Scotland, 1851, *BPP*, (1854) lix.

both cities these churches failed to keep pace with population growth between 1835 and 1851, indicated by a decline in their proportion of churchgoers: a decline from 30 to 27 per cent in Edinburgh and from 27 to 23 per cent in Glasgow. This deceleration in growth was probably greater in country areas – a circumstance reflected in the fact that only about a fifth of Scottish churchgoers in 1851 belonged to the United Presbyterian Church. But linked to this, and perhaps a causal factor, was the striking number of dissenters produced by the formation of the Free Church. The Disruption sapped energy and self-confidence from the Established Church, and perhaps induced the high number of non-returns to the 1851 census. Thus, the census underestimates the number of those attending the state church, but whether the non-returning congregations had lower than average attendances is unclear. Making a statistical compensation for such non-returns is difficult in these circumstances. But even if every denomination is credited with its own average number of attenders for each non-returning congregation, the Established Church would still have claimed less than 36 per cent of worshippers in 1851. Collectively, the presbyterian dissenters clearly outnumbered Established Church supporters and undermined the validity of the state church.

Table 1 demonstrates the sweeping transformation in the denominational structure. In 1700 the Established Church accounted for probably 95 per cent of churchgoers – including those served by episcopal clergy who were holding on to parish churches. Little had changed six decades later. Even if we accept the exaggerated estimate of 100,000 presbyterian dissenters in 1766, and allow for around 20,000 Catholics and an equal number of episcopalians, the Established Church could still claim that 89 per cent of the population was in at least *de facto* nominal adherence. The position in the second quarter of the nineteenth century is thus all the more striking, and is highlighted by a comparison with sizes of the major religious groupings in England (Table 2). The established church

Table 2 The denominational structures in Scotland and England, 1851 (% all churchgoers)

	Scotland	England	
Church of Scotland	32	47	Church of England
Presbyterian dissent	59	47	Nonconformists
Non-presbyterian dissent	9	6	Catholics and minor churches

Sources: The table is based on data in the Religious Census, Scotland, and on a tabulation by W. S. F. Pickering, in 'The 1851 religious census – a useless experiment?' *British Journal of Sociology* vol. 18 (1967) p. 392.

in each country was stabilising its numerical strength after losses to dissent, but the Church of Scotland had clearly suffered more acutely than its southern counterpart.

The rump of the Established Church had the highest growth of the three main presbyterian churches by the time membership data was collected in the 1860s. The rates of growth of the Free and United Presbyterian Churches were consistently lower than that of the Established Church for the entire period from 1860 to 1928 with the exception of the First World War. The Church of Scotland was slowly regaining ground in attracting members and adherents. In 1860 the Church of Scotland accounted for 48 per cent of presbyterian church members, the Free Church 32 per cent and the United Presbyterian Church 20 per cent; by 1891 the proportions were 53 per cent, 30 per cent and 17 per cent.[3] Though the mid-Victorian decades from 1860 to 1880 were the high point of presbyterian dissent's influence in public affairs, yet it is quite evident that within the presbyterian community the trend towards religious pluralism that had characterised the period from 1760 to 1843 was well in reverse by the 1860s.

The reversal of pluralisation was a major phenomenon within British Protestantism in the later nineteenth century. In England the Anglican Church was certainly increasing its share of Protestant church membership after the 1880s at the expense of the Methodists and most nonconformist denominations, and possibly from the 1830s. But the process was slow on both sides of the border. In Scotland the numerical decline of presbyterian dissent after 1850 proceeded at a very much slower pace than that at which dissent had grown during 1760–1840. The presbyterian dissenters remained into the 1920s a large and powerful force in Scottish church life. Moreover, they could be very strong in certain communities. Figure 1 shows the relative strength of the three main churches in the regions of Scotland in 1891. As can be seen, the Church of Scotland was dramatically weak in the north and north-west of the country, claiming the allegiance of only 3.9 per cent of presbyterians in the West Highlands and Hebrides (Glenelg), 6.4 per cent in Sutherland and Caithness, and 7.9 per cent in Easter Ross (Ross). In each of these three areas and to a lesser extent in Argyll and Moray, the position of the Established Church was overtaken by that of the Free Church. The Free Church's grip on the Highlands was remarkable, but elsewhere its support was fairly even, ranging from 19 per cent in the Borders (Merse and Teviotdale) to 30 per cent in Orkney. But in non-Highland areas support for the Established Church varied more than that of the Free Church. In the synod of Aberdeen the state church

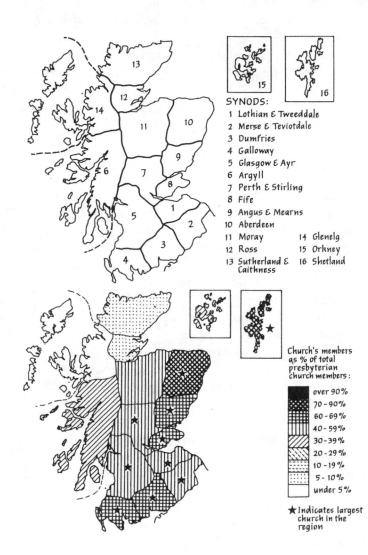

SYNODS:

1 Lothian & Tweeddale
2 Merse & Teviotdale
3 Dumfries
4 Galloway
5 Glasgow & Ayr
6 Argyll
7 Perth & Stirling
8 Fife
9 Angus & Mearns
10 Aberdeen
11 Moray   14 Glenelg
12 Ross   15 Orkney
13 Sutherland & 16 Shetland
   Caithness

Church's members
as % of total
presbyterian
church members:

over 90%
70-90%
60-69%
40-59%
30-39%
20-29%
10-19%
5-10%
under 5%

★ Indicates largest
church in the
region

(a) Church of Scotland

Figure 1. Comparative regional strength of the main presbyterian churches in 1891, calculated according to provincial synods of the Church of Scotland.

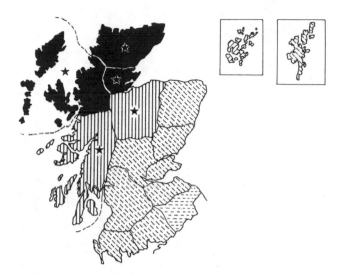

(b) Free Church of Scotland

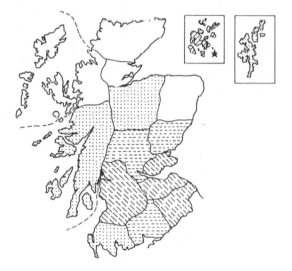

(c) United Presbyterian Church

Source. Data calculated from R. Howie, *The Churches and the Churchless in Scotland* (Glasgow, 1893), p. 38

Table 3 Non-presbyterian dissenters in Scotland, 1790–1959

	1790		1851		1914		1959	
	Adherents	% of total population	Churchgoers	% of total churchgoers	Adherents	% of total population	Adherents	% of total population
Roman Catholics	25,000?	1.6	79,723	4.6	546,000	11.4	787,170	15.5
Episcopalians	12,000?	0.8	43,904	2.5	146,073	3.0	106,478	2.1
Methodists	1,356	0.1	21,675	1.2	9,651	0.2	14,146	0.3
Jews	10?	(0.0006)	35	(0.002)	10,000	0.2	20,000?	0.4
Mormons			3,407	0.2	700?	(0.01)	784	(0.02)
Brethren					5,000?	0.1	28,000?	0.6
Seventh Day Adventists					280?	(0.006)	500?	(0.01)
Jehovah's Witnesses							2,876	(0.06)
Others	500?	(0.03)	3,243	0.2	3,000?	(0.06)	5,000?	(0.09)
Totals	38,866	2.5	151,987	8.7	720,704	15.0	964,954	18.9

Note: Figures accompanied by a ? are estimates.

Sources: A wide range of sources has been used, notably for the estimates. Most of the firm figures come from R. Currie et al., *Churches and Churchgoers: Patterns of Church Growth in the British Isles since 1700* (Oxford, 1977), and J. Highet, *The Scottish Churches: A Review of their State 400 Years after the Reformation* (London, 1960).

could claim 70.9 per cent of presbyterian members, but in Orkney only 34.7 per cent. With the Free Church taking such an even proportion of members from the Established Church at the Disruption, the vital factor in regional variation in the Lowlands was the United Presbyterian Church. The United Presbyterians were virtually unknown in Highland areas by the late nineteenth century, and were weak in the south-west and the north-east. They were more numerous in the synod of Glasgow and Ayr which held 42 per cent of Scotland's population in 1891, making their church more urban in character than the other two. But in terms of density, United Presbyterians were most concentrated in a local population in the Orkney Isles. With 35 per cent of presbyterian members the United Presbyterian Church claimed Orkney as the only part of the country where it was the largest single denomination.

This regional 'snapshot' in 1891 is not entirely satisfactory for it conceals some important features of the historical geography of religion in Scotland. In 1891 the United Presbyterian Church was the largest denomination amongst the 30,000 inhabitants of the Orkney Isles; out of 12,887 members of all churches, 4,301 (or 33.4 per cent) belonged to the United Presbyterian Church. But of these, 1,215 worshipped in one church in the islands' capital of Kirkwall, and a further 1,379 were located in another three parishes. In other words, 60 per cent of United Presbyterian members were concentrated in only four of Orkney's nineteen civil parishes, contributing to highly diverse structures of church affiliation in separate and sometimes adjacent communities. Such diversity was perhaps accentuated in an island group where isolation could sustain variations in denominational alignment. But in Lowland districts of the mainland of Scotland diversity could result from different degrees of industrialisation and urbanisation. Protestant dissenters were strongest in districts with considerable built-up areas and industrial manu-facturing, with the Free Church's support being more evenly spread than that of the United Presbyterian Church, whose membership tended to concentrate in cities and larger towns, whilst adherents of smaller denominations often attained high density in smaller industrial villages.

Throughout the growth and decline of presbyterian dissent since 1740, there has been a steady rise in the numbers adhering to non-presbyterian churches. As Table 3 shows, these churches were particu-larly weak in the eighteenth century, their members being located mostly in the Highlands, Hebrides and north-east where Scottish Catholicism and Episcopacy were largely concentrated. Diversity in church adherence is customarily associated with towns and cities, but in religious terms at least Scottish urban areas were extremely homogeneous before 1800 whilst many country districts in both Highlands and Lowlands had

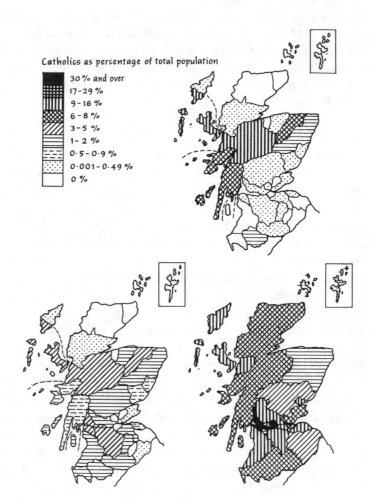

Figure 2. Density of Catholics in population in 1755, 1851 and 1984 (as % of total population)

(a) 1755, from Alexander Webster's census (adherents)

(b) 1851 (attendances on 30 March at all diets of worship, making a nominal allowance of 300 attendances for a county with Catholic chapels but no returns)

(c) 1984 (estimated Catholic population)

Sources: Based on data from R. H. Campbell, *Scotland Since 1707* (Oxford, 1965), p. 10; Census of Religious Worship, *PP* (1854) lix; and P. Brierley and F. Macdonald (eds), *Prospects for Scotland: Report of the 1984 Census of the Churches* (Edinburgh, 1985, MARC/NBSS).

significant sprinklings of non-presbyterians. In Glasgow in 1778 there were reportedly less than twenty Catholics and probably fewer than 500 episcopalians, together representing less than 2 per cent of the city's population. In the Highland county of Inverness, on the other hand, Catholics alone accounted for more than 5 per cent of the people in 1755 and it is likely that episcopalians, starting to emerge as a separate denomination, accounted for a further 10–15 per cent. During the nineteenth and twentieth centuries this situation has been reversed. By 1851 most of the minority churches had their base in cities such as Glasgow, Edinburgh and Dundee, whilst in country areas their strength tended to be much less. There are qualifications to this, however. The 1851 religious census showed that the Mormons were more numerous outwith cities, usually in small industrial villages. Indeed many of the small sects, both presbyterian and non-presbyterian, had a greater appeal in small communities which had experienced recent growth of population. The larger churches were often slow off the mark in forming congregations and erecting places for worship, and in this way proselytising minor churches could form congregations quite quickly in rural parishes changing rapidly as a result of the arrival of manufacturing industry and migrating workers.

Immigration to Scotland was the single greatest cause for the growth of non-presbyterian dissent. In 1841, 4.8 per cent of Scotland's population was Irish-born; of these, perhaps two-thirds were Catholic and the remainder episcopalian, Methodist and presbyterian. Continued high levels of immigration from Ireland in the 1840s and 1850s were followed between 1880 and 1910 by a considerable influx of Jews from Eastern Europe and Russia. Since the 1880s there have been groups of immigrants from Lithuania, Poland and Italy, and over the last two centuries steadier flows from England and the United States. This has introduced new churches to Scotland: some of them characteristically 'modern', such as the new religions of America, but others ethnic variations on the Catholic Church. In the early stages of immigration, there was a strong tendency for incomers and their churches to congregate in certain communities. Perhaps more than half of Scotland's Jewish population in 1900 lived in the Gorbals district of Glasgow. Lithuanians collected at Bellshill. The Irish Catholics and their descendants displayed the same pattern of concentration. Over a third of all the Irish-born in 1841 lived in Glasgow and its suburbs, and the bulk of the remainder lived in the neighbouring counties of Lanarkshire, Dunbartonshire and Renfrewshire. But since then, as Figure 2 shows, Catholics have fanned out from west central Scotland moving eastwards into the Lothians, West Fife and the Stirling area, northwards to Dundee, and southwards into Ayrshire and the Border counties. In some areas such as the Highlands, the proportion of Catholics has diminished, whilst in the north-east their density has stayed almost the same over the whole period since 1755. But in the rest of Scotland, Catholic population has grown. Since Irish immigration diminished considerably from the late nineteenth century, this was due almost entirely to natural increase. From Glasgow the Catholic population has overspilled, and increasingly it has moved not into other large cities but to smaller cities and towns – initially between the 1870s and the 1920s to rapidly expanding satellite towns of Glasgow and to new industrial and mining communities in central Scotland and Fife; and since 1945 to new towns (notably East Kilbride, Cumbernauld and Livingston) and other smaller communities throughout the Lowlands. This small-town growth of Catholics has been particularly noticeable in east central Scotland where their proportion in the total population stood in 1984 at 8.6 per cent for Edinburgh but 11.6 per cent for the surrounding Lothians. Even in the west in 1984, the density of Catholics was higher in Motherwell and Monklands (35.9 per cent) and Dunbartonshire (33.5 per cent) than in the city of Glasgow (30.7 per cent).

The spread of Catholicism throughout Scotland has been a product of Catholic population growth. Table 4 shows how the proportion of marriages solemnised by the Catholic Church continued to grow until the third quarter of the twentieth century whilst those of most other churches fell. Of all religious marriages, the presbyterian proportion dropped from 84 per cent in 1855 to a fairly stead rate of around 67 to 73 per cent between 1915 and 1995, whilst Catholic marriages increased to a peak of 24 per

Table 4 Marriages by manner of solemnisation in Scotland, 1855–1995 (%)

Year	Church of Scotland Free Church 1855–95 United Presbyter. Church 1855–95 United Free Church 1915		Catholic Church	Episcopal Church	Other churches	Civil marriage
1855		83.8	9.3	1.8	4.7	0.05
1875		80.5	8.7	2.5	7.3	0.9
1895		75.2	10.0	3.1	7.3	4.4
1915		58.8	10.8	3.2	6.7	20.5
1935		63.4	13.3	2.7	9.1	11.5
1955		56.0	15.6	2.4	6.8	19.3
1975		43.1	15.3	1.7	4.6	35.4
1995		36.5	9.6	1.5	6.0	46.4

Sources: Figures calculated from data in R. Currie et al., *Churches and Churchgoers* (Oxford, 1977), pp. 226–9; and Registrar General Scotland, *Annual Report* 1995.

cent in 1975. Since then, however, there has been a most striking drop in Catholic marriage; between 1975 and 1995 the number of marriages solemnised by the Catholic Church has more than halved from 6,003 to 2,948. The continued growth of the Catholic population appears to have been thrown into serious jeopardy; in 1995 the Catholic proportion of all marriages has returned to the level of 1855.

Since the eighteenth century, then, there has been significant change in the denominational affiliation of Scots. Within presbyterianism, the near monopoly of the Church of Scotland broke down from the 1730s with the rise of dissenting presbyterian churches, whose adherents by the second half of the nineteenth century outnumbered state church adherents by almost two to one. The near-monopoly of presbyterianism started to erode rapidly from the 1810s, accelerating from the 1850s as Catholicism, episcopalianism, Jewry and other religions new to Scotland expanded, and as Protestant denominations such as the Baptists and Congregationalists, which had emerged from within presbyterianism, added to the religious diversity of a modernising society. In the twentieth century, the unions of 1900 and 1929 reversed most of the presbyterianism schismaticism of the previous two centuries, but, with the sustained growth of non-presbyterian churches, denominational choice grew.

CHURCHGOING AND THE ORIGINS OF DECLINE

Statistics of religious activity should in theory be easier to collect than membership data, and should provide a more accurate guide to the social significance of religion. In practice the value of churchgoing censuses is much reduced because of the lack of consistency in manner of enumeration and the reliance placed on churchmen for counting. There is no census which can provide a reliable figure for the extent of church attendance in the population, and incompatibility between censuses limits the types of changes in patterns of religious observance which can be illustrated over time. None the less, 'snapshot' statistics can be used to draw out conclusions concerning the effects of social change.

The geographical patterns of churchgoing in 1851 and 1984 are shown in Figures 3 and 4. It must be emphasised that the two censuses are not directly compatible, in large part because the first shows *attendances* per head of population whilst the second is an estimate of *attenders* per head of population. However, the two maps suggest some interesting characteristics in churchgoing habits. In 1851 there was considerable variation within regions. In the Highlands and Hebrides churchgoing levels increased from south to north, being lowest in Argyll and highest

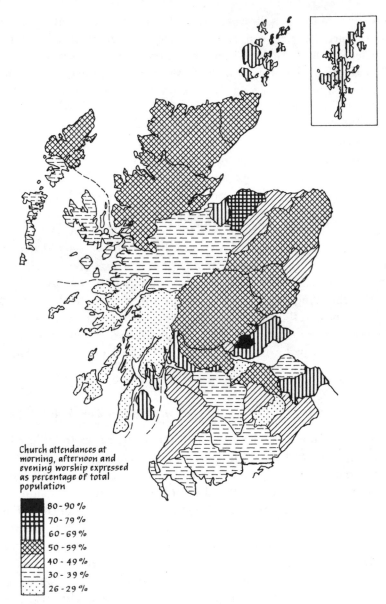

Church attendances at
morning, afternoon and
evening worship expressed
as percentage of total
population

80 - 90 %
70 - 79 %
60 - 69 %
50 - 59 %
40 - 49 %
30 - 39 %
26 - 29 %

Figure 3. Churchgoing rates in 1851, by county (church attendances at morning, afternoon and evening worship: % of total population)

Source: Figures based on data in Census of Religious Worship, 1851, *PP* (1854) lix.

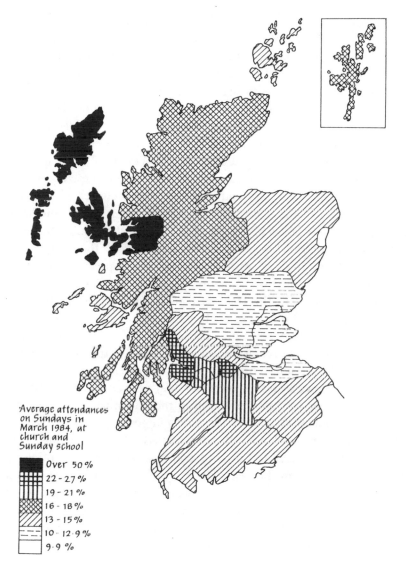

Average attendances on Sundays in March 1984, at church and Sunday school

▓	Over 50%
▦	22 - 27%
▥	19 - 21%
▧	16 - 18%
▨	13 - 15%
≡	10 - 12·9%
□	9·9%

Figure 4. Churchgoing rates in 1984, by region or sub-region (average attendances on Sundays in March 1984 at church and Sunday school)

Source: Based on data from P. Brierley and F. Macdonald (eds), *Propects for Scotland: Report of the 1984 Census of Churches* (Edinburgh, 1985, MARC/NBSS).

in the northern counties of Ross and Cromarty, Sutherland and Caithness. In the north-east and the south-east levels varied considerably: high in Moray and Nairn but low in Banff and Kincardineshire, and high in Berwickshire but low in Selkirk. There was also considerable variation in the central belt with high figures in Dunbartonshire and low figures in West Lothian, but in the south-west there was a uniformly low attendance. By contrast, the 1984 map, despite its reduced detail, shows that firmer regional patterns had evolved by the later twentieth century. The Hebrides and the Lochalsh district in the West Highlands have an extraordinarily high level of Sunday worship compared to the rest of the country; 52 per cent of adults and children attend church or Sunday school in that area. In the rest of the Highlands, Orkney and Shetland, Sunday turnout is reasonably high. But in the Lowlands there is interesting variation. The highest attendance rates are in the west central districts, and notably in those with a high Catholic population. The two districts with the highest proportions of Catholics also have the highest churchgoing rates outwith the Hebrides and Lochalsh: Dunbartonshire with a churchgoing rate of 23 per cent, and Motherwell and Monklands with 27 per cent. Edinburgh and surrounding Lothian have smaller Catholic populations and average churchgoing rates. At the other extreme from west central Scotland is Aberdeen city with a very small number of Catholics and the lowest churchgoing rate (9.9 per cent) in the country.

Despite the rather confused situation in the mid-nineteenth century, we can discern a major change by the 1980s in geographical patterns of churchgoing in the Lowlands. In 1851 levels of churchgoing were relatively low in all western Lowland counties with the exception of Dunbartonshire, whilst in the east – despite variation – the average level was significantly higher. By 1984, however, the position had been reversed with all western districts becoming areas of high attendance and eastern districts areas of low attendance; even the south-west (Dumfries and Galloway), where rates have generally been low throughout, had overtaken Lothian, Fife and Tayside. Between 1851 and 1984, there was a spectacular falling away of churchgoing in eastern Scotland – especially in the cities (notably Edinburgh, Dundee and Aberdeen) and densely-populated areas (such as Lothian and Fife). Churchgoing in the later twentieth century is strongest in two different types of area in Scotland: the isolated Hebrides where puritanical presbyterianism is strong, and the urbanised districts of west central Scotland where Catholicism is most vigorous. As far as the latter area is concerned it is not sufficient to attribute high rates of Sunday worship to Catholics alone. Church of Scotland ministers have recorded that religious antagonisms sustain Protestant observance in some proletarian communities like Lennoxtown

Table 5 Churchgoing rates, 1835–91: selected counties and towns (% total population attending church)

	1835/6		1851			1876	1878	1881	1891
	Average attendance	'In habit of attending'	Morning	Afternoon	Evening				
Scotland			25.6	16.9	5.4				
Counties:									
Aberdeenshire			29.0	11.9	8.9				
Argyllshire			14.7	8.6	2.7				
Berwickshire			43.9	13.3	5.1				
Dunbartonshire			28.3	18.1	7.8				
Elginshire			34.6	17.6	8.8				
Inverness-shire			18.7	12.1	5.4				
Kinross			48.7	39.6	—				
Ross & Cromarty			27.6	15.6	8.9				
Wigtownshire			20.5	7.4	4.7				
Burghs:									
Glasgow	24.9	40.3	20.7	18.2	3.8	19.3		18.8	
Edinburgh	23.1	46.1	25.2	24.4	5.8			21.7	
Dundee			24.2	27.0	6.9			21.9	15.9
Aberdeen			25.4	23.1	8.3		26.1		25.5
Paisley			19.6	24.7	4.9			19.5	
Greenock			27.5	32.7	6.4			19.7	
Brechin			43.6	39.4	30.1			33.1	
Montrose			23.7	24.9	17.7			27.2	
Ayr			24.2	22.9	3.0		26.0	18.1	
Inverness			35.4	21.4	14.1			19.9	

Note: The figures for years other than 1851 were not broken down by diet of worship (morning, afternoon and evening), but because of the nature of the figures and the widespread anecdotal evidence for the decline of 'twicing' after 1870, it is likely that they represent attendances at the largest diet, i.e. morning. *Sources:* Figures based on data in Royal Commission on Religious Instruction, *BPP* (1837) xxx, and (1837–8) xxxii; Census of Great Britain; Religious Worship and Education, Scotland, 1851 *BPP* (1854) lix; and R. Howie, *The Churches and the Churchless in Scotland* (Glasgow, 1893), pp. 92–108.

to the north of Glasgow, but it also seems that active religious connection is strong in the middle-class suburban areas around Glasgow: in Bearsden, Milngavie, Eastwood and Bishopbriggs. A sharp contrast in the religious habits of the people has developed between the Glasgow conurbation and east-coast cities.

Evidence such as this contributes to a major revision in the way we look upon the impact of cities and industry upon churchgoing. Until recently, it used to be commonly asserted that churchgoing in most countries (including Scotland, England and the United States) was highest in rural areas and that it was weakened by the growth of urban and industrial districts and by the increasing religious diversity (or number of denominations).[4] The Scottish evidence has contributed significantly to undermining this long-held hypothesis at the heart of secularisation theory. Table 5 demonstrates the wide range of church-going rates in town and country. On a simple level, the 1851 Religious Census showed that churchgoing levels were higher in towns than in the countryside, and that in each region of Scotland churchgoing was never less in the major city than it was in its hinterland – and in the case of Dundee and Edinburgh was higher.[5] A more advanced statistical method – regression analysis – showed that in 1851 the size of a Scottish town or city did not determine the rate of churchgoing of the inhabitants. Even the growth rate of a town's population over the preceding ten years did not influence churchgoing rates. Only the rate of population growth over the preceding *fifty* years was significant, with faster-growing towns experiencing lower churchgoing; however, this factor only accounted for 26 per cent of the variations in churchgoing rates.[6] In consequence, it is possible to state that in Scotland urbanisation was not a cause of decline in churchgoing in the mid-nineteenth century, but that towns with long-term high population growth had a partial tendency to lower churchgoing, probably because church building failed to keep pace with demand for pews until 1850.[7]

The conclusion to be drawn from an analysis of the 1851 religious census is that churchgoing was remarkably high, and was probably growing still further in the twenty-five years that followed; a similar conclusion has been advanced for an industrial area of England.[8] More remarkable still is that in a fast-growing large city like Glasgow, total church attendances represented 43.2 per cent of the total population – higher than in a quarter of Scottish rural counties – and at a time when that city had church sittings for at most 35 per cent of the population, 20 per cent below the national average. Indeed, amongst the counties with the lowest churchgoing, agricultural and Highlands districts predominated: Argyll, Dumfriesshire, East Lothian, Inverness-shire, Kirkcudbrightshire, West Lothian, Selkirkshire and Wigtownshire.

It appears that urban churchgoing rates stayed quite buoyant in Scotland during the second half of the nineteenth century. There seems to have been a steeper downward trend in church attendance amongst the smaller towns compared to the larger towns. In Glasgow, Edinburgh and Aberdeen the figures produced in the last quarter of the century were of similar proportions to those produced in 1851, whilst in the other places with the exception of Montrose there seems to have been a downturn in the rates of attendance in the thirty years after mid-century. The general impression rendered is that the growth of non-churchgoing in Victorian Scotland was exaggerated by contemporary churchmen. This leaves a real problem of identifying when churchgoing fell. Perhaps the most reliable recent census was conducted by Dr John Highet of the University of Glasgow in the mid-1950s. He showed that just over 10 per cent of the population of Glasgow attended morning worship in April 1954.[9] This was half the figure for 1851, and indicated a major fall in churchgoing habits in the city. But to locate the point within that hundred-year period when the decline originated we must revert to a variety of other types of statistical evidence of religiosity.

RELIGIOUS ADHERENCE AND 'CHURCH CONNECTION'

It is clear that the fall in churchgoing has afflicted some churches more than others. We have already noted that church attendance has tended to be higher in districts with a strong Catholic population. This pheno-menon is not confined to Scotland but has been observed in many countries; in England, for instance, attendance is high in counties with high numbers of Catholics, like Lancashire. Whilst the Catholic Church has not been immune to declining attendances, especially since the early 1970s, the decay of churchgoing in the twentieth century has been most pronounced amongst Protestants. In Scotland until the 1960s, this decay was not solely, or even primarily, a product of non-adherence. We have seen how the proportion of the population in membership with presby-terian churches continued to rise until the 1950s, indicating that *adherence* remained strong. The explanation for declining *attendance* thus lies with the membership. Until the last two decades, presbyterian churchgoing fell almost entirely because of the diminution of the habit amongst communicants. Between the 1850s and the 1950s the proportion of presbyterian church members attending Sunday worship fell from around three-quarters to one-quarter. Going to church has become less important as a criterion for maintaining church connection, and the Church of Scotland in particular condoned the progressive laxity of its communicants.

Figure 5 encapsulates all the available data on church adherence in Scotland. For each year, it shows in a stacked graph the communicants or membership or adherence of every significant church, together with

% Total Population

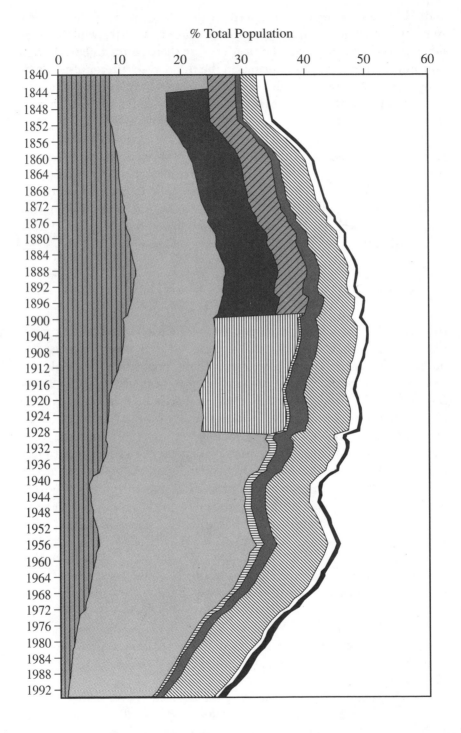

Figure 5. Church adherence in Scotland, 1840–1994

Legend

■ Muslims, Jews, 'New religions' & others, 1840–1994

☐ Methodist, Baptist and Congregational, 1840–1994

▨ Roman Catholic Church, 1840–1994

■ Scottish Episcopal Church, 1840–1994

▥ Free Ch. (1900–), F.P. Ch. (1893–), U.F. Ch. and Sun. sch, (1929–), and Ass. Presb. Ch. (1989–)

▤ U.F. Church 1900–29

▧ U.P. Church (1847–1900) and antecedents (1840–7)

■ Free Church, 1843–1900

▦ Church of Scotland, 1840–1994

▤ Presbyterian Sunday school roll

Sources: R. Currie et al., *Churches and Churchgoers: Patterns of Church Growth in the British Isles since 1700* (Oxford, 1977), pp. 128–9, 132–5, 137 (nn. 7–8), 141–4, 145 (n. 4), 149–51, 153, 154 (n. 3), 169–70, 172–4; Census of Great Britain, 1851: Religious Worship and Education, Scotland, *BPP*, 1854 lix; D. W. Bebbington (ed.), *The Baptists in Scotland: A History* (Glasgow, 1988), pp. 338–9; J. Highet, *The Churches in Scotland Today* (Glasgow, 1950), pp. 54–63, 75; J. Highet, *The Scottish Churches* (London, 1960), pp. 213–14; *The Church of Scotland Yearbook*, 1971–96; *The Catholic Directory for Scotland*, 1971–96; *Scottish Episcopal Church Yearbook and Directory*, 1969/70–1995/96; *Yearbook of the Congregational Union of Scotland*, 1971–96; *Handbook of the United Free Church of Scotland*, 1971–95; *Registrar General for Scotland, Annual Report* 1984. Original stacked graph generated by *Excel*. See Note 10 below for a technical explanation of the graph.

the total rolls of all presbyterian Sunday schools. The top line of the graph thus gives a minimum figure for the church adherence per capita. However, this can only be a minimum figure, for there are many categories of adherence excluded because of the absence of usable long-run data: excluded categories include minor churches which failed to record members (like the Brethren, the Glasites), church-like organisations (the Salvation Army and the Faith Mission), independent missions (like City Missions), and church youth organisations (including Bible classes, youth fellowships and Christian Endeavour). The value of the graph is to show the marked upward trend in church adherence in the nineteenth century, the peak in 1905 (at 50.5 per cent of population), the slow decline from the early 1930s followed by recovery between the end of the Second World War and 1956, and the unremitting and steep decline that then set in during the early 1960s. This late-twentieth century crisis will be examined in more detail in Chapter 7. However, a key factor was the crisis in the Sunday schools. By the 1890s Sunday schools had attained an enormous significance in the religious life of the country, and especially in the urban and industrial districts. In 1891, 52 per cent of all children aged 5–15 years were enrolled at Sunday schools of the major presbyterian churches and average attendance was con-sistently around three-quarters of the enrolment. Given that many children also attended worship in churches, it is possible that more children than adults were active in religious observance. Be that as it may, there was a reversal of Sunday-school growth between 1890 and 1910, as Figure 5 shows. The proportion of Sunday-school scholars amongst 5–15 year olds fell to 46 per cent in 1911, 38 per cent in 1931 and 13 per cent in 1981, whilst the absolute decline in the numbers of scholars was accentuated after the First World War by the fall in the birth rate. The consequences were severe for church growth. Churches failed to recruit from all except children of church members, and even then their success was diminishing. The fall in Sunday-school enrolment after 1890 was followed by the reduced growth in church membership after 1900. The presbyterian churches lost their most valuable outreach into the community, and through this failure in evangelisation of the young were left vulnerable to losses thereafter.

As a result churches gradually lost institutional momentum from the turn of the century onwards. Annual growth rates for presbyterian church membership were very high in the second half of the nineteenth century, varying from 1.9 per cent in the 1850s to 1.0 per cent in the 1890s. But in successive decades after 1900 the annual growth rate fell sharply: from 0.6 per cent in 1900–10 to 0.4 per cent in the decade of the First World War, reaching a mere 0.1 per cent in the 1920s.[11] The period between 1890 and 1914 was clearly critical to the churches, for it was then that church growth slowed down and churchgoing started to decline. However, Table 4 (p. 54) shows how the popularity of religious marriage remained relatively high in Scotland until the last quarter of the twentieth century; in the early 1970s, for instance, 70 per cent of Scots were marrying according to religious rites compared to 55 per cent for England and Wales. Apart from a temporary increase in civil weddings during the First World War, it was not until the years 1961–78 that a sharp downward trend in religious marriage was established. With 54 per cent of marriages still being religiously solemnised in 1995, young couples are still returning to the church to mark this rite of passage. None the less, this figure is likely to drop, and very soon funerals will be the only occasion when the majority of Scots participate in a religious ceremony.

NOTES

1. R. Mudie-Smith (ed.), *The Religious Life of London* (London, 1904), pp. 6–7.
2. *OSA*, vol. 2, p. 228.
3. Figures calculated from data in or derived by linear extrapolation from R. Currie, et al., *Churches and Churchgoers: Patterns of Church Growth in the British Isles since 1700* (Oxford, 1977), pp. 132–3; and R. Howie, *The Churches and the Churchless in Scotland* (Glasgow, 1893), p. 38.
4. H. Perkin, *The Origins of Modern English Society 1780–1880* (London and Henley, 1969), pp. 200–1.
5. H. McLeod, 'Religion' in J. Langton and R. J. Morris (eds), *Atlas of Industrializing Britain 1780–1914* (London and New York, 1986), p. 212. R. J. Morris, 'Urbanisation in Scotland', in W. H. Fraser and R. J. Morris (eds), *People and Society in Scotland vol. II, 1830–1914* (Edinburgh, 1990), p. 92.
6. $R^2 = 0.26$, t statistic $= -4.21$.
7. C. G. Brown, 'Did urbanisation secularise Britain?' *Urban History Yearbook* 1988, pp. 6–8. Steve Bruce challenged these results in a regression involving a 56% sample of towns for Britain as a whole. This made his results less reliable than the 100% datasets I used, and united the discrete Scottish and English & Welsh censuses with their different enumeration standards. His 'best-case' calculation omitted London, applied a log10 array, but even then achieved an R^2 of only 0.14. Even with extensive data manipulation, Bruce showed that town size was a poor predictor of churchgoing, accounting for only 14 per cent of the observations. In addition, he wrongly asserts that '[town] size and [religious] diversity are associated with less and not more church attendance'; his result for diversity demonstrates the reverse. S. Bruce, 'Pluralism and religious vitality', in S. Bruce (ed.), *Religion and Modernization; Sociologists and Historians Debate the Secularization Thesis* (Oxford, 1992), pp. 182–5.
8. M. Smith, *Religion in Industrial Society: Oldham and Saddleworth 1740–1865* (Oxford, 1994), p. 253.
9. The results of this census are given in J. Cunnison and J. B. S. Gilfillan (eds), *The Third Statistical Account of Scotland, Vol. 5, The City of Glasgow* (Glasgow, 1958), p. 956.

10. This graph displays the annual real or estimated membership/active adherence and Sunday-school enrolment of major churches as proportions of total Scottish population in a stacked graph format. Data are based on actual church-collected figures for most years between the following dates: for all the period for the Methodist churches, for 1858–1994 for the presbyterian churches; for 1864–1994 for the Baptist Church; for 1876–1994 for the Roman Catholic Church; for 1877–1994 for the Scottish Episcopal Church; for 1900–94 for the Congregationalist Churches; for 1947 and 1959 for the 'New Religions' (Jehovah's Witnesses, Church of the Latter Day Saints). For the period 1840 to the start of church data, an estimate of 420,000 for the Church of Scotland's communicant's roll in 1840 was combined with a weighting of denominational alignment as revealed by morning attendance in the religious census of 1851, and extrapolated back to 1840 on the basis of a 1% growth-rate per annum. The estimate of Catholic population for 1841 was set at 120,000 (cf 190,000 suggested by Currie et al. – see *Sources* opposite graph). For Muslims, the figures of 100 for 1920, 1,000 for 1945, and 14,000 for 1984 (based on proportion of Islamic marriages in Scotland in that year) were used. For Jews, estimates of 28 for 1840–51 (based on religious census morning attendance), 7,000 for 1900, and 20,000 for 1955–94 were used. All other estimates were obtained from the *Sources* opposite the graph. All gaps, including between decennial population censuses, were then filled by linear extrapolation. The series 'estimated Catholic population' was then divided by a factor of 1.75 to produce a series of notional mass attenders. The series 'U.F.C. communicants' was multiplied by a factor of 1.2 to create improved compatibility with the preceding series 'Free Church members and adherents' and the succeeding series of 'Church of Scotland communicants' roll'. (Note: This does not, however, completely eradicate the breaks in compatibility of these series at the church unions of 1900 and 1929.) The series of Free Church and Free Presbyterian Church communicants were multiplied by factors of 3.9 and 6.00 respectively to compensate for the low level of communion in those denominations. Sunday-school enrolment combines figures collected by the Church of Scotland, Free Church, U.P Church and U.F. Church for most of the period, and additionally uses the figures for enrolment for the first three of those churches given in the 1851 religious census.

11. Figures calculated from R. Currie, et al., op. cit., p. 25.

CHAPTER 4

RELIGION IN RURAL
SOCIETY 1707–1890

THE PRE-INDUSTRIAL FORM OF RELIGION

Scottish religion first took its modern shape in the countryside. Agricultural improvement and rural manufacturing refashioned the social structure and with it the church structure and from there the people – whether driven from the land or attracted by towns – carried the changes to urban society. Looking at Scotland as a whole, the transformation of the countryside seemed slow to complete, but it very often had a sudden local impact. Christian Watt, a fisherwoman from Broadsea on the Moray Firth coast, recalled of the 1840s:

> And then the whole world changed. It was not gradual but sudden like lightening. Whole gangs of men came in to reclaim the land, they ploughed bogs and stanks, everywhere was the smell of burning whins. Suddenly huge big parks were marching up the side of Mormand Hill, so greedy did they become for land.

In Christian's village, protest at these changes turned into the ecclesiastical revolt of the Disruption. The Free Church met on the boat shore, 'the whole arena of the braes black with people', giving 'an awful smack in the face to the would-be's [in the Established Church] who were left with nobody to look down on.'[1] This cleft weakened the Established Church, undermined parish unity and communal worship, and allowed dissent to proliferate. Yet, though modernisation of religion and society began in the countryside, the pace of change was slower than in the larger towns. Agricultural work was bound more to the weather than to machinery, and the ambience of rural life remained one in which old customs and superstitions lingered in the folk memory. Though dissent was a claim to 'custom', to a traditional pre-industrial form of religion being abandoned by those 'would-be's', the landed elites, it did not quickly displace the civil functionality of the rural Established Church. In the words of a popular rhyme, the Free Kirk was 'the kirk without the steeple', and not a civil institution; the 'Auld Kirk', on the other hand, was 'the cauld kirk, the kirk without the people'.

Religion of pre-industrial and rural society presents a contrast to the religion of the manufacturing towns and cities which sprang up after 1780. By today's standards both government and the economy were underdeveloped and the functions and character of religion reflected this. At a constitutional level organised religion was central to issues of national politics and to the operation of the state. At the level of the local community the church played a pivotal role as the intermediary between the state and the family, seemingly more suited to the comparative rustic stability of rural society than to the more dynamic and technologically-oriented character of industrial society. Yet we do not know what 'normal' levels of adherence were in the sixteenth and seventeenth centuries, and are unlikely to do so. The concern of the pre-industrial church and the government was not with apathy or indifference to religious ordinances but with rejection of church authority. This was particularly the case in Scotland where strong regionalism, the difficult terrain and distrust of monarchical power reduced the authority of the Crown. In the vacuum of secular government the Established Church was a vital instrument of civil power, having in its parish churches, schools, officials and ethos of popular participation the most sophisti-cated machinery available to impose stability in society. To accomplish this, religion was an obligation on the people, not a choice as it became in the nineteenth and twentieth centuries. As a result, faith and belief were of secondary importance to overt obedience to ecclesiastical law.

From this obedience derived the distinctive character of the pre-industrial form of religion in Lowland Scotland. It was represented in four major relationships which bound the people to the Established Church: economic, judicial, devotional and educational. The economic relationship between church and people was of great significance. In principle the burden of maintaining church finances rested with the landowners who formed the board of heritors in each parish. The board was responsible for the construction and maintenance of a church capable of accommodating two-thirds of the population over the age of twelve, for the provision of a manse and a glebe of four acres arable or pasture for sixteen cattle, and for the payment of the minister's stipend from the teinds – an annual tax exacted by 'teind-holders', usually landowners, equal to one fifth of the agricultural rental value of the parish. For the kirk's educational work the heritors had to provide a school, pay a schoolmaster, and ensure that all children had access to schooling irrespective of means. The board was not an ecclesiastical court but a civil one, supervised by crown commissioners until 1707 and by the Court of Session thereafter until the commutation of teinds in the 1930s. By forcing landowners of whatever religious affiliation to meet their ecclesiastical obligations, the board symbolised the established status of the Church of Scotland.

In practice heritors ensured that costs were minimised and passed on to the lower social groups in the parish. Heritors challenged claims for expenditure, kept salaries low (especially schoolmasters'), and made tenants responsible for the payment of their proportion of the teinds.[2] Landowners generally paid their portion in cash whilst tenants customarily paid in oatmeal, barley, butter, fish, kelp or other produce depending on the nature of the local economy. Tenants additionally undertook certain labour services, such as thatching the church and manse, and bringing in the harvest from the minister's glebe. These labour dues were in turn passed on to farm servants and the peasantry so that much of the work was carried out by those at the bottom end of the social spectrum. Heritors offset their expenses further by charging school fees and extracting rents for church pews. There were also charges for marriages and baptisms to be paid to the minister, the session clerk (who was almost invariably the schoolmaster) and the beadle, and the kirk session rented a mortcloth for covering coffins at funerals. Parishioners were expected to contribute according to their means to the parochial fund for the relief of the poor – a collection made under the eagle eyes of the elders on entering church for Sunday worship, by door-to-door visitation, or at a parish booth. Applicants for poor relief were subjected to lengthy and often humiliating investigation by the kirk session, and in order to qualify parishioners had to be free of scandal, to attend church regularly, and to bequeath all property to the church. Farmers made their victual payments of teinds direct to the minister and obtained a receipt as proof for the landowner; in coastal communities teinds were collected every time fish was landed. As for the minister, agricultural and commercial concerns dominated his work: supervising his glebe farm and its servants, ensuring his stipend from farmers, and negotiating with heritors for maintenance of church property. By 1800 parish clergy were in constant dispute with landowners over the paucity of glebes and the ruinous condition of manses and churches, but as far as ordinary parishioners were concerned the minister and heritors were jointly the source of heavy financial burdens which placed the church at the centre of the local economy.

Equally important was the church's judicial role. The kirk session, presided over by the minister, administered the provision of communion and other purely ecclesiastical matters, but in the seventeenth and eighteenth centuries the vast bulk of its business was the supervision of parishioners' conduct. In this the session's role straddled ecclesiastical and civil law with at best a hazy division between the two. The kirk session acted as the lowest court from which more serious cases could be referred to the civil system. Elders were often assigned portions of the parish to supervise, and they acted as 'searchers' or patrols on the lookout for instances of Sabbath desecration. But their work was not confined to moral or religious offences. They became in an *ad hoc* fashion general policemen enjoying the support of the civil courts – the baron courts before 1748 and the JPs' courts thereafter. In a few cases the minister was also the JP, as at Barras on the Isle of Lewis. A visitor there in 1802 remarked on the power thus concentrated in the minister, and on the parishioners' position: 'They submit, though sometimes reluctantly, to the decision of their pastor. From his court there are no appeals.'[3]

It is difficult to draw a clear line between civil and ecclesiastical offences. Some crimes such as adultery, fornication, witchcraft (an offence until 1736), drunkenness, swearing and Sabbath profanation were both, but in a more general sense there was no offence which sessions were unwilling to investigate. They heard cases such as theft, assault, wife-battering and even suspicious death. However, the overwhelming majority of cases in Established and dissenting kirk sessions before 1850 were for fornication and to a lesser extent adultery. Fornication was the bread and butter of session business with fines passing to the parochial fund for the poor: as one historian put it, 'the lascivious regularly providing for the needy'.[4] With fornication cases regularly taking a year – and sometimes several years – to complete, many kirk sessions were continuously engrossed with the sexual exploits of parishioners. A case usually started when an elder reported the pregnancy of an unmarried woman. The woman and, if revealed, the father would appear to give evidence, and third parties would be summoned if guilt was not admitted. Kirk session minute books recorded the voyeuristic nature of the meetings. Here is the evidence of one of three witnesses in a fornication case at Aberfoyle Church of Scotland in 1794:

> In Consequence of a summons executed by the kirk Offices of the parish of Drumen – compeared ... Hugh Mcphie servant to John McLarlan in Blarvaigh, and being solemnly exhorted to declare the truth, and nothing but the truth, he declares, that as far as he recollects, it was on the Thursday before Christian McGregor left her service /that is the Thursday before the 5th. day of Nov./ that Robert Monteath, being in his Master's house, and to sleep with him and Alex. Stewart, put off his clothes at the bed side, and then went into bed with Christian McGregor & Agnes McMurrick, who slept in the same room, and were in their bed naked: that the said Robert staid in bed with the women for a long time, – at least an hour, and then came to bed with the declarant: that he knows not whether Agnes McMurrick left the bed or not.[5]

The dissenters copied the rationale and the system of the Church of Scotland, though they lacked the civil authority to summon witnesses.

But they imposed the same magisterial interrogation and heard the same sexual details. A witness swore to an Antiburgher kirk session in Perthshire in 1776 that:

> in the beginning of winter 1774 a taylor returning from his work late at night, having left his master a little behind him met with John [Miller] and his sister in law in a bank south from Crieff, and that some conversation took place between them, by which he understood it was them. That some time after the master coming up a little east from that place, and hearing some noise among the ridges, listened a little, heard a woman saying in a mournful tone 'O! Johnie dinna' do it'; and after saw two persons rise up, and heard the woman say again 'you have given me foul cloths this night'; – and that the persons he heard were guilty together.[6]

In cases where sessions had a choice of believing either a man or a woman, they tended to believe the man. They often disbelieved the woman's evidence even when there was no contradictory account. During a sixteen-month investigation in 1795–6 neither the session of Aberfoyle Church of Scotland nor the Presbytery of Dunblane to which the case was sent up would believe Catherine Stewart's consistent story of being raped by Angus Kennedy, a married man, despite the fact that Kennedy told an elder during an interview that 'I cannot but say it was against her will'. Catherine was found guilty of adultery and fined 10/6d., a large sum for a weaver, whilst Kennedy, being a Catholic, was not summoned.[7] The session of Holyrood in Dumfriesshire believed none of the women in six cases of alleged rape in the eighteenth century, and the Stirling Presbytery of the Antiburgher Church rejected out of hand a woman's claim in 1773 that she had been raped at gunpoint and instead disciplined her for fornication.[8] If a woman denied that she was pregnant, or that she had secretly given birth, or that she had had or attempted an abortion, or that she had committed infanticide, then it was known for kirk sessions to order that her breasts be milked for 'evidence' – a demonstration of 'guilt' carried out by midwives, doctors and, in one case, by a woman's sister. The Stirling Presbytery of the Antiburgher Seceders heard a case in 1773 in which Margaret Littlejohn of Muckhart was accused of becoming pregnant by her master's son, of having unsuccessfully 'used means' for an abortion, and of child murder. Her father David, an elder, was bizarrely permitted to investigate his own daughter's case, including arranging for Margaret's breasts to be milked by her sister. He cleared Margaret of guilt, but she then absconded and her father was suspended from the eldership. Eight years later she re-emerged to be accused of having fled to Kilwinning, changing her name to Margaret Smith, marrying a 'sober man', and then, when news of her past caught up with her, of fleeing again to Perth where she was imprisoned under suspicion of child murder. On being released without charge, she returned to Muckhart where her father was found guilty of conniving in his daughter's assumed name by signing himself 'David Smith'.[9] In another case before the same Presbytery in 1790, a doctor gave evidence of a woman accused of being pregnant out of wedlock; he pressed her breasts and milk was emitted.[10] Despite being hazardous as 'evidence' of pregnancy, the technique was known elsewhere in early modern Europe.[11] The barbarity continued; if a woman refused to reveal the father of an illegitimate child, kirk sessions of both Establishment and dissent frequently ordered that she be interrogated as to his identity during the pains of childbirth.

When it came to punishment women also suffered more severely. They were convicted of fornication more often than men; in some situations they were fined more; and in the many instances of masters accused of fornicating with female servants, kirk sessions demanded an increased burden of proof and often did not even charge the master, and ministers selected and paid by heritors and patrons were tempted to give them protection against prosecution. In 1792 it took Lachlan Mackenzie, the renowned evangelical minister of Lochcarron, to reveal the scandal that Sir Hector Mackenzie, the major landowner of Gairloch in Wester Ross twenty-five miles to the north, had lived in adultery with his maid Jean Urquhart for four years and had fathered three bastard children, concealed by the bribed local minister. The local minister, Daniel McIntosh, had accepted the donation of a mortcloth and cash in return for baptising the children and keeping quiet about the laird's domestic arrangements. When the scandal broke, the shocked presbytery ordered the repentant clergyman to fine Sir Hector sixty pounds, whilst – unusually – the woman servant was not charged.[12]

In addition to being fined, and in many ways more important, fornicators and other transgressors had to 'purge their scandal' by rebuke. This took the form of standing before the congregation for up to three Sundays and being subjected to a 'rant' from the minister. This public humiliation might take place whilst standing or sitting on a special repentance stool at the side of the church or beside the pulpit, and in a few places wearing sackcloth. Not surprisingly, the male social elites found sessions willing to administer private rebuke before the session – a practice which grew in the Church of Scotland from the 1770s – whilst men and women from lower social groups had to submit in almost every instance before the 1820s to public rebuke. The minister's rant must have been one of the theatrical highlights of the eighteenth-century week, but it is now a sadly unrecorded cultural custom of presbyterian Scotland.

Between them, Established and dissenting kirk sessions were still imposing much of rural justice until the 1840s, sometimes investigating and punishing crimes like child murder, assault and theft, but above all fornication.[13] But there were important changes taking place in kirk justice in the middle decades of the nineteenth century. Offences of drunkenness, imprudent 'dealing out of intoxicating drinks' and 'walking disorderly' became more common, especially in the United Presbyterian Church and in the Free Church. Moreover, punishment changed. In urban congregations public rebuke was giving way to private rebuke around 1800, but in rural churches the traditional form was only receding in the 1850s. By then, police forces were expanding, and kirk-session justice had lost much of its original role. Instead of policing society through purging scandal, sessions between 1840 and 1870 were increasingly suspending or ejecting the wayward from congregations. Doune Free Church suspended a man in 1843 for telling his elder that 'if he did not get his Child baptised he would get it done by the Episcopal Church for one shilling'. Two men at Laurencekirk in the north-east were summarily struck off the roll of their United Presbyterian Church in 1849 for being seen in a drunken fight which 'made such an exhibition as to draw a crowd around them, thereby bringing a scandal on the body'.[14] This policy shift gave way by the 1870s to the disintegration of kirk-session justice with even fornication cases virtually stopping. The all-inclusive, communal role of church justice of pre-industrial religion was replaced by an urban-style theory of the church as a private and 'respectable' club.

The devotional and educational links between church and people in rural society were predicated upon the economic and judicial ones described above. This was not a libertarian society in which people had a choice as to whether they adhered to a church. In over a thousand parish theocracies kirk sessions imposed a compulsory culture of conformism. Parishioners were rarely forced to attend church. But in an environment in which the church represented a whole range of institutions and values – the Protestant state, law and order, the dutiful payment of church taxes, parochial education and correctness in sexual morality – neither the activity of going to church nor the passivity of not going indicated anything about the extent of religious observance generally. The communion season, for instance, was a highly popular event in seventeenth- and eighteenth-century Scotland, but it was more often an annual holiday than a holy event; thus, rarely more than 20 per cent of parishioners came forward to receive the sacrament. Truly 'religious' communions were infrequent and suppressed. The religious revivals at Cambuslang and Kilsyth in 1742 were deprecated by landowners for the loss of farm work which they caused. As a result, communions were held with decreasing regularity as the agricultural revolution proceeded. By the 1780s the lapsing of communion was the norm, and some parishes had not held the ceremony for sixteen years. As T. C. Smout concluded, 'active popular participation in religion was thus clearly not seen as socially desirable, but as socially dangerous'.[15]

Such evidence as exists suggests that religious observance at other times of the year was just as poor. There was exceedingly limited church accommodation in rural parishes before the arrival of dissenting meeting houses, yet there was little pressure upon it until late in the eighteenth century. Large numbers of churches, and probably the majority, were in very poor structural condition with rotting thatched roofs, rising damp and earthen floors through which it was not unknown for scraping feet to reveal corpses. Larger churches in towns were often disused or semi-derelict with worshippers meeting in cordoned-off naves or aisles; this was the case at churches in Aberdeen, Dornoch, Dunblane, Dunfermline, Dunkeld, Elgin, Haddington, Jedburgh, Kirkwall, Perth, St Andrews and Stirling. Such conditions were in part the result of presbyterian irreverence for pre-Reformation Catholic churches, but were also both cause and consequence of low church attendance in pre-industrial Scotland. An Argyllshire minister echoed a common observation when he wrote in 1790 that 'with us of the church of Scotland, many of our country kirks are such dark, damp and dirty hovels, as chill and repress every sentiment of devotion'.[16] Neither the civil nor the ecclesiastical authorities were overly disturbed by this situation. They were quite content for the church to accommodate a representative congregation so long as its judicial authority was observed by the community as a whole.

The parish-school system should be seen in the same light. Education was regarded from John Knox onwards as an important means of inculcating acquiescence to the reformed kirk and its authority, and the church undoubtedly contributed to high literacy in Scotland. But we should not exaggerate Scotland's educational prowess, and nor should the parish-school system be seen as the product of high-minded principles of open-access learning. Education was part and parcel of the control of the people exercised jointly by the state and the church. The schoolmaster was a key officer of the local church customarily holding the posts of precentor and kirk-session clerk. He was paid by the heritors and his educational work was inspected by the presbytery. The curriculum depended heavily on the Bible and the catechism, and prepared children for a life of obedience to the kirk. Even the state take-over of parish schools in 1873 did not divert control from the local church and the landed classes. With elected school boards dominated by clergy and local elites, education like religious observance remained an adjunct to the wider relationship between church and people which maintained social order in rural communities.

This relationship was different in some respects in the pre-industrial towns of Scotland. Most town churches were managed by town councils which financed their ecclesiastical operations by charging seat rents or, as in Edinburgh and Montrose, by also imposing an annuity tax on property. The board of heritors was replaced by the town council which paid clerical stipends entirely in cash, thus depriving urban clergy of a central role in the local economy. Similarly, urban kirk sessions lost much of their power to burgh magistrates in the seventeenth and eighteenth centuries. Even the supervision of moral and religious law tended to be dealt with by the city authorities. In Glasgow in the 1780s Sabbath profanation by cattle drovers was countered by municipal decree, and the city's Sabbath 'searchers' were organised by the magistrates using volunteers drawn from the incorporated tradesmen. Moreover, there were no parish schools in most towns since royal burghs used their influence to be excluded from statutory educational provisions, and instead built their own and more exclusive high schools.[17]

Despite this apparent 'secularisation' of urban institutions, there is little evidence to suggest that church attendance was appreciably worse in towns. Church buildings were perhaps in better repair, though not always, and there was a growing economical use made of the large city churches. In each of the towns of Edinburgh, Glasgow, Dundee, Aberdeen, Perth and Stirling by 1780, multiple congregations assembled for worship in different sections of the principal kirk; in Glasgow Cathedral one congregation met in the choir, a second in the nave and a third in the crypt. Moreover, there was a relatively high expenditure on the construction of new churches in the seventeenth and eighteenth centuries. In Glasgow the ratio of number of churches to number of inhabitants (indicated by rough censuses by the magistrates) improved from 1:2936 in 1660 to 1:2133 in 1708 to 1:1545 in 1740, and only fell again to 1:1712 in 1780 with the onset of rapid commercial expansion.[18] This seems to have been a common pattern for British towns which, given the larger seating capacity of most town churches, indicates that urban populations were just as well provided with pews as rural inhabitants.[19] As in the countryside the entire population was not expected to attend church. Municipal authorities allocated pews to various organisations and social groups to create balanced congregations: pews were reserved for universities, incorporated trades, merchants' houses, councillors, inmates of charity hospitals and schools, and the poor. The middle ranks and others in the social elites rented more comfortable and expensive pews. In this way, municipal councils followed the same policy as rural landowners in using churches to symbolise social cohesion whilst at the same time discouraging religious enthusiasm.[20]

In the pre-industrial form of religion the church was the primary focus for community identity. The rites and practices of popular religion were centred on a communal experience which enveloped all, including the casually apathetic and the non-churchgoer. With religious taxes and session justice as the fundamental ties between church and people, there was no need to enforce church attendance. In so far as it was measured at all, religiosity was gauged negatively by demanding avoidance of misdemeanour rather than positively by demanding evidence of enthusiasm or inner piety. But though dissenting churches created parallel church systems to that of the Established Church, ultimately the puritan presbyterians were undermining the basis of traditional religion. Whilst traditional values associated with communal worship and kirk discipline were re-stated by the dissenters, the role of religion was decreasingly one of uniting parishes. Increasingly religion became the focus for social division and the fracturing of rural communities.

THE IMPACT OF ECONOMIC AND SOCIAL CHANGE IN THE LOWLANDS

The agricultural and industrial revolutions created varied consequences for rural religion. Rapidly growing population from the 1740s had within five decades put great pressure upon church accommodation in most districts, and with this growth came an accelerating movement of people in search of industrial work or six-monthly contracts of farm service on enclosed and enlarged farms. Heritors felt little obligation to provide new churches for this expanding and shifting population, and a system of reserving pews for tenants and renting out the remainder to the more prosperous residents spread rapidly across the Lowlands between 1720 and 1800. Whilst general change in agricultural society was spread out over many decades, the sudden advent of these new arrangements in a parish church often ruptured the religious bonds of traditional rural paternalism.

The effects of social change showed themselves quickly in the parish church. The increasing wealth of the landowning classes led to the erection of 'laird's lofts' in most rural churches in the eighteenth century. Some of these lofts were palatially furnished with external staircases, ante-rooms and fireplaces, creating a marked social segregation from the more spartan facilities enjoyed by the rest of the congregation. The separation of social groups was increased by the erection of 'common lofts' and by heritors requesting the local sheriff to sub-divide the ground floor of the church between them according to the valuation of each heritor's land in the parish. The legality of this process was never successfully contested, but it led to the erection of fixed pews in replacement of the stools which worshippers had formerly brought to church. The ostensible reason for 'pewing' was to aid the poor fund: capital in the fund paid for erection of pews which were then rented out to provide a steady income. But the system introduced a novel and acute separation of social ranks. In most parishes heritors reserved at least half and sometimes all the pews for their own tenants with the result that the increasing non-agricultural population had to compete for a small number of seats. In addition, a legal judgment of 1787 released heritors from any obligation to build new churches for 'a fluctuating population, which may be here to-day, and away to-morrow',[21] and ministers found themselves preaching increasingly to the prosperous and to the larger tenantry. But it was not just the poor who felt excluded. Whilst tradesmen and tenants accepted the system as a source of status, promoting virtues of thrift and self-reliance, disquiet arose amongst them – and even amongst many heritors – because they were paying directly to the church but having decreasing say in congregational government. As patrons started to exercise their right to choose the minister after 1730, it was amongst the independent small landowners, skilled artisans and merchants that pressure to dissent sprang up.

The starting point for dissent in rural parishes varied but was almost universally a product of conflict – either with aristocratic patrons or with the class of large landowners. In some parishes the cause was the abandonment in the parish church of 'reading the line' of psalms by a precentor for the benefit of the illiterate; this was prevalent on the east coast in parishes stretching from Berwickshire northwards to Aberdeen-shire. In other places it was a simple lack of accommodation and the refusal of heritors to build extensions, lofts or new churches. Elsewhere the cause was increasing pew rents. Occasionally it was a failure of a patron to fill a ministerial vacancy – an act interpreted as an anti-presbyterian way of saving money. But by far the most frequent reason was opposition, often violent, to the settlement of an unpopular minister chosen by an aristocratic patron. The act of opposing a presentation involved barring the minister and presbytery officials from entering the church. Often only the main door was nailed up or filled by a human barricade, leaving the minister, as with the Rev. Micah Balwhidder in John Galt's novel *Annals of the Parish* to enter unceremoniously through a window. Kenneth Logue has argued that this partial obstruction demonstrated a belief on the part of the protesters that an induction was only valid if carried out after entry had been made through the correct door; any other entrance was symbolically and technically contrary to custom.[22] Protesters were defending the traditional right of the popular 'call' to a minister, and it was through ruling-class disregard for this right that cause was given for secession from the jurisdiction of an improper Established Church.

The spread of patronage disputes followed the diffusion of agricultural improvement. In the central Lowlands, the south-east, Fife and the Dundee area they reached their greatest frequency and violence between the 1750s and 1770s. In Perthshire, Easter Ross and the north-east they occurred mainly between the 1790s and 1850s. But in many parishes, protests occurred repeatedly. The passions have often been seen as narrow ecclesiastical disputes, but they had much wider significance. For a Scottish peasantry noted for the apparent passivity of their response to economic change, patronage disputes were the most significant equivalent to rural protest in the rest of the British Isles. For religious unrest was not directed at presbyterianism or even theocratic church government. Disputed control of the church was emerging from a wider social contest over religious and secular values in the new capitalist environment.

In rejecting a new parish minister and forming a dissenting church, rural protesters were snubbing the interlocked social and ecclesiastical elites: the aristocratic patron (or the Crown where it was patron), the board of heritors dominated by the large landowners or their factors, and often also the kirk session and its eldership of larger farmers. As early as the 1740s Thomas Gillespie, the founder of the Relief Church, was inveighing against 'patrons, heritors, town-councillors, tutors, factors, presbyteries' and those 'whose station or office afford them weight or influence in the matter of settlement of ministers'. 'Satan,' he wrote, 'tempts legislators to invade the prerogative of the Lord Jesus.[23] The protesters and dissenters were defending the theory of 'twa kingdoms' and the people's direct bond or covenant with God which conferred on them rights and privileges in the church. Thus, they were not revolutionaries. They unwaveringly supported the Hanoverian succession and the British constitution. Indeed, ramshackle battalions of Seceders assisted in 1745 in the military defence of Stirling and Edinburgh, and marched to the battlefield of Prestonpans to defend Protestantism from the 'popish' and episcopalian marauders of Bonnie Prince Charlie's Jacobite army.[24] But the dissenters would not endorse the prevailing party in church and state, because it was 'unworthy' and because it was withdrawing from them traditional rights and customs.

In most parishes it was the Antiburgher Seceders who were in the vanguard of social and religious dissent from the rule of the gentry. John Ramsay, a Perthshire landowner, considered them the instigators of class antagonism in the early nineteenth century.

Not many years ago, in walking upon the highroad, every bonnet and hat was lifted to the gentry whom the people met. It was an unmeaning expression of respect. The first who would not bow the knee to Baal were the Antiburghers when going to church on Sunday. No such thing now takes place, Sunday or Saturday, among our rustics, even when they are acquainted with gentlemen. It is connected with the spirit of the times.[25]

Ramsay here records the transformation of traditional Sabbatarianism into a display of social as well as religious dissent. In the new context of contracted farm service and waged labour, the Sabbath became not merely a day of rest but a day of freedom from the control of land-owners, factors, farmers and the loom. By going to the parish church, with its serried ranks of authority figures, parishioners submitted to an extension of this control. John Younger, a Borders shoemaker of the early nineteenth century, heard his minister 'horse-rattling us into obedience to Pitt, Castlereagh and Peel Government as "ordained of God"'.[26] In the 1840s, by which time the Free Church symbolised plebeian protest, Christian Watt in the north-east wrote:

The Kirk had become an organisation to suppress the working class. Several folk had been evicted from crofts on the side of Benachie. The Aberdeenshire folk banded together right away, – it must stop forthwith. Ministers preached that it was God's will to go if told so, but folk had had enough. If you had no profession you were of no consequence to a minister, save only to fill the kirk on Sundays.[27]

In this context the Sabbath, and especially the walk to worship in a dissenting meeting house, was central to the culture of the puritan presbyterians. The rigour of the walk, occasionally as long as thirty miles, expressed the intensity and meaning of dissent. As John Younger wrote, the Sabbath was 'the kindly interference of heaven with the stern conditions of our lot in the scale of humanity', and the walk to church was the freewill declaration of independence in a society where other freedoms were being circumscribed:

There is no walk that a working man can take on the surface of his native earth like a walk to his place of worship. Here the harassments – the toils and anxieties of his everyday life, appear as if cleared away before his footfall. Here he feels more certainly than at other times the true dignity of his own existence and ultimate destination![28]

In the small Ayrshire weaving village of Fenwick in the 1840s the strongly Seceder community observed a strict Sabbath. Fenwick was a noted stronghold of Chartism and one of the local leaders, a radical republican and opponent of the Established Church, recorded in a handwritten pamphlet:

At this hour, this hour of Sabbath evening quiet, it may be said that almost every dwelling has become a family sanctuary, every hearth an altar, every home a temple of praise. Pass along that long range of thatched dwellings, and your ear will often catch the evening song of devotion, as it rises from poor and humble men to the throne of the Eternal.[29]

As class consciousness developed, the dissenting churches became the focus of plebeian identity. The Sabbath was incorporated into proletarian culture, and keeping its sanctity became not a test of civil conformism but a statement of class unity and independence.

A consequence of this was a rigid division made by dissenters between work and religious observance. The Burgher kirk session at Leslie in Fife held David Miller, a maltman by trade and a prospective elder, to be in scandal in 1742 by obeying his master's instruction to work and by selling a horse; since he 'had not observed the last fast day appointed by the Presbytery, but was openly employed in his ordinary business, and in Merchandising that day', his ordination was suspended until his scandal was purged. A farmer in the same congregation three years later was found guilty of setting his non-Seceder servants to ploughing on a fast day – and, worse, of paying them – despite his defence that they were 'not of our way of thinking'.[30] The fast day was an important institution in Seceder culture, generally not involving fasting but rather a harsher form of Sabbatarianism. Manifestos were issued to account for the occasion. The manifesto for Stirling Seceders' Fast Day on 19 February 1783 bemoaned:

> conformity to the world in sinful customs, particularly in promiscuous dancings; levity of spirit, and uncleanness of various kinds; injustices in matters of trade; lying, backbiting, and covetousness, ... and the late unfavourable harvest ... with the many other spiritual strokes we are lying under – while there is no suitable viewing of the Lord's hand in these strokes ... [We entreat God] to break the snares of Satan that are spread for entangling his people; ... that he would overthrow Mahometism, Popery, Prelacy, with all that stands in opposition to the kingdom and interest of Christ; bring in the Jews, and spread the gospel with power among the heathen, and thus introduce the more eminent glory of the latter days.[31]

Seceders held roughly twice as many fast days as the Established Church: six per year compared to three in the late eighteenth century. Apart from New Year and occasions such as the monarch's birthday, Scotland has generally not observed national holidays until the twentieth century, in large measure because such holidays in other countries are usually 'popish' saints' days. In this situation the growth of dissenters' fast days represented a claim to time off from work. This was apparent between 1840 and 1887 in the transformation of fast days into Scotland's distinctive system of local holidays which still survive today.

The presbyterian dissenters saw economic struggle for survival as a unifying element in their faith. Commercial crime such as smuggling was sternly dealt with, as was sharp practice towards the poor. At Inverkip on the lower Clyde in 1814, the Antiburgher church gathered its own evidence from housewives and traders to add ecclesiastical punishment to that of the civil courts upon a baker, Archibald Laird, for selling underweight loaves of bread.[32] Maintaining their congregations was a financial headache. Many in rural areas could not provide a glebe for the minister, and a considerable proportion were in persistent trouble with church authorities until the 1840s for failing to pay full stipends. Perhaps two-thirds of Antiburgher congregations in Stirlingshire and southern Perthshire in the late eighteenth century had no resident ministers but instead received 'sermon' when they could afford it. The Comrie congregation in the 1770s paid 9s. per sermon, and by 1800 there were so many congregations in Scotland 'paying-as-they-heard' that the national synod set a scale of charges: 12s. 6d. for a sermon to under 300 worshippers, and 15s. to over that number. Between 1800 and 1840 Secession presbyteries negotiated stipends with congregations before authorising the appointment of a minister, and often insisted that pay rose *pro rata* with the membership. But the low level of ministerial stipends attracted men of low standard. The Antiburgher minister at Falkirk between 1774 and 1781 made free use of his sermons to rant at will at members of his flock, especially the elders, and was eventually forced to resign from the Church. Archibald Willison, also an Antiburgher minister, was accused by his brethren in 1806 of a catalogue of offences: habitually plagiarising sermons, drunkenness, abandoning his congregation in Montrose, stealing eight notebooks from a fellow minister and using their contents in a sermon, and being 'in habit and repute an evil speaker, liar and tale-bearer'. But such was the shortage of clergy that he was permitted to move to Denny in Stirlingshire where eleven years later he was found guilty of fornication and deserting his post again, and was finally deposed.[33] The ministers preached in the broad Scots tongue for which they were ridiculed by the refined and anglicised ministers of the Established Church's Moderate Party. Dissenting clergy were poorly qualified before the 1840s. By 1800 the Burghers had no doctors of divinity; as one minister of that Church commented: 'their ministers have been too poor to purchase the title, and too illiterate to deserve it'.[34]

However, the rustic image of the Seceders was never totally accurate. From the outset presbyterian dissenters were drawn from a wide cross-section of Lowland rural society. In West Calder parish in Midlothian in 1790 just over a third of parishioners adhered to dissent; out of a population of 968, 169 were Burghers, 142 Antiburghers, seven belonged to the Relief Church and three to the Reformed Presbyterian Church. As Table 6 shows, West Calder dissenters were spread throughout the social structure though with a weighting towards the higher groups: dissenters made up 37 per cent of the eleven landowning families, 40 per cent of the tenant farmers and portioners, but only 21 per cent of cottagers and day labourers. The same social spread is also evident in Jedburgh and Strathaven Burgher congregations also analysed in Table 6. What is noticeable, though, is the high proportion of farmers in the eighteenth century; but in Jedburgh by 1825–35 this class had disappeared from the congregation to be replaced by increased numbers of tradesmen and by the new group of hinds, or married servants who lived on enlarged farms. As the society was becoming increasingly polarised, so dissent grew stronger amongst skilled farm workers rather than tenants or small landowners. The arrival of the Free Church in 1843 added a further dimension to rural social polarities. As the evidence from Forgue in the north-east and Bowden in the south-east suggests, the Free Church of the rural Lowlands began as very much a denomination of the manual workers. If inclined to dissent, the landowners, medium and large tenantry and rural professionals were by then strongly aligned with 'older' dissent – the Seceders and Relief Church (which united as the U.P. Church in 1847) – leaving the Free Church as an ecclesiastical

Table 6 Social composition of rural dissent in the Lowlands, 1737–1859 (%)

	Burgher Churches			West Calder Parish		Free Churches	
	Jedburgh		*Strathaven*	*Total population*	*Dissent*	*Forgue (Huntly)*	*Bowden (Melrose)*
	1737–45	*1825–35*	*1767–89*	*1790*	*1790*	*1843–9*	*1843–59*
(Numbers)	*(40)*	*(72)*	*(88)*	*(968)*	*(321)*	*(82)*	*(116)*
Landed and professional	40	15	63	52	59	21	20
Skilled tradesmen	37.5	59	30	14	17	26	35
Farm workers and unskilled	22.5	26	2	24	18	53	45
Others			5	11	4		

Note: Data for Burgher and Free churches relate to fathers' occupations in baptismal registers. Data for West Calder relates to occupations of heads of household.

Sources: Figures calculated from data in Jedburgh Church, Baptismal Register, SRO CH3/350/3; Strathaven Burger Church, Baptismal Register, SRO CH3/289/1; *OSA.*, vol. 18, pp. 190–5; and from P. L. M. Hillis, 'The sociology of the Disruption' in S. J. Brown and M. Fry (eds), *Scotland in the Age of the Disruption* (Edinburgh, 1993) p. 51.

home for the skilled tradesmen, the small tenantry and the landless. If the Seceders had been the church of the aggrieved and disinherited of rural society in the 1740s, then it was the Free Church that assumed this mantle in the 1840s.

There were two critical occupational groups in dissent. Firstly, tradesmen – such as wrights, smiths, coopers, masons, bakers, butchers, carpenters and shoemakers – shared with farm servants an hostility towards the landed classes, yet were also the small entrepreneurs and respectable artisans who supported the new ethos of commercial capitalism and the virtues of hard work and independence it encouraged. Secondly, textile workers, especially weavers, were located in hundreds of planned villages set up by landowners to absorb dispossessed small tenant farmers, and became strong adherents of dissent and notably the Antiburgher Church. By the early nineteenth century, textile villages – whether based on handloom weaving in the home or on cotton mills – were centres also for the Methodists, Burghers, Baptists and Relievers. Individual villages and towns acquired their own religious complexions: the Burghers and Relief Church at Inveresk, Antiburghers and Relievers at Blairgowrie, the Antiburghers at Buchlyvie and so on. The larger factory villages often bred feverish religious enthusiasm; Deanston and Doune in Perthshire had by 1866 seven churches representing six denominations – the Established, Free, United Presbyterian, Wesleyan Methodist, Episcopal and Roman Catholic churches not to mention small groups of Brethren and Mormons. Parishes specialising in bleaching and calico printing were strongly Seceder; this applied to Slateford near Edinburgh, Cardross, Balfron, Renton, Tibbermuir and Scone. Mining and metallurgical villages like Lochgelly and Dysart in Fife, Cambusnethan, Inveresk, West Calder, Saltcoats and Ardrossan were also strongly Seceder.

The artisans and textile workers of such villages promoted urban-style culture and social divisions in the countryside, allowing the ambience of industrial society to permeate Lowland rural life. They were also the vehicle by which, from the 1830s, the decay of dissenting presbyterianism began. The first major impulse was the decline of handloom weaving which reduced the strength and vitality of rural dissent. Their ethos of an oppressed yet proud occupation withered and with it went the last major vestige of covenanting culture in the Lowlands. The United Presbyterians became increasingly the rural bourgeoisie, and though the Free Church became in some measure the new focus of rural plebeian culture, both grew intolerant of intemperance and the 'rough' culture of the emerging rural proletariat. But more important than shifts within rural dissent was the steadily improving position of the Established

Church in the second half of the nineteenth century. Despite the popular passions aroused by and centred on patronage, pew-renting and the other sparks to dissent in earlier decades, the 'Auld Kirk' in most country parishes retained the adherence of about one-third of the population even at the peak of disaffection in 1850. The parish church enjoyed a permanent place in the social landscape, its enduring status connected by law and custom with the perpetual elements in country life: land-ownership and the heritors' board, the harvest and the teinds, education in the parish school, and burial in the parish churchyard. It had retained the loyalties particularly of landowners (even when they might live in England and frequent the Anglican Church), their retainers and their tenant farmers, and with rural de-population building up from the 1860s self-supporting dissenting congregations started to become unviable.

By 1890 the major denominations were noting a loss of energy in country kirks: church-building was past and many parishes were clearly 'over-churched'. The elements of growth and social fragmentation which had focused religious energy and enthusiasm were now gone and were replaced in many parts by decline and congregational insolvency. Even in rural Aberdeenshire, where the established status of the Church of Scotland had been used in mid-century as 'a stick with which to beat landlords and capitalist farmers',[35] the Free Church lost its identification with anti-landlordism as the issue was moved into the political and trades-union spheres. In any event by 1874 the system of patronage, the cause of so much of the schism in presbyterianism, had been abolished by parliament. The secular significance of the Establishment-dissent split was dissolving, and the arrival of modern occupations (in the post office, banks and shops) and rural local government (county councils in 1889 and burgh councils in many small towns around that period) were realigning the Lowland countryside to city culture and city ways. The countryside was breeding civic ways, and in the process the stature of rural religion in the Lowlands was altered and brought within an urban framework.

THE HIGHLANDS, HEBRIDES AND NORTHERN ISLES

Religion in western and northern Scotland underwent equally significant change to that in the Lowlands, only it had a different starting point and a different outcome. As in the Lowlands religion became the focus of an oppressed culture of puritanical presbyterianism. But whilst the English-speakers in the northern isles of Orkney and Shetland as well as in some coastal communities on the adjacent mainland came strongly under the influence of Lowland churches, the Gaelic-speakers of the Highlands and Hebrides maintained cultural and religious isolation. The landowning class looked to the south and to England for the social identity conferred by the Episcopal Church, but the crofters appropriated imported presbyterianism and turned it into the vehicle for sustaining introverted Gaelic culture during the economic transformation of the 'Clearances'. The result was crofting society, a system of near-subsistence farming and fishing in which puritanical religion conferred cultural insularity and remarkable resilience to an oppressed peasantry divorced from the lairds and from the benefits of modern capitalism. In 1760 this part of Scotland held over a quarter of the country's population. By 1890 it held less than a tenth and by 1940 under seven per cent. Rapid population growth in the eighteenth century went into reverse after 1860 as streams of emigrants abandoned, or were forced to abandon, homes and livelihoods.

The Highlands and Hebrides were the last parts of the British Isles to be properly Christianised. The efforts of missionaries before AD 1000 were dissipated by successive waves of settlements, and by 1700 there was a varied culture of Celtic, Norse and superstitious customs. A lengthy liturgy of rituals prevailed: the worship of saints like St Bride and St Maelrubha; magical practices involving sacrifice of bulls and tampering with milk; tales of fairies, beasts and 'waterkelpies'; and reverence for the poetry, song and second sight of seers. The Reformation had had only a localised effect in the Highlands because of shortage of clergy and lack of enthusiasm, and whilst Franciscan missionaries from Ireland had initiated a Catholic revival in a few isolated districts after 1619, and whilst episcopalian clergy served nobles' houses, the Lowland Established Church had made little headway by the beginning of the eighteenth century. Jacobitism and the need to impose civil order on the turbulent clan society led to a prolonged effort by church and state to presbyterianise the north-west after 1715. But the problems were immense. The presbyterian form of church government seemed unsuited to both the clan system and the crofter-landlord society which replaced it after 1770. Highland terrain was unsuited to parochial supervision by ministers and elders. Parishes were of colossal proportions and generally devoid of roads and bridges, in many cases until the 1840s: Kilmalie (Fort William) measured sixty miles by thirty; Harris, covering seven inhabited islands, was forty-eight miles by twenty-four; and the parish of Applecross was so large and inaccessible that its proportions were still unknown by the minister in 1790. Boards of heritors rarely existed in the early eighteenth century; payment of teinds and parish schools were uncommon; and as ecclesiastical units parishes were of purely token significance, bearing little relevance to the realities of parochial supervision and church attendance. In addition the Church had few Gaelic-speaking clergy and came to rely in the seventeenth and eighteenth centuries upon itinerant missionaries and teacher-catechists. This brought its own peculiar problems. Tacksmen or middle-ranking farmers applied for such posts for extra income, and many were of dubious character. One Church of Scotland catechist was accused by his employers in 1792 of magical practices including 'recourse to certain herbs and an Iron key which were thrown into another's milk in order to restore the fruit of it'; to confound his inquisitors, the catechist defended himself by claiming 'that he did actually restore the fruit of the milk'.[36]

It is not surprising, perhaps, that presbyterianism was looked upon initially by Highlanders as an alien intrusion. Parish churches and schools of the Edinburgh-based Scottish Society for the Propagation of Christian Knowledge (SSPCK), with its pro-English language policy, were supported by the government Commissioners for Forfeited Estates who until 1784 tried to suppress Jacobitism, paganism, episcopacy and the clans in almost equal measure There was a vigorous government-backed drive to force heritors to erect churches and manses between the 1740s and 1770s, but communities disliked the new demands for teinds and labour services and the confiscation of excessive amounts of good arable to form enticing glebes for incoming Lowland clergy. Presbyterian ministers were left in no doubt that they were unwelcome intruders. The minister of Gairloch in the 1710s, John Morrison, having no church, manse or glebe, was forced to rent land to farm but had to leave through poverty when Jacobite rebels stole his cattle. Before going, according to local legend, he was attacked whilst walking beside Loch Maree, stripped naked, tied to a tree, and left for hours to be bitten by the rampant midges.[37] Aeneas Sage of Lochcarron had his house set alight four days before his induction in 1727 as the first presbyterian minister in the parish, and he carried arms thereafter, narrowly avoiding at least one further assassination attempt.

The presbyterianising of the Highlands was achieved by the cultivation of a simple puritan code – including strict Sabbath observance. The eldership developed into a prestigious office which ministers held out to loyal supporters who, as the so-called 'Men', became the first lay leaders of the new crofting communities. Venerated for godliness and given privileges of speaking at communion 'enquiry' meetings and of discussing Scripture at fellowship meetings, the coming of 'the Men' signified a wider puritanisation of Highland presbyterianism in which Episcopal and Moderate clergy were branded as 'the ungodly' and the less numerous evangelical ministers were accorded the status of prophets. Evangelical clergy actively pursued 'unworthy' colleagues: Aeneas Sage accused his neighbouring minister at Applecross of rum-smuggling in 1754, the minister of Lochbroom was disciplined in 1798 for being repeatedly drunk in the pulpit and embezzling kirk session fines and the poor fund for seven years, and Sage's successor, Lachlan Mackenzie, had his own schoolmaster deposed for fornication in 1821.[38] The crusade of fearless evangelical pastors unseated many patently idle ministers from their parish sinecures.

Such changes within the Highland church were but reflections of rapid social transformation. Improving landowners cleared estates in some areas to make way for mixed farming and in others for large-scale sheep farming. In the latter, the population was moved to coastal townships where inhabitants turned to crofting, fishing and the collection of seaweed to make kelp. In both instances the collapse of the old traditional order of the Highlands and the sense of betrayal thrust a wedge between lairds and people, driving the latter to evangelicalism. Religious revivals were reported with increasing frequency after 1790. Accounts spoke of crofters who 'see visions, dream dreams, revel in the wildest hallucinations', and Lewis folk in the 1820s were said to be 'seized with spasms, convulsions, fits, and screaming aloud'.[39] Those affected, certainly before 1810, were not merely the poor but also the prospering. Indeed, Lachlan Mackenzie was quite explicit that it was amongst the improving tenants, those granted extended twenty-five year leases, that made for 'a great appearance of religion in Lochcarron'.

The social chasm opening in Highland society by the end of the eighteenth century was being matched in religion. The poet James Hogg acutely observed on a visit to Lochalsh parish in the west Highlands during the communion season of 1802 that the 'common people' of the parish and surrounding areas thronged in the fields to hear two visiting Gaelic-speaking ministers preaching whilst 'the more genteel people' met in the parish church to listen to the minister Alexander Downie. Downie spoke little Gaelic, was 'a good shot but a wretched preacher', and was often absent from his parish, allegedly residing sixty miles away, probably on one of his large farms on the island of Skye. He owned several properties in the west Highlands on which he was a noted improver in sheep and cattle breeding, and in addition had a large stipend, a glebe, a lucrative army chaplaincy, and was on a par with the social elites of Highland society.[40] Though Downie later sided with crofters in a dispute with the heritor over the inadequacy of the parish church, the trend for the crofting people to hold separate church services became widespread from the 1790s. The sense of oppression, of deprived rights and privileges, was powerful and crucial to crofter mythology, and the religion of the 'Separatists' provided the focus for their grievances and for their new identity.

A vital and often underrated factor in exciting Highland puritanism was the work of Lowland missionaries. They came from a variety of denominations and movements, and all found a ready response amongst both the middle and lower ranks of the north and north-west. Between 1797 and 1808 the Haldane brothers' Society for the Propagation of the Gospel at Home sent dozens of lay preachers, divinity students and visiting English evangelicals like Charles Simeon and Rowland Hill into the Highlands preaching an open evangelical gospel tinged with Painite ideas about the dignity of man. Vast expanses of the north could be covered by itinerant preachers, and popular religious enthusiasm was easily ignited. Between the 1790s and 1830s the lower and middle ranks of Highland society welcomed any and all evangelical preaching, and the role of the Seceders was particularly important. Two of their missionaries reported in 1819:

> A spirit of religious inquiry has been excited, chiefly by the labours of pious and zealous individuals, who have been in the habit of itinerating from place to place; so that the people, having got a tasting of doctrine, with which they were formerly unacquainted, are ardently longing for more. Provided they can only be permitted to enjoy it, they care not from what quarter it comes, or by what instrumentality it is conveyed. When a preacher goes amongst them, who has the character of being an evangelical preacher (no matter to what denomination he may belong), the people flock to hear him, and listen with gladness to the message he delivers.[41]

Some of these southern dissenters stayed on in the Highlands, but more generally native preachers emerged to spread the puritan gospel and to appropriate it to native Gaelic culture.

The missionary explosion in the Highlands and Hebrides after the 1790s extended also to the Orkneys and Shetlands. The people here were culturally different from the rest of the north, being English-speakers drawing heavily upon Scandinavian customs and religious practices. None the less, the economies of these islands were a mixture of the Highland and the Lowland, combining crofting and fishing with more sophisticated commercialism and craft industry in the ports of Kirkwall, Stromness and Lerwick where there were strong associations with, amongst others, the Hudson's Bay Company. Like the crofter-fishers of the Highlands and the Moray Firth coast, the islanders of Orkney and Shetland proved to be receptive to the millennialist gospel brought by southern missionaries. The Haldanite movement enjoyed considerable success after 1798, leading to the foundation of strong Baptist and Congregationalist churches in some of the smaller islands and isolated parishes. In the Shetlands the Methodist Church had its most successful appeal anywhere in Scotland, and a separate synod was founded there. With the arrival of commercial herring fishing from the late 1870s, these evangelistic churches boomed amongst both fishers and the larger groups employed at the curing stations. But the most striking success of all fell to the Seceders who swept through Kirkwall and adjacent parishes in the south-east of Orkney around 1800, and later spread out to some other parishes. Lowland dissenting churches were more success- fully founded in the Orkneys and the Shetlands than in the Highlands and Hebrides, but there were many isolated islands and parishes in which crofting-fishing communities with low incomes sustained a staunch puritanism akin to that of the Gaelic-speaking areas.

The growth of commercial herring fishing and the continuation of older trading links created a modernising economy in the Northern Isles. The benefits were fewer in the Highlands and Hebrides. Evictions and the collapse of the lucrative kelp industry after 1810 induced enduring immiseration amongst the crofting community. Evangelical puritanism had been linked by Lachlan Mackenzie in the 1790s to 'the spirit of industry', but it was soon synonymous with poverty and hostility to landlords and factors. An unsympathetic Edinburgh magazine reported in 1814:

> Many of the converts became emaciated and unsociable. The duties of life were abandoned. Sullen, morose, and discontented, some of them began to talk of their high privileges and of their right, as the elect few, to possess the earth ... The landlord was pronounced unchristian because he insisted on his dues.[42]

Evangelicals started to be associated with discontent, and the clearances were occasionally met with religious protest. In Assynt parish in Sutherland in the early 1810s, the clearance of peasants from their traditional farms and houses was marked by violent opposition to the induction of a Moderate minister, leading to the dispatch of troops from Edinburgh and the prosecution of several parishioners for mobbing and rioting. Emigration increased, drawing off many of the formerly prosperous small tenants from Protestant areas. The government sponsored a General Assembly churchbuilding programme (the Telford churches) which tended to increase the religious segregation of crofters from the landlords. The Ten Years' Conflict between 1834 and 1843 brought southern evangelical clergy canvassing support for the Evangelical Party, heightening tensions and the sense of conflict in the Highlands. Patronage disputes increased in the Highlands and Islands and religious revivals erupted in Easter Ross in 1839, spreading as far as Skye, Harris, Mull and Kintyre. When the Disruption took place in May 1843, it was no surprise to find the crofters being swept *en masse* into the Free Church.

The significance of the Disruption in the Highlands was enormous. On the island of Lewis 98 per cent of the people left the Established Church, in Sutherland reportedly 99.8 per cent, and in all but the Catholic areas and a few of the larger towns like Inverness the figure was rarely less than 90 per cent. Practically everyone seceded except landowners' families, their domestic servants, factors and estate workers, together with some of the small number in the professions: or, as a Free Church publicist put it, 'all who are not the creatures of the proprietor, and have not stifled their convictions for a piece of bread'.[43] Rarely can such a cataclysm have befallen a major Christian church. The crofters were candidates for revolt, but instead adopted the dignity of religious schism as their protest. The Free Church may have been a creation of the Lowland bourgeoisie, but the Gaels claimed it for their own: 'Her principles,' one minister said, 'have been riveted in their souls'.[44]

The impact of the Disruption upon the Highlands was dramatically heightened by two factors: eviction and the potato famine starting in 1845. Hugh Miller, a prominent Free Church journalist, witnessed an impoverished congregation of his fellow brethren meeting for worship a few weeks after the Disruption near Helmsdale in Sutherland. They met near the crowded cottages and small patches of cultivation to which they had been recently cleared by the Duke of Sutherland. The 700 people, he wrote, 'were expelled from their inland holdings, and left to squat upon the coast [and] occupy the selvage of discontent and poverty that fringes its shores'; he commented that he had 'rarely seen a more deeply serious assemblage, never certainly one that bore an air of such deep dejection'.[45] In an effort to stifle organised peasant opposition, the Duke of Sutherland and other landowners refused sites for Free Church buildings and threatened crofters who sheltered seceding clergy with eviction. Within five months of the Disruption the Free Church General Assembly described a 'conspiracy against the Free Church on the part of the landed proprietors', and four years later a House of Commons Select Committee was appointed to investigate. Against a background of disturbances, especially in Ross-shire, and 'rioters' being charged when factors tried to prevent open-air preaching, Thomas Chalmers sought to assure English MPs that the Free churchmen were not revolutionaries:

> I believe that the upper classes very honestly thought ill of us. They looked upon us as so many radicals and revolutionaries; and I have heard some of the higher classes, for whom I have the greatest respect, associate with the Disruption the idea of a coming revolution. I have myself heard them speak so; but I believe that the experience of our being a far more harmless generation than they had any conception of previously, has gone a considerable way to mitigate that feeling; and I trust that the mitigation will go on.[46]

Free Church congregations were driven to extraordinary lengths to find meeting places because of the concentration of landholding with the large estates. At Sunart on the west Highland peninsula of Ardna-murchan, Sir James Riddell's refusal of a site forced the Free Church congregation to the novel solution of using a moored ship as a church for many years. Elsewhere sites were generally negotiated in the 1850s and churches built, but the landowners' obstruction imprinted the Disruption in crofter mythology as a great social as well as ecclesiastical revolution.

Though many Free Church ministers were critics of evictions and the landowners' treatment of their poorer tenants, the Free Kirk was above all, in Chalmers' word, a 'harmless generation'. The puritanism of the crofters was not opposed to the new social order created by the Clearances. It welcomed the new values of hard work and self-reliance that improvement implied, and opposed old Highland customs and the clan system. As James Hunter, the historian of the crofting community, has put it, there was in the puritanism of 'the Men' 'a more or less conscious attempt to come to terms with the realities of a social and economic system dominated by landlordism rather than by clanship'.[47] The Free Church did help mould a crofter political consciousness, even a 'theology of liberation', and a sense of righteousness in the crofter cause. However, when the next great struggle in the 1880 won the Crofters' Act of 1886 and security of tenure for Highlanders, support from the southern Free Church was muted, indicative of the widening gap between Lowland and Highland sections in the Church. The Church in the Lowland cities and towns was moving swiftly towards a liberal, middle-class theology, breaking its by now token adherence to hell-fire preaching and aggressive puritanism. In 1892 the Free Church formally abandoned Calvinist doctrine, and in 1900 combined with the United Presbyterian Church. To the crofters these developments were the abandonment of traditional presbyterianism, and the result was schism: the Free Presbyterian Church, formed in 1893, and the larger Free Church which refused to join the 1900 union. Just as the Crofters' Act, for all the benefits it brought, cemented the society to an unchanging economic structure, so the ecclesiastical breaches of 1893 and 1900 welded the crofting community to a similar fixed religious structure. The Lowland-Highland union within the Victorian Free Church was an anomaly from the outset, and its dissolution between 1893 and 1900 was probably inevitable.

The Highlands and Hebrides were the Scottish kirk's first 'foreign' mission, and a 'dry run' for the great work in Africa and Asia. It was also the most successful mission venture. It was presbyterianism rather than military force that suppressed clan customs and superstitions, and absorbed the Highlands into both Scottish Lowland culture and the British state. From the 1810s, the churches used the Gaelic language and helped its survival into the late twentieth century. Throughout the presbyterianising of the north and north-west, the key element had been the southern influence. The gospel brought was a Lowland one, carried by missionaries steeped in covenanting history and the dissenting struggles of the Secession, Relief and independent churches, bringing the Highlands within the church system of the Lowlands. The irony was that by 1900, after a century and a half of converting the Highlands to puritanical presbyterianism, the south abandoned it and left the Gaelic-speakers of the north as the last upholders of the religious heritage of the seventeenth-century Lowlands.

NOTES

1. D. Watt (ed.), *The Christian Watt Papers* (Edinburgh, 1983), pp. 24, 47.
2. A. A. Cormack, *Teinds and Agriculture: an Historical Survey* (London, 1930), pp.128–9.
3. J. Hogg (ed. W. F. Laughlan), *Highland Tour* (Hawick, 1981), p. 111.
4. C. Larner, *Enemies of God: The Witch-Hunt in Scotland* (London, 1981), p. 56.
5 Aberfoyle Church of Scotland, Punishment Book, 14 September 1794, SAS CH2/704/4.
6. Stirling Antiburgher Presbytery, MS minutes, 9 April 1776, SAS CH3/ 286/1.
7. Aberfoyle Church of Scotland, Punishment Book, 5 January 1794 to 19 April 1795, SAS CH2/704/4.
8. H. Kirkpatrick, 'Holyrood Kirk Session minutes 1698 to 1812', *Transactions of the Dumfriesshire and Galloway Natural History and Antiquarian Society*, third series, vol. lv (1980), p. 121, Stirling General Associate [Antiburgher] Presbytery, minutes, 6 January 1773, SAS CH3/286/1.
9. Stirling General Associate [Antiburgher] Presbytery, minutes, 6 April, 7 June and 29 June 1773, 1 August 1781, 14 May 1782, SAS CH3/286/1 and 2.
10. Ibid., 2 March 1790, SAS CH3/286/2.
11. A small number of women can produce large quantities of milk without pregnancy (hyperprolactinaemia), and many women can secrete small amounts at the breast after vigorous massage. I am grateful for medical advice on galactorrhoea to Professor A. A. Calder of University of Edinburgh's Centre for Reproductive Biology and Professor Peter W. Howie of University of Dundee Medical School. On the use of milking breasts in Germany, see A. Rowlands, '"In great secrecy": the crime of infanticide in Rohenburg ob der Tauber, 1501–1618', *German History*, vol. 15 (1997).
12. Church of Scotland Presbytery of Lochcarron, minutes, 3 and 5 April 1792 and 1 April 1794, SRO CH2/567/3.
13. Two recent scholars attribute 'the disintegration of kirk session discipline' to 1780, which is at least a half century too early. L. Leneman and R. Mitchison, 'Scottish illegitimacy ratios in the early modern period', *Economic History Review*, vol. xl (1987), pp. 44–5
14. Doune (Bridge of Teith) Free Church, kirk session minutes, 11 November 1843,

SAS CH3/78/1; Muirton U.P. Church, kirk session minutes, 7 November 1849, SRO CH3/816/1.

15. T. C. Smout, 'Born again at Cambuslang: new evidence on popular religion and literacy in eighteenth-century Scotland', *Past and Present* 97 (1982), 118.

16. *OSA*, vol. 8, p. 352.

17. Royal [Argyll] Commission on Education in Scotland, Second Report, *BPP* 1867, vol. xxv, p. xlv.

18. Calculated from census data in G. MacGregor, *The History of Glasgow* (Glasgow, 1881), pp. 253, 291, 315, 365. Data on churches from diverse sources.

19. See for instance M. Smith, *Religion in Industrial Society: Oldham and Saddleworth 1740–1865* (Oxford, 1994), p. 36.

20. C. G. Brown, 'The costs of pew-renting: church management, church-going and social class in nineteenth-century Glasgow', *Journal of Ecclesiastical History*, vol. 38 (1987), pp. 348–51.

21. The Tingwall judgement, quoted in *Statement of Facts and Case for the Heritors of Neilston relative to Church Accommodation in the Parish* (Glasgow, 1826), p. 118.

22. K. J. Logue, *Popular Disturbances in Scotland. 1780–1815* (Edinburgh, 1979), p. 169.

23. T. Gillespie, *A Treatise on Temptation* (Edinburgh, 1774), pp. 145, 202.

24. *Scots Magazine*, September 1745, p. 439.

25. J. Ramsay, *Scotland and Scotsmen in the Eighteenth Century, vol. 2* (Edinburgh and London, 1888), p. 557.

26. *Autobiography of John Younger, Shoemaker, St. Boswells* (Kelso, 1881),p. 354.

27. D. Watt (ed.), op. cit., pp. 24, 47.

28. John Younger, *The Light of the Week: or the Temporal Advantages of the Sabbath Considered in Relation to the Working Classes* (London, 1849), pp. 19, 26.

29. James Taylor quoted in T. D. Taylor (ed.), *The Annals of Fenwick* (Ayrshire, 1970), p. 12.

30. Leslie Associate [Burgher] Congregation, kirk session minutes, 25 March and 8 April 1742, 7 January 1745, SRO CH3/319/1.

31. Stirling General Associate [Antiburgher] Presbytery minutes, 11 February 1783, SAS CH3/286/2.

32. Greenock Greenbank [Antiburgher] Church, kirk session minutes 30 December 1814, 13 and 27 January, 10 February 1815, and 2 February 1816, SRO CH3/812/2.

33. Stirling Antiburgher Presbytery, MS minutes, 30 July 1806 SAS CH3/286/13; D Scott, *Annals and Statistics of the Original Secession Church* (Edinburgh 1866), pp. 267–70.

34. J. Peddie, *A Defence of the Associate Synod against the Charge of Sedition* (Edinburgh, 1800), p. 7.

35. I. Carter, *Farmlife in Northeast Scotland 1840–1914* (Edinburgh, 1979), pp. 160ff.

36. Church of Scotland Presbytery of Lochcarron, MS minutes 3 and 5 April 1792, SRO, CH2/567/3.

37. J. H. Dixon, *Gairloch* (Edinburgh, 1886), pp. 65–6.

38. J. MacInnes, *The Evangelical Movement in the Highlands of Scotland 1688 to 1800* (Aberdeen, 1951), p. 52, Church of Scotland Presbytery of Lochcarron minutes, 29 August 1798, 8 February and 9 April 1821, SRO CH2/567/3. Many authorities cite erroneous dates for Mackenzie's career: he was inducted to Lochcarron in 1782 (not 1776), and his oft-cited year of death (1819) is premature as his name appears in the presbytery *sederunt* in 1821.

39. Quoted in J. Hunter, 'The Emergence of the Crofting Community: The Religious Contribution 1798-1843', *Scottish Studies*, vol. 18 (1974), p. 106.
40. Downie's story is told more fully in C. G. Brown, 'Protest in the pews: interpreting presbyterianism and society in fracture during the Scottish economic revolution', in T. M. Devine (ed.), *Conflict and Stability in Scottish Society, 1700–1850* (Edinburgh, 1990), pp. 94–5.
41. Quoted in J. McKerrow, *History of the Secession Church* (Glasgow, 1841), pp. 639–40.
42. Quoted in J. Hunter, *The Making of the Crofting Community* (Edinburgh, 1976), p. 97.
43. H. Miller, *Sutherland: as it was and is; or How a Country May be Ruined* (Edinburgh, 1843), p. 11.
44. Convener of the Gaelic Committee quoted in *Discussion in the General Assembly of the Free Church of Scotland on the State of Sutherland and Ross Shires* (Glasgow, 1843), p. 8.
45. H. Miller, op. cit., p. 11.
46. Evidence given before the Select Committee of the House of Commons on Sites for Churches (Scotland), 12 May 1847, quoted in *The Free Church Magazine*, August 1847, p. 254.
47. J. Hunter, op. cit., p. 101.

CHAPTER 5

THE CHALLENGE OF THE CITIES 1780–1890

CIVIC ADMINISTRATION AND RELIGION

'We are apt to think that Churches are prospering,' the Rev. Thomas Chalmers, the leading light of the Free Church, told English MPs in 1847; 'but if they are so, then it would appear that that prosperity is consistent with a phenomenon altogether contemporaneous with it, and that is the palpable increase, from year to year, of a profligate, profane, and heathen population.'[1] Chalmers was responsible, more than any other individual in Britain, for cultivating the notion that urbanisation caused the decline of religion. When preaching in Glasgow in 1817, he had warned that:

> on looking at the mighty mass of a city population, I state my apprehension, that if something be not done to bring this enormous physical strength under the control of Christian and humanised principle, the day may yet come, when it may lift against the authorities of the land, its brawny vigour, and discharge upon them all the turbulence of its rude and volcanic energy.[2]

In his most influential book, he wrote in 1821 that 'in our great towns, the population have so outgrown the old ecclesiastical system, as to have accumulated there into so many masses of practical heathenism'.[3] His alarmist language of 'home heathens', 'paganism' and 'dense irreligion' conveyed his central idea that in cities the working classes were alienated from the churches, morality and social order. It was an idea that infected the British ecclesiastical and political establishments, and was the basis for the declaration of an 'emergency' of non-churchgoing by the Census of Religious Worship of 1851. If religion had formerly been the basis of social order in town and countryside, its collapse in the new industrial centres was regarded not merely as an ecclesiastical problem but as threatening the entire stability of civil society.

Cities were the cause of international ecclesiastical alarm – whether it was the scale of metropolises like London and New York or, as in Scotland and the north of England, their sudden appearance within predominantly rural regions. Scotland urbanised more rapidly than anywhere in Europe: in 1700 only 5.3 per cent of her population lived in towns of more than 10,000 people, but by 1850 the figure was 32 per cent, higher than the whole of continental Europe.[4] Only in England and Wales was there a comparable experience, and the rapidity of change, especially between 1800 and 1830 (when Glasgow, Liverpool and Manchester each almost tripled in size), shocked and alarmed clergymen and social commentators. In most existing Scottish burghs, effects started to be noted between the 1770s and 1790s. The Edinburgh bookseller William Creech recorded of the capital's residents:

> In 1763 – It was fashionable to go to church, and people were interested about religion. Sunday was observed by all ranks as a day of devotion; and it was disgraceful to be seen on the streets during the time of public worship ... In 1783 – Attendance on church was greatly neglected, and particularly by men; Sunday was made by many a day of relaxation ... The streets were far from being void of people in the time of public worship; and, in the evenings were frequently loose and riotous; particularly owing to bands of apprentice boys and young lads.[5]

A minister in Stirling noted something similar in 1790: 'There is generally no room in churches for the accommodation of the poor', he recorded, causing them to 'loiter away the days of public solemnity, in sloth and vicious indulgence at home.'[6] A Glasgow contributor to the *Statistical Account* of the 1790s spoke of a recent decline in the 'strict severity and apparent sanctity of manners': 'There is now a great deal more industry on six days of the week, and a great deal more dissipation and licentiousness on the seventh.'[7] Most Established Church ministers welcomed the coming of industry, but there was general agreement that the beneficial effects of industrial employment could not develop in a vacuum of moral and religious influence. In towns and cities, the old parochial system of the Church of Scotland was under strain, and the maintenance of religiosity became a major challenge.

Industrial urbanisation brought immediate changes to the nature of the churches' role – changes not merely in terms of the need for more churches and clergy for rising city populations, but qualitative changes in how organised religion operated. For example, the employment of children in the new cotton-spinning factories, and the general growth of child labour which this encouraged, led to the older week-day education provided by charity schools being unsuited to the needs of the plebeian young. In 1785 the Rev. William Porteous of the Established Church advised the town council of Glasgow to expand charity schools to serve the child workers in the new cotton factories; but two years later he acknowledged the failure of this design when, within five days of the city's first and very violent cotton strike, he proposed that Sunday schools were needed to educate 'apprentices' on their one day of rest.

Councils all over Scotland agreed to this innovation immediately, and Sunday schools became the first of the many forms of religious voluntary organisation to emerge over the next hundred years. The original Sabbath school in Aberdeen in 1787 was set up 'for the instruction of poor children in reading English, learning the principles of the Christian religion, and psalmody', and by keeping children at 'exercises' virtually continuously from 8 a.m. to 7 p.m. it was hoped that Sunday games and burglary of residents' homes during divine service would be eliminated.[8]

It is noteworthy how the early attempts to adapt urban religion to the industrial age were co-ordinated by town councils. Since they owned most burgh churches and had since the Reformation taken responsibility for the religious life of the citizens, town councillors and magistrates continued for several decades to manage Established Church responses to the new society. Practically all the Sunday schools set up in Scottish cities in the 1780s were municipally patronised, signifying how civic administrators continued to use the Church of Scotland as an arm of local government. Poor relief was a statutory duty shared between town councils and the Established Church, and urban growth after 1780 brought such levels of underemployment and poverty that varieties of novel schemes were tried out. Thomas Chalmers became the doyen of poor-relief innovation, getting the approval in 1819 of his employers, the town council of Glasgow, to create a new parish in the mushrooming industrial east end of the city in which he sought to re-create a rural parish in an urban setting. The town council agreed to remove St John's from the statutory system of poor relief based on the rates, and allowed Chalmers to substitute it with a system of voluntary relief, backed up with intensive Sunday-school and evangelistic endeavour to encourage family self-reliance, in which church collections were distributed with great parsimony to the poor after the most rigorous examination by church elders. Although the St John's experiment made Chalmers a famous figure in the evangelical world, it was largely a failure: in part because of the shortage of lay helpers and in part because it did not reduce poverty.[9] Indeed, one of his clerical opponents publicly proclaimed that Chalmers perpetuated paupers' suffering by keeping huge balances of unspent poor funds, the product of church collections which 'were not the contributions of the parish, but of the admirers of your eloquence, who flocked from all quarters of the town and country to hear you.'[10] The experiment collapsed some time after Chalmers left in the 1820s, but he tried a similar scheme of parochial supervision in the West Port district of Edinburgh twenty years later, and other partial imitations were tried elsewhere. A national campaign by Chalmers in the 1840s against the poor-relief system was finally unsuccessful, but the ideas behind it were very popular amongst middle- and lower-middle-class groups who not only found rates a heavy burden but who believed strongly that worth and status in modern urban society were to be gained by financial self-reliance.

Town councils had secular matters of pressing concern. From the 1840s insanitation, poor housing, the provision of public utilities like water and gas, and the suppression of disorder and crime took up an ever increasing amount of council time and expenditure. But interestingly, town councillors were almost always church elders, and they applied a strongly religious policy to the improvement of the urban environment. Indeed, Victorian social policy rested heavily on evangelical foundations with church committees and pressure groups fostering public debate about civic government. Such was the influence of evangelical thinking on social policy that it can be argued that evangelicals dictated when and in what manner state intervention was necessary. Though not united on such 'political' matters, evangelical ministers and leading laity were frequently influential in promoting social reform and civic improvement: for instance, in the provision of free access to public parks in Edinburgh and Glasgow; in slum clearance and sanitary legislation in the 1850s and 1860s; in the formation of a state system of education in 1872; in licensing of public houses; and in the organisation and administration of public works schemes for the unemployed, especially in the 1840s.

Town councils accepted evangelical solutions to urban problems. The municipal response to proletarian unrest, as in Glasgow in 1811–13, tended to be the planning of 'large plain churches' for working-class districts. Evangelical councillors grouped together, sometimes across party lines, to press for city-improvement acts and municipal take-over of private water and gas companies. The Glasgow City Improvement Act of 1866, which set about the demolition of city-centre slums, originated in a secret philanthropic scheme run by twenty-two wealthy citizens and councillors and financed by the Clydesdale Bank under the inspiration of a Free Church minister, Dr Robert Buchanan. His missionary work in the wynds of the Tron parish convinced him in the 1850s that improvement in the working classes' religion and morals was dependent in some measure on 'breaking up the denser quarters of the city, [and] of letting in upon them the light and air of heaven'.[11] In 1857 and 1858 Buchanan led the Glasgow presbytery of the Free Church into staving off a ratepayers' reaction against the costs of a mammoth project to bring clear Highland water from Loch Katrine, and, as the unofficial chaplain to civic improvement, gave the teetotal toast at the celebration banquet to the joint stream of water and the gospel: 'Let that living water be made to circulate through all the dwellings of the city.'[12]

This conjunction of religious and municipal designs produced other co-operative activity. In the 1850s and 1860s municipal sanitary departments turned to congregational parish missionary societies to distribute leaflets on hygiene and sanitation during the fever epidemics of typhus and cholera, and Sunday-school teachers were used by councils to provide the best information on the extent of literacy and attendance figures at day, evening and Sunday schools. Perhaps most commonly, though, was the way in which the churches and religious organisations turned to the councils for enforcement of moral and religious laws. In 1850 the Sunday-school teachers of Glasgow inundated the council with petitions to close public houses on the Sabbath and to restrict the number of licences issued. The council acceded and, like Edinburgh at the same time, adopted a restrictive licensing policy which was engrossed in Scottish legislation in 1853.[13] Licensing courts represented how municipal administration became increasingly puritanical in the second half of the nineteenth century. The Sunday running of trains became a *cause célèbre*, creating a national rumpus in the 1840s which largely prevented it, and another in the 1860s which, much to the chagrin of the dissenters, permitted it;[14] even so, Sabbath trains remained limited in Scotland until the mid-twentieth century. From the 1830s onwards municipal authorities pressurised many industries and employers to reduce Sunday labour; as their own contribution art galleries and museums were closed on the Sabbath to reduce 'profanation'. By 1904 a university research student was noting that Glasgow councillors used their powers 'in a narrow and puritanical manner', going so far as to censor pictures from art exhibitions in the city.[15] In this way the civil magistrates in modern burghs continued to be called upon to act for the benefit of the churches' moral and religious code.

But the religious role of civic authorities narrowed after 1832, mainly because of the electoral power of the presbyterian dissenters who objected to municipal ownership of Established churches. The fundamental link between church and burgh inherited from pre-industrial times was town councillors' role as urban heritors, providing the Established churches in most towns and employing the clergy. In towns like Edinburgh and Glasgow this could amount to up ten churches and ministers being under the control of the council. Initially, town councils sought to sustain the municipal monopoly of church provision by building new churches, but so rapid was growth of population in cities like Glasgow, Edinburgh and Dundee that town councils could not find the funds with which to build sufficient numbers. Very quickly the shortage became evident in Glasgow when demand for pews forced the council in 1782 to raise seat rents to keep pace with prices in other kirks.

To continue meeting the demand, the council in the 1810s removed seats reserved for the poor and discontinued the practice of allocating sections of low-rent seats for the use of the working classes. Consequently, the middle classes came to dominate in these congregations whilst the working classes were only allocated two new council churches erected in the east end in 1819–20.

Evangelicals in the Church of Scotland abhorred the way in which town councils raked in profits from inflated pew rents whilst leaving thousands unaccommodated at Sunday worship. In 1833 Thomas Chalmers initiated a philanthropic scheme to provide Scotland with two hundred extra churches, and this started an exodus of the middle classes from city-centre churches. The Disruption of 1843 accelerated the process with, in Glasgow, over 3,000 worshippers leaving and unlet seats being rented for half price. A similar trend occurred in Edinburgh where congregations objected between 1810 and 1835 to increases in seat rents imposed by the town council, and extension churches built in the late 1830s caused an outflow of worshippers and a fall in seat rents.[16] Various attempts were made from the 1840s – largely by Free Church and dissenting town councillors – to dispose of council-run congregations of the state church, but the power of the Established Church blocked this until its disestablishment in 1925.

By the 1840s, then, the principle that ecclesiastical affairs were part of civic administration was considered to be an anachronism. But town councils had played a crucial role in the early stages of rapid urban growth and industrialisation. They brought together ecclesiastical, educational, philanthropic and medical agencies to develop and adapt civil administration to the rapidly changing environment. Rural parishes and small towns with no burgh administration were less fortunate. In textile, mining and metallurgical communities which sprang up between 1785 and 1830 ecclesiastical and civil administration was often chaotic. The parish church, the parish school and parochial poor relief were utterly inadequate to cope with rapid growth of population. In such places the only civil authority was the heritors' board and the kirk session, both of which were quickly trammelled by the advent of industrialism. In the new iron and coal town of Airdrie to the east of Glasgow, which doubled in size in the 1830s, the heritors could not provide adequate church accommodation, and Sunday attendance rate by 1851 was 23 per cent of the population – the second lowest amongst the fifty-three Scottish burghs.

Though a link between the Church of Scotland and burgh councils continued into the twentieth century, it was by the 1830s ineffective as a response to urban growth. So many urban dwellers were dissenters that councils could not politically justify spending money on erecting churches for one denomination. Thomas Chalmers' dream of creating in towns a 'godly commonwealth' based on an Established Church was effectively dead, and his acknowledgement of this was one reason for him leading Evangelicals into the Free Church of 1843. However, as already noted, presbyterians of all denominations continued to seek the support of town councils in enforcing religious morality upon the citizens. The Free and U.P. churches in particular strove to implement Chalmers' vision of a godly society in towns, wanting civic government to be a democratic 'agency' of evangelicalism. The town council was to be one agent of a wider evangelical movement based on the moral and religious preoccupations of the new urban middle classes.

EVANGELICALISM AND THE RISE OF THE MIDDLE CLASSES

An immediate effect of the growth of industrial cities was to widen the gap between urban and rural sections in the presbyterian churches. For the landed classes the Church embodied the principles upon which the country had been managed for generations: patronage (in church and state), deference, and the power and stability vested in heritable property. The middle classes of the burgeoning cities, on the other hand, developed a new social system and culture based on independent values: competition, self-reliance and status through hard work rather than inheritance. For all that Thomas Chalmers was the hero of the Scottish middle classes – his funeral in 1847 attracting reputedly one hundred thousand mourners to line the streets of Morningside and Lauriston in Edinburgh's south side[17] – his ideals were grounded in a rural society of landed interest and paternalism. As a high Tory paternalist and a rural romantic, he sought in towns what he called 'the formation of a well-conditioned peasantry'.[18] The urban middle classes, products of city prosperity and opportunity, demanded separate recognition: the extension of the franchise, the reform of government policy on the basis of *laissez faire*, and equality with the landed classes in matters of religion. More than that, the middle classes brought to the churches an aggressive and enthusiastic commitment which conflicted with the rural elites' stress on religion as a sedate instrument of civil government. The cities were transforming ideas about what religion should be.

The distinguishing feature in the social identity of the new middle classes was evangelicalism. It was not so much a theological system as a framework of response to the emergence of modern urban society. It was not limited to any one denomination, nor was it the sole preserve of the middle classes, for it enveloped the values which governed the urban social system. But the middle classes, as a broad yet remarkably united social elite, were the masters of its development. Spurning theological debate, it called citizens to action in the name of God, the economy and the individual. The call was an evangelical summons: to individual enquiry and to evangelisation. The urban church became unlike the rural one in that it became decreasingly 'laid on' by the state and by the elites. Building a church and inculcating the gospel truths had to be undertaken by voluntary effort and 'Christian liberality'. The effect was to turn the cities into the vibrant focus of aggressive Christianity with endless and very successful appeals for money for building churches, manses and mission stations, for mounting foreign missions, and for the publication of tracts. Evangelicalism demanded personal commitment through voluntary effort in Sunday schools, Bible classes, tract distribution, home visiting, the temperance soirée, and hundreds of other related activities. What one historian has termed an 'associational ideal' developed, defining both the urban church and urban society more widely, and distinguishing it from rural and pre-industrial society.[19] Just as churches were no longer institutions of the state but 'free societies of believers', so the auxiliary organisation became the hallmark of the commitment, belonging, belief and social activity of the churchgoer. Religion adapted to urban society more than anything by inventing the voluntary organisation, for which church people developed an obsession between the beginning of Queen Victoria's reign and the outbreak of the First World War. Through it, the Victorian middle classes had their outlet for 'respectable' and 'useful' leisure.

Arguably the most innovative centre for religious voluntary organisations in the English-speaking world was Glasgow, dubbed by one evangelical in the 1830s as 'Gospel City'.[20] The key inspirer was again Thomas Chalmers, whose solution 'for reclaiming the people of our cities, to a habit of attendance on the ordinances of Christianity' was 'the home mission' which he formulated as 'an aggressive operation upon the inhabitants themselves'.[21] In an important sense, the formation of the dissenting congregation was the first step in the development of the voluntary organisation, and the most obvious product of the evangelical call to action was the construction of churches. The Relief Church was initially the most popular denomination for dissent in Scottish towns; it had already claimed a firm control of middle-class groups in some small towns like Jedburgh and Campbeltown, and in Glasgow it opened five churches between 1792 and 1806. But in Dundee the largest dissenting group at the end of the eighteenth century was the Glasites, whilst in Stirling and Edinburgh the Seceders were proving the most popular amongst a range of evangelical denominations. In Glasgow after 1815 the Secession Church took over from the Relief as the leading dissenting denomination. However, Scottish urban dissent changed in the mid-1830s with evangelicals paying for two hundred extension churches within the Established Church; when the Free Church was formed in 1843, these congregations 'came out' virtually *en masse*, lost their churches in a House of Lords ruling, and then raised money all over again to provide replacements. Church building then mushroomed between 1850 and 1880 as it did in most British cities, financed by the economic boom of the mid-Victorian period.

Church extension was only one part of a much wider evangelical social policy, providing an overarching moral and religious interpretation of the cities' social problems which, from the evangelical point of view, were all interrelated products of spiritual failure of the individual. Evangelicals progressively isolated moral shortcomings and developed agencies to tackle them: from 1787 Sunday schools (and from the 1810s mission schools) to attack illiteracy which prevented reading of the Bible; from the 1810s tract distribution to provide moral and Scriptural guidance; from 1829 temperance (and, from 1836, teetotal) societies to turn the working classes from drink; from the 1810s penny savings banks to encourage thrift and reduce improvidence; from the 1840s sanitary benevolent societies to distribute advice on hygiene, and model lodging houses to improve morality and sanitation; from the 1850s co-operative building societies to promote the spirit of self-improvement. After 1850 the agencies became progressively refined according to occupation, sex and age: railwaymen's missions, mill-girl prayer groups, mothers' kitchen meetings, the Bands of Hope to promote teetotalism amongst young children, the Glasgow Foundry Boys' Religious Society and its imitator the Boys' Brigade (founded in Glasgow in 1883) for teenage boys, the Girls' Guildry for teenage girls, the YMCA and the YWCA for young adults, and so on. After 1850, such organisations were often attached to congregations, but many were independent and interdenominational – such as the City Mission, an organisation which originated in Glasgow in 1826 but which then spread to virtually every British and Irish city and to North America. The list and variety of organisations was seemingly endless, providing the working classes with an inescapeable onslaught of evangelical religion.

The development of these organisations between 1780 and 1890 followed the course of evolving evangelical methods. After 1796 Sunday schools became largely the preserve of evangelicals in the dissenting churches and grew with great speed after 1814 to be the largest religious voluntary organisation of nineteenth-century Scotland. By 1850 more city children were at Sunday school than day school and the scholars were almost exclusively working-class. Until the 1840s Sunday-school teachers were generally organised in interdenominational district societies, but thereafter congregations took over the management of Sunday schools and made them the central institution of home-missionary and evangelisation activities. Sunday-school teachers were the backbone of evangelicalism. In the 1810s and 1820s they distributed tracts which inundated working-class districts. They found this enterprise had its shortcomings because, as the Glasgow Religious Tract Society noted in 1815, 'It is extremely difficult for such a Society to determine what measure of success may have attended their exertions, as Tracts are in general circulated in quarters, from which no future information concerning the result is received.'[22] To facilitate contact with working-class adults, city missions were established to send divinity students into the slums to visit the working classes in their houses between once and twice every four months with the aim of 'diffusing and increasing amongst them a knowledge of evangelical truth'.[23] These interdenominational organisations were joined from the 1840s by congregational missionaries attached to the Free, U.P., Congregationalist and Evangelical Union churches, co-ordinating the multi-layered evangelistic work of the congregation. The mainstay of district visitation were the Sunday-school teachers, some 3,000 of them in Glasgow alone in 1850 and over 10,000 by 1890. They more than any other group displayed the vigour of Victorian evangelicalism, and were instrumental in enlarging the scope and extent of religious organisation.

The unifying feature of this home-mission work was the 'aggressive system' popularised by Thomas Chalmers. In his first urban parish of the Tron in central Glasgow in 1814–19, he gathered around him innovative evangelicals who developed the first infant school, as well as Sunday schools, day schools, and home visitation of all households. It was the last which was the distinctive feature of the 'aggressive system' so widely adopted by world Protestantism in the second half of the nineteenth century. One agent of the Glasgow City Mission, working in the east end of the city in the early 1850s, recalled 'starting out at six o'clock every Sunday morning, running from street to street, knocking at the doors and rousing the careless, and thus getting together, and keeping together, their Bible Class.'[24] The working classes became increasingly badgered by such missionaries. Parents were constantly the target of pressure to send children to Sunday school, and by 1850, when Free Church congregational missions were operating in the central slum areas of the major cities, home visitation was occurring at least once a month and sometimes more often. By the 1870s the 'aggressive' system was the norm, with every middle-class congregation having an evangelisation association and usually a mission station where the working classes were encouraged to strive for financial independence and full congregational status. As increasing numbers of full congregations were sanctioned in the 1860s and 1870s, they too commenced evangelisation work and duplication of effort became a major problem. Inter-denominational rivalry arose and in Glasgow, the biggest mission centre, a Home Mission Union was formed in 1885 which allocated small districts with as few as 180 families to each subscribing congregation which then carried out monthly visitation. In this way the whole city was covered, and problems of 'poaching' by one congregation on another's mission district were ironed out.

This mammoth panoply of religious voluntary organisations became the vehicle for implementing social reform amongst the working classes and the poor, and for improving the quality of urban life generally. Individual agencies tackled specific problems or obstacles to social and religious salvation. Until 1850 agencies were predominantly educational, but thereafter teetotalism and revivalism heightened the emotional character of redemption. Urban revivalism first emerged on a large scale in New York in 1858 and enthusiasts in the Free and United Presbyterian Churches immediately anticipated and worked for its arrival in Scotland. It came in 1859–62 after a trade depression, and in the major industrial districts of Scotland religious prayer meetings were conducted in factories and offices and in the wynds and closes of Edinburgh and Glasgow. The revival was to some, especially in the Established Church, 'rude' and threatening, causing high absenteeism from work. There were opponents even within the dissenting churches; there were 'good people' in the Free Church who felt that if prayer meetings continued until midnight 'all the arrangements of society would come to an end'. But there were reports of 'the appearance of greater earnestness and prayerfulness throughout our churches' and it was noted that the revival was 'most conspicuous among those classes of society who hitherto have been the least accessible to any religious influences whatever'.[25] Over the next thirty years the stress of evangelisation was to re-create this revivalism, and to link it with the taking of the 'pledge' of total abstinence. Middleclass involvement in the Moody-Sankey revival of 1873–5, especially amongst office-workers and students, reinforced the focus on the conversion experience, and diverted enthusiasm from 'secular' social reform.

By the 1890s the range and variety of church activities was enormous. St Mary's Free Church in Govan had Sunday schools with 1,137 children, Bible classes with 493 scholars, 155 Sunday-school teachers, an average of 469 children attending 'Sabbath Forenoon Meetings' watched over by 77 monitors, a Literary Society with 185 members, male and female fellowship associations with 213 members, Christian Endeavour societies with 251 members, a Company of the Boys' Brigade with 58 officers and boys, Gospel Temperance Meetings with 420 members, a Penny Savings Bank with 19,000 transactions annually, and branches of the YMCA. And to watch over, recruit and maintain working-class members, the congregation provided 292 Home Mission workers to undertake door-to-door visitation on a monthly basis. Few congregations by 1890 were offering a less varied range of activities, and many encouraged more. The evangelical call to action was answered by the Victorian middle classes, and with the 'soirée' (born out of the temperance movement), middle-class leisure became a commitment to the evangelisation of the cities.

The work of the Victorian religious voluntary organisation relied on voluntary helpers. Though not all middle class, they tended to be drawn from those in secure, white-collar occupations; middle-class women, denied job opportunities owing to the prevailing domestic ideology, participated in great numbers as Sunday-school teachers, home visitors and tract distributors. The middle-class motivation for this work was complex. Often hostile to state intervention in the rescue of social casualties, the moral and religious crusades of evangelicalism were an attractive solution to the urban condition. They provided an active response to fear of revolution, notably after the 1848 revolution in Paris; as one Glasgow minister said in a publicity speech to the Glasgow middle classes:

> I have often shuddered in traversing the wynds of Glasgow to think that we have there in abundance the very materials with which the St. Antoines and the St. Marceaux of Paris have, again and again, fed the flames of its frequent revolutionary conflagrations ... Surely, however, humanity and religion do not need such an argument to summon them into the field.[26]

Victorian religious organisations made great play in their publicity material of successful businessmen who had started as hard-working typesetters or weavers or foundrymen, or shifted from a landed background into commerce and industry, and who were committed evangelical workers. Sir Michael Connal (1817–93), founder of numerous voluntary educational associations for young men and later chairman of Glasgow School Board, kept a diary with classic entries of the evangelising philanthropist. At the age of 21 he recorded:

> 1838, November 6th: Visited two poor women, as a member of the Stirlingshire Charitable Society; one a Mrs. Buchanan, a poor object, five children just out of scarlet fever, three stairs up in a back land in the High Street; dreadful poverty, suffocating smell, rags, filth; these sights should make me more and more active doing good.[27]

He kept up his evangelical work throughout his life, recording in his diary Bible classes he conducted with working-class lads of Glasgow's Gallowgate, and visits to their homes:

> June 29th, 1847: It is good to go to the houses of the poor and see how they struggle through with their difficulties. It puts to flight every shadow that may have hung upon one's spirits. Visited an Irishman – a very specious fellow; I shall keep my eye on him.[28]

Like Connal, Edward Bailey (1836–1912) specialised in work amongst young men between the ages of twelve and eighteen, but his 'clientele' were predominantly middle-class children in Edinburgh's suburb of Morningside. After thirty years running his own oil-field company in the United States, he returned to Edinburgh to devote his retirement to the Guild Bible Classes of the Church of Scotland. Of the Guild he wrote in 1893:

> Much is now being said about lapsed masses and non-churchgoing; let it be ours to see that those who are now rising from boyhood to manhood are preserved from lapsing into such irreligion. It is easier to preserve the boy than to reform the man. Such a commission our Lord has committed to Scotland's Guildsmen. Shall we rise to the duty, or sit supinely by as our predecessors have done, and permit the evil to go on at an ever-increasing ratio?[29]

Through responding to the call to action, evangelicalism was for the Victorian middle classes a source of identity, affirming separateness from the older landed elites and from the working classes: the dressing in 'Sunday best' clothes, the sense of belonging conferred by the family name inscribed at the end of the rented pew, the visible 'givings' to church missionary funds of one kind or another, or for the more wealthy the sponsoring of an evangelist or even an entire mission church in 'the slums'. The work of volunteers, and more especially of the growing army of 'home missionaries' from the 1840s onwards, was publicised for middle-class sponsors, affirming bourgeois values and separateness through the power of mission work to improve society. One full-time missionary, his salary paid by a businessman, recalled:

> One Sabbath morning, at seven o'clock, I had one of the most deeply interesting and fruitful of all my Classes for the study of the Bible. It was attended by from seventy to a hundred of the very poorest young women and grown-up lads of the whole district. They had nothing to put on except their ordinary work-day clothes, – all without bonnets, some without shoes. Beautiful was it to mark how the poorest began to improve in personal appearance immediately after they came to our class; how they gradually got shoes and one bit of clothing after another, to enable them to attend our other meetings, and then to go to church; and, above all, how eagerly they sought to bring others with them, taking a deep personal interest in all the work of the Mission.[30]

Table 7 Social Composition of John Street Relief/United Presbyterian Church, Glasgow, 1822–57 (%)

(Numbers)	1822–32 (161)		1853–57 (148)	
1. Professional, commercial and manufacturing	6		10	
2. Lower middle class (clerks, shopkeepers, factors, spiritdealers, etc.)	11		27	
3. Skilled working class (except major textiles)	66		45	
(a) Metal, wood, furniture and building		29		27
(b) Butchers, bakers, fishmongers, millers		21		7
(c) Engineers, engine-drivers, printers, shoemakers		9		10
(d) Clothiers, tailors		7		1
4. Major textiles	9		5	
(a) Foremen				1
(b) Weavers, spinners, calico printers, etc.		9		4
5. Unskilled	9		13	
	101		100	

Source: Figures based on data on fathers' occupations in Baptismal Register, John Street Relief/U.P. Church, Glasgow, SRO CH3/806/12.

The power of religion to reform was, for the churchgoing middle classes, apparently evident within congregational life. Urban society was a highly mobile one both spatially and socially: just as suburban movement became a permanent feature from the 1810s onwards, so was the upward social mobility of migrants and their offspring. Congregations were rarely if ever purely composed of the middle classes, but as towns and cities grew in size between 1750 and 1900 there was a strong tendency for congregations, especially of the dissenters, to become more socially differentiated. Table 7 indicates the dominance of skilled working men in John Street Relief Church in Glasgow in the 1820s; two-thirds of occupations on the baptismal roll were from this group. But within thirty years a significant shift had occurred. Skilled tradesmen fell to 45 per cent whilst middle-class groups rose from 17 to 37 per cent. One result was the creation of a mission congregation under the superintendence of the John Street kirk session. The growth of both the higher- and lower-middle classes in the John Street congregation was indicative of the tendency for newer congregations to rise in status as their members moved up the social scale in terms of occupation and prosperity. As a result dissenting churches, as edifices, developed rapidly between 1780

Table 8 Proportion of brides and grooms unable to sign marriage books in religious ceremonies, 1871 (%)

	Men	Women
United Presbyterian Church	3.8	11.8
Free Church	6.7	15.7
Church of Scotland	7.0	16.5
Episcopal Church	9.8	20.9
Roman Catholic Church	46.0	61.7

Source: Figures based on data in *Census 1871 (Scotland)*, vol. 1, xlii–xliii.

and 1890 in size, style and cost as congregations built new churches in progressively more suburban districts. The Secession congregation in Irvine in Ayrshire first assembled in 1807 in a back-street malt kiln, then moved in 1845 to a more pretentious church with a vestry and a hall, and after paying off the debts within a few years moved to another new church in 1862. In this way the United Presbyterian Church, which the bulk of the Secession and Relief Churches became in 1847, had in the later nineteenth century an overpowering air of commercial prosperity vastly different to the more puritanical and petit-bourgeois character of the urban Seceders at the start of the century. As one reflection of this, the highest rates of literacy amongst brides and grooms in 1871 were to be found with those marrying in United Presbyterian churches (see Table 8).

In an important study of Aberdeen, Allan MacLaren has demonstrated how increasing differentiation and social mobility within the middle classes was an instrumental factor in the formation of the Free Church in the city in the mid-nineteenth century. His analysis of the elders who left the Established Church at the Disruption of 1843 shows that an aspiring and socially dynamic breed of commission agents and merchants was crucial, for they were far more numerous amongst those who 'went out' than amongst those who stayed in. At the period of the Disruption this group was challenging the established middle classes of the city and the Established Church which they controlled. These 'insolent social upstarts' displayed their entrepreneurial vigour and recently acquired wealth by changing house and business very rapidly, moving westward within the city to new developments at some distance from the older and more staid middle-class streets. Their walkout at the Disruption was an integral feature of their emergence, their new Free churches being located beside their new residences. In the Victorian period, according to a local comment in 1902, 'the height of a merchant's ambition in Aberdeen was a house in Crown Street and a seat in the Free West Church'.[31]

A study of nine presbyterian congregations in Glasgow at the same period provides much support for MacLaren's analysis.[32] Peter Hillis found that lower-middle-class groups were more common amongst the dissenting churches (making up 19 per cent of the membership) than the Established churches (9 per cent). As in Aberdeen, Hillis found the kirk sessions of all the Glasgow congregations he studied dominated by the higher social groups. In the Established churches 71 per cent of elders were high-status middle class, 14 per cent low status, and only just over 2 per cent working class; in the dissenting churches 78 per cent of elders were high status, 19 per cent low status and 4 per cent working class. The eldership was in the nineteenth century, as it perhaps has always been in the cities, a preserve of those who had attained success in business and with it the standing and financial means with which to lead congregations.

But the authors of these two studies disagree fundamentally about the extent of middle-class dominance in the churches as a whole. MacLaren identifies kirk-session discipline as the key. He maintained that it was concerned especially with moral offences amongst the lower classes, and notably fornication and drunkenness. Whilst elders were liable to censure for business irregularities, few of the middle-class membership were disciplined or even investigated for moral offences. Hillis on the other hand sees church discipline as applied equally to middle- and working-class members, and more generally discounts the notion of working-class exclusion from the churches. But individual congregations varied enormously in social composition, even within the same denomination, and the social make-up of a congregation tended with time to rise. In such circumstances, it would be unwise to see the social composition of presbyterianism as static or uniform.

RELIGION AND THE MAKING OF THE SCOTTISH WORKING CLASSES

Allan MacLaren has argued from his research in Aberdeen that working-class church membership was low. He notes aspects of congregational management which deterred working-class admission: pew rents, the need for fine clothes, segregation of social classes between pews, and more generally a patronising and offensive bourgeois attitude towards lower-income groups evident in kirk-session discipline and elders' supervision of working-class members. He cites the case of a Free Church kirk session which denied communion to a member who had 'accommodated in her house, for a short time, a female of disreputable character'; in another instance an hotel waiter was told 'to abstain from such an objectionable occupation in future'.[33] MacLaren's work stresses both the repugnance of middle-class churchmen for working-class life and culture, and the role of the churches as a primary agency for extending bourgeois control over the proletariat.

Contemporary evidence from the period is not hard to find in support of MacLaren's general argument. The working classes tended to be progressively excluded from many city congregations as the building of new churches fell behind the rise in population between 1780 and 1850. In Edinburgh in the 1790s the Church of Scotland initiated separate evening services for servants and 'the common people', whilst in Glasgow between 1780 and 1820 special diets of worship were arranged for the working classes on Thursday and Sunday evenings. Even this division did not satisfy ministers and middle-class congregations who continuously asked Glasgow town council to discontinue the special services – mostly on grounds of hygiene. In the 1830s, many Established Church ministers identified rising seat rents as the cause of diminishing working-class adherence, and the inter-denominational Glasgow City Mission in 1826 observed that high seat rents could be the only explanation for the fact that one-quarter of all pews in the city were unoccupied. The process of social segregation was continuous throughout the century as new congregations were established and as the wealthier members moved on within a few decades to finer and more opulent churches. When, in the 1860s, the minister of Cambridge Street United Presbyterian Church in Glasgow led wealthy merchants and manufacturers to a more palatial church in the west end, a scribe chalked on the door of the new building on its opening day:

> This Church is not built for the poor and needy,
> But for the rich and Dr. Eadie.
> The rich may come in and take their seat,
> But the poor must go to Cambridge Street.[34]

But there is also considerable evidence of large working-class sections in city congregations. Peter Hillis's analysis of seven Glasgow congregations between 1845 and 1865 indicates an average working-class membership of 61 per cent. Established Church congregations had the highest proportion, averaging 79 per cent in three of the older parish churches in the city and long-settled suburbs; in four newer dissenting congregations the proportion was 54 per cent. Further division of the working-class membership into the skilled and unskilled showed that the former were more prominent in dissenting congregations (making up 80 per cent of the working-class communicants) than in Established Church congregations (where the figure was 69 per cent). The Royal Commission on Religious Instruction noted of Edinburgh in the mid-1830s that dissenting congregations were 'generally composed of the poor and working classes'.[35] Similarly in Glasgow the commissioners found that in all but the Episcopal churches and the older parish churches of the Establishment the city's congregations were 'composed, in great measure, of the poor and working classes, the proportion of these being in few cases below one-half, while in the congregations of the Dissenting denominations, it is, for the most part, above two-thirds'.[36] Yet by the 1860s and 1870s, many of these congregations – especially of the Secession and Relief Churches – were to have a reputation for wealth and solid middle-class status. Clearly, a significant social transformation occurred in many urban congregations during the first three-quarters of the nineteenth century.

The seeds for this change were evident in the Royal Commission's report in the 1830s. The commissioners found that all but the Baptist churches charged seat rents. In Edinburgh they noted that 'although 9–10ths of the Dissenters' seat-rents are above 5s. a-year, yet their Congregations are generally composed of the poor and working classes, and that the rate of seat-rent is in most cases fixed by vote of the congregation.' Furthermore, the Royal Commission remarked on a standard feature of seat-renting: namely, that lower-priced seats had a low occupancy rate compared to higher-priced seats. There was a 'dislike of the people to occupy low-priced or gratuitous sittings, avowedly set apart for the poor'. In part this was because these seats were of an 'inferior nature', being invariably located in the awkward back pews at the rear of the gallery; and in part because of reluctance of people to take seats which were given 'on sufferance, from which they are liable to be displaced at pleasure'. In Edinburgh's churches in 1836, 88 per cent of expensive pews priced between twenty and forty shillings were let; but this occupancy rate fell to 76 per cent for mid-priced seats between nine and eighteen shillings, and to 60 per cent for cheaper seats at between two and eight shillings.[37] A stigma attached to occupying low-priced and free seats, with the result that those amongst the lower-income groups who were drawn to church-going in the presbyterian churches tended to have strong economic aspirations and to be upwardly mobile in the social structure. The ability to pay for pew rents, and perhaps to forgo other expenditure, became a mark of those who wished to distance themselves from the 'rough' working class and to lay claim to social respectability.

The dissenting denominations appealed to artisans for a number of reasons. In the first place church accommodation was offered at a price they could afford and, as the Royal Commission pointed out, one that could often be decided by congregational democracy. In the 1830s, this meant that the more evangelical congregations tended to have lower seat rents, resulting in dissent being strongest in working-class districts. Another appeal for artisans was that the pricing system for seats in self-managing dissenting churches was the mechanism by which the lower working classes were excluded and for giving those congregations, before 1850 at least, a socially homogeneous composition and identity. In the Established churches in Edinburgh in the 1830s, 7 per cent of sittings were offered at the very low price of three shillings or less, whilst the Secession churches offered less than 1 per cent; more revealing is the fact that the occupancy rates for these cheap seats was over 50 per cent in the Establishment but only 3 per cent in the Secession. Dissenting culture in the cities was designed to demarcate between 'rough' and 'respectable', and the narrow range of seat prices reflected the high degree of social uniformity achieved in the first half of the nineteenth century. This social homogeneity was evident in the appeal of dissent to tradesmen like wrights, smiths, shoemakers and butchers, but also to shopkeepers, miners and metallurgical workers. Two large occupational groups in dissent before 1850 were the weavers and spinners, who were attracted not only to the Secession and Relief Churches but also to the Methodist Church (as in Kilsyth), the Baptist Church, the short-lived Chartist Church of the 1840s, and Irish immigrants to the Catholic Church.

As the industrial revolution moved in the 1840s and 1850s into the era of steam-power and heavy industry, skilled artisans became both more numerous and more conscious of their own identity as a social group. Sometimes referred to as 'the aristocracy of labour' in the mid-Victorian period, artisans were by no means all alike, but a culture of religious respectability was strong amongst them. They were particularly numerous in urban congregations of the Free Church. One such was John Sturrock, a millwright in Dundee who started a diary when he was in his mid-twenties so that 'I may be able to form an estimate of how I have spent my leisure time, whether I have been trifling it away or turning it to any particular advantage'. He recounts in daily entries the life of a fastidious, hard-working and (mostly) teetotal bachelor, given to church attendance usually twice every Sunday, and entertainment from 'crack' with friends, walks around Dundee and discreet courting of his future wife. Leisure time, by his own standards, had to be 'to advantage' which he got from reading *The English Mechanic* and attending drawing classes and religious lectures. At the time of writing his diary, he was 'sermon-tasting' widely amongst Dundee Free Church congregations, trying to decide which to join:

February 1865

Sat. 4. Spent the afternoon at the newspapers. Went in the town at half past six and got home again a little past eight. Then wrote a little and read a little at Scott's *Poems* before going to bed.

Sun. 5. Lay till nine o'clock as usual and went to Free St. Andrews in the forenoon and afternoon. Happened to see an old acquaintance, Bythinia Emers, at church in the forenoon, with whom I went along the Nethergate a bit. Went and heard the Rev. George Gilfillan's monthly lecture in the evening on the religious aspect of Ireland. Got home about eight o'clock and read a while at the *Sunday Magazine* before going to bed.

Mon. 6. Working till ten o'clock tonight and will be for all the week.

Sat. 11. Got off at two o'clock and spent the afternoon at the newspapers. Then went in the town and happened to meet Elizabeth Packman, with whom I went along to her mother's and stopped till about ten o'clock. Then took a look at Crabbe's *Poems* which I bought tonight and also a Valentine for somebody. Got to bed about twelve o'clock.

Sun. 12. Got up at half past eight, half an hour earlier than usual. Went to Free St. Andrews forenoon and afternoon, and heard a sermon in the evening by the Rev. Dr. McGavin on behalf of the Young Men's Christian Association on 'Young men – their Obligations and Blessings', and which the Rev. Doctor handled in a very eloquent and impressive manner. Happened to meet Helen Wright as I was coming home, with whom I turned and went a short way in the Nethergate. Got home a little before nine. Read a chapter and psalm and went to bed about ten.

Tues. 14. Took this evening to myself and went to the Scottish Reformation Society's annual festival or soiree, where I enjoyed myself nicely and was so highly pleased with the proceedings and object of the society that I intend to join it the first opportunity. Got home about eleven o'clock.[38]

Sturrock exemplifies, even if in extreme form, the respectable artisan, frugal and thrifty, shocked at the smell of alcohol and tobacco smoke, for whom Sabbath sermons were stimulants to personal reflection and, occasionally, self-remonstrance. Piety and churchgoing were pivotal in his life and culture, and in October 1865 he finally joined Free St Enoch's Church. Another young artisan in the same decade, Peter Taylor, was a newly-married railway engineer in Kilmarnock, living in a tenement of young couples working in the same industry. 'Every house nearly having little children,' he recalled, 'we could not go to the church prayer meeting, so we had one of our own in each other's houses week about. I have carried my first-born in his cradle upstairs, and Maggie coming up behind with the Bible. Ach, it was not only grand, it was glorious.'[39]

Despite the importance of prospering artisans in the presbyterian churches, it would be wrong to overlook the sustained popularity of religious culture amongst more depressed working-class occupations. Alexander Somerville, the son of a Borders farm servant, moved to Edinburgh in 1828 and found work as a sawyer. Though clearly a cynic about ecclesiastical reputation, he nonetheless found religious 'treats' to be entertainment:

> One of the chief intellectual treats which I enjoyed was that of going, on Sundays, to hear the most celebrated of the Edinburgh ministers preach. I was disappointed in every effort to hear Dr Chalmers ... But the greatest entertainment of an intellectual nature was enjoyed in attending the sittings and listening to the debates of the Synod of the United Secession Church, which met in May. On more than one occasion their debates lasted until daylight in the morning ... and [I] proceeded from the gallery where I had listened direct to work in the saw-pit ... I remained there ... from the fact that many of the debaters were ministers ... whose reputations for piety and ministerial ability stood high, and whose very names were always uttered by my father and others like him with accompanying expressions of veneration; and whom I could now look upon face to face, at least I could look down from the gallery upon their heads, grey heads, bald heads, and wigs; and as they debated I wondered at the grey heads, the bald heads, and the wigs.[40]

Even for cynics, there was a sense of being a party to a common presbyterian culture, irrespective of social class. Nor was the religiosity of the common people purely an 'intellectual' one. Covenanting and predestinarian theology could mix in a volatile cocktail with salvationist evangelicalism (sometimes promoted by American evangelists) to produce strong religious feelings and outbursts of revivalism. As early as 1807 a clergyman wrote: 'In Scotland weavers in Glasgow, Paisley, Perth, Dundee, etc., are among the first to join any new sect set up, the effect no doubt of their sedentary life and the melancholy monotony of their occupation.' Thus, he went on, 'where a great number of weavers are gathered, there new and gloomy notions of religion prevail'.[41] The forlorn and self-remonstrating attitude of some working-class congregations produced a reverence for covenanting history and at least a partial adherence to predestinarianism. Belief in the Elect became a compensation for perceived oppression and economic distress, especially amongst occupations prone to cyclical or seasonal depression. A Glasgow weaver's poem of 1838 went: 'Religion cheers the weaver in his cot/ ... And charms with heavenly hope our humble lot.'[42] Christian Watt, the fisherwoman from the north-east, went through a 'crisis of life' in the 1850s as catastrophe piled upon catastrophe: she lost five brothers at sea, open fields were enclosed by large landowners, fish prices plummeted, and she became pregnant out of wedlock with the likely prospect of being summoned before the Established kirk session on a charge of fornication. Her memoirs recall her anger. She told the landowner and his wife: 'How any of the wealthy ... have the sheer hard neck to enter any church and call themselves christians! God will spew them out of his mouth.' Though a Congregationalist, she planned to 'wreck the session' by demanding to appear 'in the body of the kirk not the vestry', and then 'start on one elder, a Fraserburgh businessman who had in the past been known to frequent bawdy houses in Aberdeen'. Writing later in her life, her faith in redemption was placed in a proletarian predestinarianism: 'Many are called but few are chosen; before your first sark [shirt] gets over your head God knows who are going to be his.'[43]

At the same time, however, the differences between Arminianism and predestinarianism could become blurred, in depressed communities and occupations as in prospering ones. Conversion experiences – Christian Watt had two – became increasingly of a salvationist variety, and revivals were especially common before 1859 amongst weavers, miners and ironworkers in small industrial towns. In Christian Watt's Congregationalist denomination the debate on the extent of the Atonement came into the open in the mid 1840s with the Arminians defecting in large numbers to the newly-formed Evangelical Union. But in a more general sense, predestinarianism waned amidst the growing evangelical fervour of the times. A revival in 1859–62 was particularly important in this respect, attracting mass assemblies of the working classes: allegedly 15,000 to a rally at the mining village of Dreghorn in Ayrshire and 10,000 to another at Huntly in the north. Workers started prayer meetings in factories: notably amongst female powerloom weavers at Bridgeton and Pollokshaws in Glasgow but also amongst railwaymen, policemen and others. Revivalist preaching quickly became a norm for evangelical ministers, though the quality of the methods was highly variable. A Church of Scotland minister, not unsympathetic towards revivalism, was critical of the style of a Free Church colleague at work in Lauder in Berwickshire in 1859:

> Instead of preaching the Gospel he indulged in realistic descriptions of revival scenes where people were 'struck down', and strong men 'felled to the ground like oxen' . Following on this, he asked all to engage in prayer. For a few minutes he remained silent, until one felt the tension of suppressed excitement, and then he began, 'O Lord, *do* it – do it now.'[44]

Mission stations mushroomed in working-class districts of the larger cities: the most famous perhaps were the Wynd Mission in Glasgow and the Carrubber's Close Mission in Edinburgh. But these were merely the frontrunners in a missionary explosion amongst the Scottish industrial classes with which the evangelical churches – mainly the Free, United Presbyterian, Methodist and Congregationalist Churches – tried to keep abreast.

From church reports in the 1860s and 1870s, it is difficult to avoid the conclusion that working-class interest in organised Protestantism was growing and being better satisfied with faster church building, a phenomenally-wide range of religious voluntary organisations, and more attractive religious worship. American evangelists such as Charles Finney and Edward Payson Hammond introduced the distinctive revival service: short sermon, joyous hymns, and the call to the 'anxious' to come forward. The stress in working-class presbyterianism shifted markedly to the sureness of salvation and the joyousness of the conversion experience, and away from an older emphasis on prolonged and serious contemplation of sin. Preaching of hell-fire and damnation diminished, giving way to the American-style offer of the open gospel exemplified in the preaching of Dwight Moody in the 1870s, 1880s and early 1890s. Between 1873 and 1880, working-class mission congregations urged the kirk sessions of their parent middle-class churches to 'sanction the introduction of instrumental music' in the form of the harmonium popularised by Ira Sankey.

Religious voluntary organisations for the working classes also grew enormously from the 1870s. The Bands of Hope for instance offered a new and partially secularised version of the Sunday school which attracted a mostly proletarian membership, whilst Sunday-school scholars were, between 1870 and 1890, more and more the children of middle-class church members. The Bands provided not only a teetotal religion but 'respectable' leisure. In Dundee the Band of Hope organised a whole range of pursuits including marches, parades, rambles and river excursions, and through such secular attractions continued to grow: the number of Bands in Scotland rose from seven in 1871 to 570 in 1887 and to over 700 in 1908 with 147,000 members. The Catholic Church had its own League of the Cross which, despite a much smaller juvenile section, had a membership of over 30,000 in the Archdiocese of Glasgow by the end of the century. In all denominations, the trend in the last quarter of the nineteenth century was towards meeting all the leisure needs of young and old alike: through respectable activities in temperance pubs and hotels; Christian reading-rooms and libraries; football competitions organised by denominations, Sunday-school unions, the Boys' Brigade and temperance organisations; outings and picnics for the under-twelves; militaristic and jingoistic uniformed organisations for youths both male and female; and for older youths and adults prayer meetings, gospel assemblies (both temperance and ordinary), games rooms (in Catholic churches) and woman's guilds. Though caused by the revivalism of the 1860s and 1870s, the explosion of religious leisure harmonised working-class religion to an increasingly secular world of shorter working hours, the half-day and then full-day Saturday off. By combining the offer of sport and pastime with an evangelisation effort unmatched before or since, the Scottish working classes were subjected between 1870 and 1890 to the peak of the Chalmers 'aggressive' system.

The growth in the churches' outreach to the working classes included the Catholic community. The essence of the Catholic Church's problem was keeping pace with Irish immigration to the new industrial districts of west-central Scotland, and there was a distinct shortage of chapels and priests in the early decades of the nineteenth century. But in the second half of the century enormous strides were made in building chapels and in recruiting priests, of whom an increasing proportion were from Ireland or the Irish community rather than from the Catholic areas of the Highlands and the north-east. The result was a substantial rise in religious observance amongst Catholics leading to, by the middle of the twentieth century, their predominance in most Lowland districts with high rates of churchgoing. It is commonly observed that the Catholic immigrants were uniformly poor and that they joined the lower echelons of the Scottish working classes. There were certainly high proportions of Catholics in unskilled and low-status skilled occupations like navvying, labouring, spinning, weaving and mining. Perhaps a quarter of weavers were Catholic after 1815, and there were large numbers in unskilled metal-working. Whilst upward social mobility by Irish Catholics has probably been underestimated in Victorian Scotland, it remains likely that they were more uniformly proletarian in character than any other religious group. This certainly seems to be the conclusion from Table 8 (p. 109) which shows that shortly before the introduction of compulsory education Catholic brides and grooms had significantly higher rates of illiteracy than those in the main Protestant churches.

But it would be wrong to regard the Irish Catholic community as uniformly poor, and equally wrong to overlook the extent to which the Church induced a social (and ethnic) hierarchy amongst its active worshippers. Many thousands of Catholics paid seat rents, in some cases substantial sums on a par with presbyterians. A decade after its opening in 1816, St Andrew's Church (now Cathedral) in Glasgow was raising £600 a year from seat rents. Native recusant Catholics of aristocratic pedigree were paying as much as £5 for a seat in an Edinburgh chapel in 1815, but even ordinary worshippers at Glenlivet in the north-east were in 1829 paying between four and twelve shillings a year – an identical range of prices to that found in most Seceder congregations. Pew-renting spread quickly amongst Catholic chapels in the 1810s and 1820s, and was used by many Scots-born priests to segregate the 'respectable' from the 'rough'. A priest in Paisley was so strict over non-payment of rents in the early 1810s that many worshippers stopped attending, and in response to the problem Bishop Scott of Glasgow suggested in 1812 that 'seat-minders' be appointed to regulate the immigrants: 'The Irish must be treated in a different manner from our Scots people, or they never can be helped on the way to salvation.'⁴⁵ Friction between Irish and Scots, both laity and clergy, persisted until at least the 1860s, but in industrial districts the Irish character of the Church came to dominate, leaving only northern dioceses with a strong tradition of native Scottish Catholicism.

Assimilation to urban and industrial society brought increasing attunement to the ideals and values of self-help and 'improvement', and created in the Catholic Church virtues and institutions very similar to those in the presbyterian churches. Churchgoing was increasingly associated with prosperity, fomenting the practices of pew-renting and of wearing 'Sunday best'. An Ayrshire priest noted in the 1830s: 'The Irish will not come out on Sunday and go to chapel unless they can be clothed and appear like natives. They will not go in ragged clothes as they went in Ireland.'⁴⁶ Poverty was an important factor in keeping Catholic attendances in Glasgow low between 1830 and 1860. There were other signs of assimilation to the new urbanism. In 1842 the Catholic teetotal pioneer Father Mathew administered the pledge on Glasgow Green to a mixed assembly of Protestants and Catholics, reputedly 40,000 in number. But the temperance cause seems to have languished in the Scottish Catholic Church during the mid-Victorian decades only to be revived after 1887. In the large Archdiocese of Glasgow in that year, there were only twenty-two branches of the Church's temperance organisation the League of the Cross, with a membership probably in the region of 1,000. As a result, Archbishop Eyre organised an executive committee of laity and clergy which within four years had created an extra 106 branches and a total membership of 30,000. Games rooms were a common feature of chapel rectories by the 1870s, providing 'respectable' alternatives to the public house and street gambling; in many cases, though, gambling (especially cards) and boisterousness were merely switched to church premises, and, as one priest noted, the men 'would play at their games even if Benediction was given in the Church, near them'.⁴⁷

Whilst promoting the ideals of urban society and thus Irish integration into the industrial milieu, the Church came to represent a wider segregation of Catholics from Scottish presbyterian life and culture. The Church formed the core of a set of distinctively Catholic cultural associations and practices. Separate Catholic schools developed during the century, and the Church provided its own versions of Protestant organisations like the Boys' Brigade. Observance of saints' days became in the presbyterian environment an act which marked out Catholics in Scotland in a much more prominent way than it did in Anglican England. Irish nationalism, though discouraged by Church authorities, was promoted by some priests and in a more general fashion could not fail to be associated with Catholicism. High degrees of Catholic inter-marriage (80 per cent in Greenock in 1855) and residential segregation in 'wee Dublins' slowed down social assimilation. Economic assimilation was restrained by concentration in certain occupations, factories and pits. In 1851, 52 per cent of unskilled workers in Greenock were Irish-born, and amongst dock labourers this rose to 65 per cent; even forty years later nearly half the unskilled in the town were Irish-born, which taken with second- and third-generation immigrants probably created an occupation dominated by Catholics.[48] In Coatbridge in 1861, 60 per cent of unskilled metal workers were Irish. Moreover, partly through the use of immigrants as strike-breakers and partly through sectarianism, Catholics were generally isolated from the trades-union and Labour movements before 1890. The hostility of both middle- and working-class presbyterians, and discrimination in employment, lay at the root of Catholic isolation. Antagonism between 'Proddie' and 'Pape' was not new to Scotland, but the arrival of Catholic and Protestant Irish after 1800 brought an enlivened culture of sectarianism. Working-class Protestant missionaries such as the inimical Harry Long of Glasgow agitated for resistance against the attempts 'to bring this land under the sway of the Romish Pontiff, and wrest from us the dear bought and invaluable liberties which we possess'.[49] Many presbyterian ministers, prominent laity and manufacturing companies subscribed to sectarian missions in the second half of the nineteenth century, and sectarianism developed into an intrinsic element of the industrial culture of Scotland. This culture was not to diminish after the 1880s but rather harden, and whilst it was not entirely unique within mainland Britain, it had none the less an unmatched muscularity and transcendence of social class.

The working classes were a large and varied component of Scottish urban society in the nineteenth century. This section has stressed the ways in which the working classes participated in religion, but the Victorian middle classes and the churches – mainly the presbyterian ones – were obsessed with the 'unchurched', the 'lapsed masses', the 'sunken portion'. They spent vast time, energy and money on the great 'home mission' in seeking – from their point of view – to 'reclaim' the 'lapsed' to organised religion. Yet, the evidence clearly demonstrates that the Scottish proletariat were not uniformly, nor even generally, alienated from religion. If the vast majority of the working classes did not go to church, it remained the case that the vast majority of the churchgoers were working-class. The upper working classes seem to have been the largest single social group in presbyterian congregations throughout the period, and the unskilled lower working class still laid strong cultural claims to their religious heritage. Victorian churchmen had a tendency to perceive those they preached to as 'middle-class' since they strove to dress appropriately, to pay their seat rents and contributions to church funds, and more generally to uphold the values and ideals which sanctioned elevation in the society. It was unskilled occupations like 'labourer' and 'carter' which tended to be grossly under-represented in lists of presbyterian church members. Church-going was undoubtedly low where they were most congregated in 'slum' districts and in new industrial villages as yet unreached by organised religion. One commentator remarked in the 1820s of one community outside Edinburgh: 'Demand and supply were admirably well-balanced in the village of Niddry: there was no religious instruction, and no wish or desire for it.'[50] But social mobility, especially from one generation to the next, and increasing evangelisation and church-building in the period from 1850 to 1890, meant that opportunities to gain admission to a church were widening as the nineteenth century progressed.

The first hundred years of industrialisation and urbanisation had produced remarkable changes in the role of religion. In both town and country the advent of dynamic social capitalism had dissolved the communal bonds which held the people within the ambit of the Established Church, and local elites had to acknowledge that their measured manipulation of popular religion through the board of heritors, the kirk session and pew-control was redundant. It was redundant not because religion had become less popular but because of the reverse. The new urban society had spawned religious values which were adaptable to different status groups and cultural environments. On the surface these values constituted unifying ties between churches and social classes, but their relevance lay in adaptability to different work and life experiences. Adherence to sabbatarianism, teetotalism and self-help might be shared by miners, millworkers and wealthy merchants, but such virtues were as much statements of group independence and solidarity as of inter-class discourse and unity. Thus, it is quite legitimate to regard religion as providing an ideology of social uniformity and as offering a venue for social contest. But this did not cause proletarian piety to wither. Those rejected as not 'respectable' by churches, and even by peers as was Christian Watt, did not then reject the values by which they had been adjudged failures. The judges became in Christian's words 'that bunch of hypocrites' and were the unworthy purveyors of a stolen heritage and culture. 'You missionaries tell us that carters and factory lassies hae souls as well as ither folk,' said one Glasgow slum dweller to an evangeliser in the 1850s: 'For my pairt I aye thocht they had, – why is it, man, you canna tell us something we dinna ken?'[51] For those of the lower working class and the poor, with little or no access to economic and social 'improvement', resentment bred fierce alienation from patronising proselytisation. In that particular form of alienation lay a threat for the future of the churches.

NOTES

1. *Free Church Magazine*, August 1847, p. 250.
2. T. Chalmers, *A Sermon delivered in the Tron Church on the occasion of the death of Princess Charlotte* (Glasgow, 1817), p. 31.
3. T. Chalmers, *The Christian and Civic Economy of Large Towns* (Glasgow, 1821), p. 342.
4. J. de Vries, *European Urbanisation 1500–1800* (London, 1984), pp. 39, 45.
5. *OSA*, vol. 6, p. 609.
6. Ibid., vol. 8, p. 292.
7. Ibid., vol. 5, p. 535.
8. *Scots Magazine*, February 1787, p. 99.
9. R. A. Cage and E. O. A. Checkland, 'Thomas Chalmers and urban poverty: the St. John's experiment in Glasgow 1819–1837' *Philosophical Journal*, vol. 12 (1976); see also S. J. Brown, 'The Disruption and urban poverty: Thomas Chalmers and the West Port operation in Edinburgh 1844–47', *RSCHS*, vol. 20 (1978).
10. A. Ranken, *A Letter Addressed to the Rev. Dr. Chalmers ...* (Glasgow, 1830), pp. 12–13, 18.
11. R. Buchanan, *The City's Spiritual Wants* (Glasgow, 1871), p. 6.
12. Quoted in N. L. Walker, *Robert Buchanan D.D. An Ecclesiastical Biography* (London, 1877), pp. 511–13.
13. *Glasgow Herald*, 26 April 1850; Glasgow Town Council minutes 7 and 28 March and 25 April 1850, GCA c.1.1.65; *Scottish National Sabbath School Union, Annual Report*, 1905, p. 21; the Public Houses (Scotland) Act, 1853 (known as the Forbes Mackenzie Act).
14. C. J. A. Robertson, 'Early Scottish railways and the observance of the sabbath', *SHR*, vol. 57 (1978).
15. M. Atkinson, *Local Government in Scotland* (Edinburgh, 1904), pp. 160–1.
16. C. G. Brown, 'The costs of pew-renting: church management, church-going and social class in nineteenth-century Glasgow', *Journal of Ecclesiastical History*, vol. 38 (1987); J. Begg, *Seat Rents Brought to the Test of Scripture ...* (Edinburgh, 1838), pp. 45–6, 68–9.
17. H. Miller, *Edinburgh and its Neighbourhood* (London and Edinburgh, 1875), p. 222.
18. T. Chalmers, *Christian and Civic Economy*, p. 25.
19. S. J. D. Green, *Religion in the Age of Decline; Organisation and Experience in Industrial Yorkshire 1870–1920* (Cambridge, 1996), pp. 181–329.
20. *Autobiography of a Scotch Lad* (Glasgow, 1887), p. 30.
21. T. Chalmers, *Christian and Civic Economy*, pp. 113, 129.
22. *Glasgow Religious Tract Society. Annual Report 1815*, p. 5.
23. Glasgow City Mission, *[First] Annual Report*, 1827, p. 3.
24. J. G. Paton, *Missionary to the Hebrides: An Autobiography* (London, 1889), pp. 60–1.
25. *Wynd Journal*, 22 October 1859; United Presbyterian Church, Presbytery of Glasgow minutes 26 September 1859, SRO, CH3/ 146/52; R. Buchanan, *Assembly Addresses* (Edinburgh, 1860), p. 13.

26. R. Buchanan et al, *Spiritual Destitution of the Masses in Glasgow* ... (Edinburgh, 1851), p. 9.

27. J. C. Gibson (ed.), *Diary of Sir Michael Connal* (Glasgow, 1895), p. 24.

28. Ibid., p. 66.

29. Quoted in W. Grant, *Edward Bayley: His Work Among Young Men* (Edinburgh, 1913), p. 201.

30. J. G. Paton, *Missionary to the Hebrides*, pp. 59–60.

31. Quoted in A. A. MacLaren, *Religion and Social Class* (London and Boston, 1974), p. 82.

32. P. Hillis, 'Presbyterianism and social class in mid-nineteenth century Glasgow: a study of nine churches', *Journal of Ecclesiastical History*, vol. 32 (1981), pp. 47–64.

33. Quoted in MacLaren, op. cit., p. 129.

34. Quoted in Hillis, op. cit., p. 54.

35. Royal Commission on Religious Instruction, Scotland, First Report, *BPP* (1837), xxi, p. 29.

36. Ibid., Second Report, *BPP* (1837–8), xxxii, 17.

37. Quotations from, and figures calculated from data in, First Report of Commissioners for Inquiry into Religious Instruction, *BPP* 1837, xxx, pp. 26–7, 29.

38. C. Whatley (ed.), *The Diary of John Sturrock, Millwright, Dundee 1864–5* (East Linton, 1996), pp. 29, 51–2.

39. Peter Taylor, *Autobiography* (Paisley, 1903), p. 121.

40. A. Somerville, *The Autobiography of a Working Man* (London, orig. 1848, 1967 ed.), pp. 72–3.

41. James Hall, quoted in D. B. Murray, 'The social and religious origins of Scottish non-presbyterian Protestant dissent from 1730–1800', unpub. Ph.D. thesis, University of St Andrews, 1977, p. 214.

42. Quoted in N. Murray, *The Scottish Hand Loom Weavers 1790–1850* (Edinburgh, 1978), p. 165.

43. D. Fraser (ed.), *The Christian Watt Papers* (Edinburgh, 1983), pp. 24, 56, 68, 93.

44. Quoted in S. Smith, *Donald Macleod of Glasgow* (London, 1926), p. 76.

45. C. Johnson, *Developments in the Roman Catholic Church in Scotland, 1789–1829* (Edinburgh, 1983), pp. 142–5.

46. Quoted in A. Ross, 'The development of the Scottish Catholic community 1878–1978', *Innes Review,* vol. xxiv, (1978), p. 33.

47. Information on temperance in this paragraph, including the quotation from Father M. I. Dempsey, was compiled from materials in 'Temperance' box, Roman Catholic Archdiocese of Glasgow Archive.

48. R. D. Lobban, 'The Irish community in Greenock in the nineteenth century', *Irish Geography*, vol. 6 (1971).

49. *Glasgow Protestant Missionary Society, Annual Report* (1880), p. 5.

50. H. Miller, *My Schools and Schoolmasters* (Edinburgh, 1856), p. 312.

51. J. McCaffrey (ed.), *Glasgow 1858: Shadow's Midnight Scenes and Social Photographs* (Glasgow, 1976), p. 14.

CHAPTER 6

THE 'SOCIAL QUESTION' 1890–1939: THE CRISIS OF RELIGIOUS IDEOLOGY

THE DECAY OF EVANGELICALISM

In 1886 the Evangelistic Association of Queen's Park Free Church in the growing middle-class suburbs on the south side of Glasgow was setting about with enthusiasm the task newly assigned to it by the city's inter-denominational Home Mission Union – the monthly task of visiting every family in its small mission district a mile away in the working-class Gorbals. This was the decade in which Thomas Chalmers' 'aggressive system' reached its peak of operation; so many congregational and city missionary organisations were at work that Scottish cities were divided into mission districts of as little as 180 families. The Queen's Park Association had a good band of more than forty visitors drawn from the church membership, working in tandem with other agencies of the congregation: Sunday schools, the Band of Hope, the Penny Savings Bank and the tract distribution service. But things started to go wrong. By 1892 attendances by district visitors were well down, threatening the whole operation, and in order to preserve its work the Association amalgamated its mission district with that of another congregation, Renfield Free Church. Three years later the tract distributors of Queen's Park had all but given up, and the Evangelistic Association took over the service to prevent it from collapsing. But the Association itself was in a bad way. It had no funds to buy hymn books for poorer worshippers at mission services, and in 1896 there was such a desperate shortage of voluntary workers that no planning meetings were held for ten months. By 1900 the organisation was in tatters. The secretary was accused of not doing his job, the treasurer had no idea of the income and expenditure for the year, and the annual subscription to the Home Mission Union had not been paid. The missionary stated openly that there was much to discourage the volunteers, and in apparent acknowledgement of decay, the Association's minutes petered out ten months later.[1]

From the end of the 1880s a crisis in evangelicalism threatened the urban churches. This crisis was not unique to Scotland. Its urban shape

found in Glasgow, Edinburgh and Dundee has been widely documented
in London, Reading, Sheffield, Halifax and other cities south of the
border, and many of the themes – such as changing leisure habits, the
rise of socialism and the labour movement – had international bearings.[2]
There were many ramifications, and they were felt most acutely in the
powerhouse of nineteenth-century religion. the dissenting evangelical
churches. For, above all, this was a bourgeois crisis of faith – not in
Christianity, but in Christian mission. There was an outward preser-
vation of the evangelical values of self-help, thrift and 'respectability',
and if pressed on the point there would probably have been few in the
middle orders in society who would have openly disavowed evangelical
orthodoxy. But the manner and extent of its social transmission, its place
in the middle-class firmament, and the goals it was expected to achieve
in the society of late Victorian and Edwardian Scotland did change very
significantly.

The decay of evangelicalism had a theological and intellectual dimension. The dominance of evangelical enterprise in the early and mid-
Victorian years had rested on certainty not only in the social relevance of
evangelical visions but in their uniqueness for reforming society and
removing social ills. Evangelicalism had operated, and could only operate
with any real power, as a single hegemonic ideology unchallenged by
contesting ideologies. Because of this, it had been able to incorporate
methods of social reform like the municipalisation of public utilities, the
compulsory purchase of slum property, and increased state spending
generally which in the later twentieth century was alien to modern
evangelicalism. Even at their most conservative in 'religious' matters,
pre-1880 evangelicals were radicals and innovators in social policy. The
Rev. James Begg, severe Calvinist and scourge of worship reformers in
the Free Church, was yet the leading Scottish advocate, lay or clerical, of
municipal and philanthropic housing improvement, writing in 1866 that
the sixth and eighth commandments placed 'our obligation to promote
sanitary and social reform on the strongest foundation on which they can
rest, viz., the direct commandment of God.'[3] Not only did this type of
evangelical call to 'secular' reform tend to disappear after 1880, but the
certainty of the biblical imprimatur for it withered.

From within the churches, evangelical certainty was dissolving because
of the cumulative effect of liberalisation of presbyterian standards, the
modernisation of worship, and most crucially because of the inexorable
advance of biblical criticism. Although Darwinism had been perceived as
a threat to evangelical Christianity by Dwight Moody who had preached
and written against it during his Scottish tour of 1873–4, Scottish popular
opinion was little affected by evolutionism until the 1890s. In the same

way, secularism was comparatively weak in Scotland, being as far as presbyterians were concerned not a rational and ordered 'unbelief' but rather a pragmatic opposition to religious traditions. The irony was that the publicisers of evolution theory and its undermining of Biblical truth in Scotland were not initially scientists or rationalists but presbyterian ministers. It was the 'Higher Critics' of the theological colleges, especially in the evangelical Free and United Presbyterian Churches, who absorbed Darwinist ideas and tried to adapt biblical interpretation to modern science. It was doubt within the churches themselves between 1890 and 1910 which caused public debate, press commentary, and a popular literature described by one commentator as 'atheistical sixpenny books at railway stalls'. One book dating from 1906, entitled *The Religious Doubts of Common Men*, takes the form of a correspondence between a poorly-educated Aberdeenshire farmer of sixty-five years of age and an educated lawyer conversant with recent publications in Bible research. The farmer writes to his old school chum in the hope that he will not 'flee up in a panic like oor meenister when I touch him up on the Higher Creeticism':

> My reading has been limited to the daily newspaper, an agricultural periodical, and a Sunday magazine. But I have read enough and I have heard enough to satisfy myself how great a change has taken place since I was a boy in the view which all educated people, and even the ministers of the Gospel, take with reference to the Bible, and the very foundations of the Christian religion. I am indeed in sore perplexity. My faith in the truth of all that I was taught in childhood and youth, as to the history of the world, as to the five books of Moses, as to the inspiration of the sacred writings, and even as to the New Testament and our blessed Lord and Master Himself, has been so shaken that I do not know what to believe ... I long for a simple faith, which I can hold firmly by when death approaches me. It maddens me to think that I may be taken away surrounded by doubt and darkness. I get no help whatever from the minister of this parish ... all that he can say is that we are passing through a transition period, as he calls it, that we at present see darkly and imperfectly, and that by and by the light will break in upon us and faith revive.[4]

Such unease did not necessarily create widespread unbelief, but tended rather, during a period when popular Christianity was charged with doubt, to undermine confidence in Christian values as an agent of social and individual improvement. The first casualty was not churchgoing but the spreading of the Word – the mission to the 'unchurched'.

Between the 1850s and the 1880s middle-class 'pastimes' had been centred on the promotion of 'improving' agencies – on propagandisation rather than passive pursuits. The middle classes of the mid-Victorian period had gone into the slums and evangelised the working classes. Those who had developed into wealthy businessmen and entrepreneurs had gone on to act as patrons and benefactors of missions and religious voluntary organisations, becoming the 'vice-presidential class'[5] of religious organisations – the trustees and chairmen. The lower ranks of the middle classes acted as Sunday-school teachers, Band of Hope leaders and mission-district visitors. What occurred between the 1880s and the outbreak of the First World War was the withdrawal of both these groups from evangelisation.

The withdrawal of the 'vice-presidential class' was caused by the changing nature of industrial organisation in the late nineteenth century. Family firms outgrew the single factory where the owner had combined business management with patronage of community and church organisations as industry concentrated in larger, often limited-liability firms with impersonal management. A celebrated example was John Campbell White, Lord Overtoun (1834–1908), who in the 1860s inherited a booming chrome manufacturing concern at Shawfield near Glasgow. He built up and broadened his business interests, as well as his philanthropic and religious undertakings, becoming amongst other things a major benefactor of the Free Church (paying for the erection of churches and the stipends of ministers and missionaries) and of religious organisations like the Glasgow United Evangelistic Association, the Bible Training Institute and the Glasgow Medical Missionary Society (of each of which he was president), and the National Bible Society, the Colportage Society and the Boys' Brigade (of each of which he was vice-president). During a strike at the chrome factory in 1899, Keir Hardie lambasted Lord Overtoun for the poor health conditions there, the low wages and long hours worked by his employees, and for the hypocrisy of a self-proclaimed Sabbatarian making Sunday a day of labour. Overtoun and the Free Church were embarrassed, but Overtoun's defence was that he was no longer active in management, having moved to distant Dunbartonshire and devolved responsibility to two nephews. Overtoun was an evangelical of the old breed, a man who had conducted his own Bible class for many years, but his nephews did not follow his evangelical example. Another member of the 'vice-presidential' class was Sir Michael Connal (1817–93) whom we encountered in the previous chapter – a Glasgow merchant and head of a shipping company who, like Overtoun, was a prominent member of the Free Church with a particular interest in education. Inspired by Thomas Chalmers, he had operated Bible classes for youths in the east end of Glasgow for much of the Victorian period, confronting what he described as the 'roughness' and 'low domestic state' of the working classes; it was, he recorded, 'wholesome but not always pleasing to visit the poor'. But in the early 1890s, near the end of his life, he perceived the fundamental collapse of the evangelical design. His Spoutmouth Bible Institute was failing to attract working-class lads, and in a mood of depression in 1892 he wrote in his diary: 'The "Spout" in a state of transition – the future is very dark – I believe it has done good.'[6]

The withdrawal of the 'vice-presidential' governors from the evangelical mission was matched further down the social scale. The late nineteenth century witnessed a tremendous expansion of white-collar occupations in both public and private sectors. Like earlier generations of presbyterian dissenters, these 'new' middle classes were upwardly mobile, aggressively 'respectable', and were often the children of dissenting skilled working-class parents. But unlike their parents, they found little with which to identify in fading ecclesiastical disputes like the Disruption a half century earlier. They were profoundly *petit-bourgeois* or lower-middle class, and more keen to distance themselves from proletarian society than to reform it. It was this social group that ended evangelicalism's hegemonic grip of Scottish urban society. Starting in the late 1870s, they began to migrate from inner-city districts to new suburban estates of spacious terraced housing and elegant tenement flats: suburbs like Edinburgh's Marchmont and Morningside, and Glasgow's Hyndland, Jordanhill, Cathcart, Pollokshields and Bearsden. The dissenting churches, and especially the Free Church, responded: in Glasgow alone between 1895 and 1900, the Free Church built thirteen new churches and the United Presbyterians six, whilst the Church of Scotland had a net loss of one. The result in the dissenting churches was burgeoning suburban churches and ailing inner-city ones. The middle-class exodus left many churches in central urban districts in a parlous state by the late 1890s and brought the threat of widespread congregational insolvency. The result was very sudden pressure in the 1890s for denominational union between the Free and U.P. churches, and when union was achieved in 1900 a wave of rationalising closures of churches followed: within months fourteen congregations in Glasgow had merged and a further set of closures ensued two years later.

The suburban exodus of the 1880s, 1890s and 1900s changed the nature of bourgeois religion. The middle classes became commuters on the new trams, retreating from the inner-city areas their parents had evangelised. The suburban churches symbolised their prosperity and their cultural concerns, with new-fangled church halls constructed to act as the busy recreation centres of suburban leisure. Pursuits and organisations catered for all ages and tastes. Religious leisure was moving rapidly away from being 'useful' or, as John Sturrock the Dundee millwright had put it in 1865, 'to advantage', and towards petty amusement and self-indulgence. One United Free Church minister in 1901 mocked a new Christian agency arrived from America – the 'candy-pull': 'This agency, if that be the correct word, is a party of young men and women who meet for the purpose of pulling candy.' He abhorred what it represented:

> The centre of thought has, in fact, shifted ... from the worship of God to the service of men ... visible in the building, more concert-room than church, where a number of good people meet in high spirits and in kindly fellowship to move one another to good works, and to sing hymns. The ancient fear of God seems to have departed entirely ... a Christian will not need to go outside the Church for culture or amusement. If he wants relaxation, entertainments must be provided for him at his Church, so that he need not go into worldly society ... His literary and debating society and drawing-room and concert must be under one roof ... The Church triumphed by her faith ... if she sinks into a place of second-rate entertainment, then it would be better that her history should close ...[7]

Suburban churches of the 1890s and 1900s were built with multiple church halls – as many as five – to cater for the new plethora of pastimes. At St Matthew's Church of Scotland in Morningside in Edinburgh, the following activities were on offer: Sunday schools with 441 children, five Bible classes with 120 teenagers, Young Men's Guild (with Fellowship and other sections) with 202 members, Woman's Guild with 463 members and ten different activities, a Self-Help Society, junior and senior Literary Societies (with drama sections), Golf Clubs for men and ladies with over a hundred members, together with curling, holiday 'retreats' and a clutch of summer picnics. The minister of this congregation regarded these activities 'as links in the chain of full Church membership'.[8] But there was one stark difference between the associational ideal in St Matthew's and that in inner city congregations like Free St Mary's, Govan, cited in the previous chapter: the former was aimed virtually entirely at the middle-class members of the congregation and their children. What was entirely absent was mission work in working-class areas.

So, the middle classes retreated to their suburban churches and withdrew from evangelisation. The collapse of Queen's Park Free Church Evangelistic Association at the start of the chapter was duplicated in most of the suburban congregations of Scotland in the 1890s and 1900s. Really quite quickly, middle-class evangelicals became less willing to undertake their established duties: entering working-class streets, knocking on doors of tenement flats up gloomy staircases, and enquiring as to the 'religious state' of the occupants. There was waning interest in asking the traditional and fundamental evangelical questions, and there was embarrassment about the very recent heritage of religious 'enthusiasm' and revivalism. One middle-class Free Church congregation tried in 1899 to withdraw the Sankey revivalist hymnbook from use in its working-class mission station – only to instigate a revolt amongst mission worshippers.[9] The most serious decline in religious voluntary work took place in the Sunday schools where the number of teachers peaked in 1895 with some 50,000 operating in the Scottish presbyterian churches. But the numbers started falling in the Free Church from 1890, in the United Presbyterian Church from 1895, and in the Established Church from 1907, and by 1910 there had been a net loss of 4,000 from these churches; during a twelve-month period in 1905–6, the United Free Church lost 300 teachers in Glasgow alone. As congregations moved to suburban areas, mission Sunday schools in inner-city areas collapsed as teachers switched to the more pleasant task of supervising scholars from the neighbourhood.

These changes had several consequences for the relationship between the working classes and the churches. In the first place evangelisation was increasingly left to the care of full-time missionaries and 'Bible women' who were being recruited in significant numbers in the last quarter of the nineteenth century from working-class converts of religious revivalism. Evangelistic association records during this period give a strong sense of 'social distance' and diverging interests between middle-class churchgoers and the missionaries they employed; as at Queen's Park Free Church in Glasgow, these missionaries were by 1900 having to conduct most of the work themselves unaided by lay district visitors. As mission work contracted, it started to be controlled, as in the business world, on a national basis by general assembly committees in Edinburgh.

But the home mission expansion of the Victorian period had generated a large number of committed working-class evangelicals, and in the 1880s and 1890s many of these emerged within an independent evangelical sector. Mostly controlled by the working classes themselves, and increasingly shorn of the 'vice-presidential' class , this proletarian Protestantism became a characteristic of urban religion in Scotland between the 1880s and 1950s: organisations like the United Evangelistic Associations of Glasgow and Dundee which ran 'Tent Halls', the City Missions of the major cities, the United Working Men's Christian Mission, the Working Men's Evangelistic Association, the Protestant Missionary Society of Glasgow, the Salvation Army, temperance friendly societies such as the Rechabites and the Independent Order of Good Templars, County Scripture Unions, the 'Pilgrim Tents' and the Faith Mission, together with various groups of the Brethren. This professionalisation and proletarianisation of the 'home mission' represented a narrowing of the power base of evangelicalism as a whole, giving it – certainly as far as suburban churches were concerned – a sectarian and 'extremist' image. Its impact on working-class communities will be examined later in the chapter.

Evangelicalism had a further problem. The period between 1870 and 1914 witnessed the growth of organised commercial leisure on an undreamt-of level: the music hall, variety theatre, organised rules sport, the cinema and many other forms of recreation. Attendances at Sunday schools and mission stations were starting to fall whilst 'secular' leisure was booming. Participant football also became enormously popular, and religious organisations (notably the Bands of Hope and the Boys' Brigade) had by the early twentieth century organised their own teams, leagues and knock-out cups. The churches were being drawn inexorably into competition with commercial and secular leisure. In 1887–9, a fad for orchestras and brass bands swept through Established and dissenting congregations. More fundamentally, the collection plates were dispensed with in many mission stations to permit them to compete, and to be seen to be competing, with secular alternatives. One mission hall for boys in the Townhead district of Glasgow had a sign outside its door in the 1890s which proclaimed boldly:[10]

NO Charge for Admission
Long Sermons
Collections

Religious organisations were starting to compromise with secular pursuits, moving from 'improving' educational classes in religious instruction, or from revivalism, to sport, outings and militaristic youth movements. Goal displacement was occurring: voluntary organisations' religious goals were being displaced by secular pursuits originally introduced as mere enticements.

Finally, evangelicalism was failing not merely because the mission to the 'unchurched' lost bourgeois assistance, but also because it lost proletarian acceptance. The middle classes lost heart with the evangelical mission in large part because systematic proletarian rejection of paternalistic religion emerged at the turn of the century. The Established Church, having lost the evangelical initiative to the dissenters during the mid-Victorian period, was the first to realise the problem. In 1884, the assistant minister at Edinburgh's Tron Church discounted the ability of either missionary work or charity to 'raise such of the masses as are in no condition either to be reasoned with or preached to'.[11] In 1888, the Rev. Donald Macleod from Glasgow was appointed convener of the Church of Scotland's Home Mission Committee with a remit to catch-up on the evangelisation work of the Free and U.P. Churches. As part of this effort in 1892, he organised an extensive 'religious carnival' of amusements and concerts for the Glasgow working classes in the East End Exhibition

Centre. He reported to the assembly that the result was a 'bitter disappointment' with few of the working classes attending:

> I am sorry to say that what occurred has made me fear that the gulf which separates class from class in our great centres of industry is wider, and the class feeling deeper, than we had dreamed. I fear that the very name of our Association as being for the Social Improvement of the People gave offence, and that inference on the part of those who are called 'the upper classes' is resented. I believe that to gain success you must act somehow through the working classes themselves. You must get them to move; or, still better, you must have it done by bodies like the Corporations of our great Cities, which represent the whole community.[12]

His last sentence hints at a new ecclesiastical polity. By 1893 he reported to the assembly that mission work had merely resulted in religion being 'handed over to the monied classes' whilst the poorer classes were segregated by 'sending down bands of workers to Mission Halls and Mission Churches, whose very names are stamped with separateness'.[13] Known for his scepticism with evangelicalism, he was elected moderator of the general assembly of the Church of Scotland in 1895, and used his moderatorial address to strike up the theme of religious crisis: 'Let us be certain that these larger discussions are reaching into the very heart of society around us; they are entering our warehouses and offices, and clerks at the desk are accustomed to exchange doubts respecting matters which a few years ago were regarded as stable as the everlasting hills.' In the space of six years, he noted the very sudden appearance of 'a stormy and dark cloud over the horizon of our faith'.[14] In careful, coded language, he urged the Church to develop a new social conscience with which to meet the greatest of all challenges to the churches: the rise of organised labour.

THE CHALLENGE OF LABOUR AND THE LOSS OF 'SOCIAL PROPHECY'

Until the last decade of the nineteenth century the centrality of religion to industrial and urban society, and thus the basis for Victorian church growth, had lain in the ubiquitous relevance of evangelicalism to modern class relations, social mobility and the solution of social problems amongst the 'residuum'. Religion held the key to social salvation by offering on the one hand an ethos of individualism which permitted 'improvement' to the receptive, and on the other an evolving agenda for social action for the rescue of the degenerate through a combination of evangelisation, legitimate philanthropy and selective intervention by the state. Evangelical values were the bedrock on which personal worth was fixed, and they delineated the means – the only means – for advancement by individuals, social groups and the country as a whole. In early- and mid-

Victorian Britain social mobility, progress and prosperity had been seen almost without challenge in terms of personal 'improvement' through combined endeavour in the religious, moral and economic spheres.

But around 1890 this hegemonic evangelical grasp of public ideology started very suddenly to slip. The decline of the home mission was merely one element in the great 'social question' – a complex national issue subsuming themes like the physical and moral fitness of Britain as a Christian and imperialist power, class divisions represented in the rise of trades unions and labour political parties, and the role of the state in ameliorating poverty, low wages, poor housing and industrial disputes. The period between the late 1880s and the 1920s witnessed a growing awareness of inequality through the work of social investigators like Charles Booth and Seebohm Rowntree and royal commissions on the poor law and housing. Intensive debate arose on the causes of social problems and on the ethics of permitting their continuation. The churches were stunned. 'The Social Question', wrote a United Presbyterian minister from Dumbarton in 1893, 'being the greatest national question of our time, is at bottom a religious question, affecting the whole status, spirit, and health of modern society.'[15] A major change was under way, not only in the functions of the churches and evangelical agencies, but in the perceived role of religion in society generally.

It was in the late 1880s that the crisis of faith erupted with evangelical-based social policy. In 1884, a Conservative MP speculated to a meeting of Church of Scotland elders that 'there must have been some great fault – some gross neglect of duty – on the part of ourselves and others who have comfortable surroundings and live in the enjoyment of Christian civilisation'.[16] A lecture four years later by Glasgow's medical officer of health to the literary society of Park Established Church on 'Life in One Room', an account of the overcrowded housing in which over a quarter of Glasgow's population lived, instigated commissions of inquiry into the links between housing, poverty and nonchurchgoing and led to the formation of the Christian-socialist movement in the Church of Scotland. Some Established churchmen exploited the failure of evangelical social policy to attack the dissenters; a parish minister from Argyll harangued the 'millionaire congregations' of the United Free Church: 'A Church conducted on ordinary commercial principles is not a Church of God.'[17] Donald Macleod told the commissioners of the general assembly 'to distinguish between nonchurchgoing and irreligion' and 'to consider how we can best bless the people'.[18] This was to be an issue which agonised the presbyterian churches for over twenty years.

'The poor worker is having his revenge', wrote Keir Hardie, the

Scottish Labour leader and MP in 1898, '... by not attending church.'[19] The undermining of evangelical thinking was nowhere more apparent than in the ideological change within the labour movement. Radicals and Chartists of the first half of the nineteenth century had been strongly imbued with evangelical precepts, and derived from puritanism the values which bred solidarity and class consciousness in many industrial communities and occupations. As we have seen already, mid-Victorian artisans like John Sturrock affirmed the relevance of evangelical self-help ideology, resulting in broad trades-union agreement with the churches and the middle classes on the economic system and its social conventions – including thrift, teetotalism and Sabbatarianism. Trades unions supported church candidates at school board elections in the 1870s and 1880s and joined with the churches in opposing the Sunday opening of art galleries and the Sunday running of trams. However, church and labour had very little contact before 1890. Despite an ideological consensus on many issues, there was significant antipathy between trades unions and the churches because of fundamental disagreement on the righteousness of combination and holding strikes. Church and labour vied for 'moral righteousness'. In the early 1880s, for example, the general assemblies of the Established and Free Churches criticised the railway servants' union for holding meetings on the Sabbath; the Glasgow trades council retorted that the kirks should be 'denouncing the great amount of unnecessary [Sunday] work now done by public companies in our midst, the shareholders of which are, we believe, in many cases, strong stoops in the Church'.[20]

But church-labour relations were radically transformed in the late 1880s and 1890s. The rise of unions for the semi-skilled and the unskilled worker enlarged the scope of industrial combination and, irrespective of the effectiveness of strike action, offered a widely available alternative, or at least addition, to evangelical 'improvement'. Labour representation emerged after 1890 on town councils, school boards, parochial boards and in the House of Commons, providing for the first time an effective challenge to the ideology and policies of competitive individualism. Despite the slow electoral progress of the labour movement before 1914, the interests of the working classes became quickly associated with the outlook it represented and the policies it promoted. In an important sense, its lack of success in the polls accentuated the ideological transformation because the 'social question' became seen by many, especially in the churches, as an ethical issue rather than a political one. Social inquiries in Scotland were largely initiated by the Established Church: notably the Glasgow Presbytery Commission on the Housing of the Poor in Relation to their Social Condition of 1888–91, and the general assembly Commission on the Religious Condition of the People of 1889–96. In carrying out such inquiries the churches were brought into contact for the first time with trades unionists, Labour activists and left-wing intellectuals, and were driven to reassess evangelical thinking. This produced from the Church of Scotland's most radical presbytery, Glasgow, the conclusion in 1888 that 'existing agencies and methods have not hitherto proved adequate to cope' with poverty and poor housing.[21] What emerged in Glasgow in 1888–94 was a small band of non-political Christian socialists, including the Rev. Donald Macleod, which sought a new social theology incorporating ideas drawn from a nexus of social reformers and representatives of organised labour. The issue was not one of overturning the existing political parties but of creating a consensus in favour of increased social action by public authorities. Churchmen went beyond traditional evangelicalism, which viewed social problems as the products of immorality, to regard poverty, insanitary and overcrowded housing, and ill-health as in themselves immoralities which could not be countenanced in a Christian country. Therefore, it became necessary and ethically justifiable for churches to work with the labour movement and to pronounce upon issues of the day. As one minister said, 'we are at a point of social pressure where to keep silence is little less than immoral'.[22]

The new social theology produced a deluge of books of biblical reinterpretation between 1890 and 1918 – the majority written by Established Church ministers but with other contributions by dissenting presbyterian clergy; very little was produced by Episcopalian or Catholic clergy. The starting point was the strike of London dockworkers in 1889 which spread to other ports and attracted national attention of an unprecedentedly sympathetic nature. A United Presbyterian minister wrote immediately after it:

> Who were the spokesmen of these miserable dockmen in making a righteous demand? Not the ministers of Jesus Christ; not the magnates of the religious world, but a few socialists who, amid the starving multitudes, kept themselves and the sufferers in such moderation and self-control as to be the admiration of the world.[23]

In the new social theology, strikes and other social protests acquired a legitimacy not recognised by churches before. A leading Christian socialist in the Established Church commented in 1908: 'Social unrest itself is a good sign, a mark of vigorous life, not of decadence. It is a divine discontent with social wrong.'[24] But churchmen regarded it as 'the bitterest drop to us that social progress is mainly effected by men opposed to our churches and our religion', and sought to sustain their relevance to 'social prophecy' by mixing socialism with Christianity:

'The fact is that socialism needs to be Christianised, and that Christianity needs to be socialised.'[25]

The principle of the new social theology was that 'the objective of all social effort is the realisation of the Kingdom of God on earth'.[26] Reward in this world through social justice became emphasised, and led clergy to attack *laissez faire* and big business. Speculators were denounced as 'the hungry parasites of our industrial order',[27] and the proper stewardship of wealth was promoted as a means of balancing the respective rights of entrepreneurs and workers. Compromise was sought between the basic tenets of evangelicalism, in which religious and economic salvation was perceived as arising from the individual as a 'free moral agent', and the need to regulate capitalism in order to reduce exploitation: 'Individualism is only a half truth, solidarity is the other half.'[28] Various ideals were drawn into the theology: that of co-operativism represented by David Dale, Robert Owen, the Rochdale pioneers, and the Scottish Co-operative Wholesale Society whose educational work was supported by many Christian socialists in the Edwardian period; the garden-city movement of Ebenezer Howard; and perhaps most importantly municipal socialism which between 1890 and 1914 was a popular and virtually apolitical trend in world-wide city government, and turned Glasgow Corporation into what one minister described as 'the mecca of the municipal reformer'. The new social theology derived much from evangelicalism – its concern for cities, its 'call to action', and its enthusiasm. The Christian socialist vision was for churches and society 'to be alit with civic ideals, to be alive with civic ardours, to be aglow with civic pride and patriotism'.[29] Indeed, unlikely as it may seem, it derived continued inspiration from Thomas Chalmers; his 'godly commonwealth' remained the objective, only it was to be a municipal community driven by collectivist action.[30]

But Christian socialism differed from evangelicalism in several important respects. It rejected the primacy of religious conversion with its attendant moral virtues as the source of social salvation; those virtues were to be the outcome of social reform, not its cause – though this left unresolved the conflict between the socialist aim of freedom from economic want and the evangelical principle of freedom from state restriction (which even the Christian socialists acknowledged was necessary for the cultivation of those virtues). It differed also in that it was overwhelmingly a movement of clergy, and lacked any real base amongst the laity. Its call to social service – to running baby clinics, undertaking sociological investigations and to providing homes and holidays for 'slum' children – was one which was answered more by professionals and by institutions rather than by the church membership.

The new social theology gave rise to the formation between 1890 and 1914 of a church-labour group, based mostly in Glasgow but with outposts in Edinburgh and Dundee, and composed of less than a hundred individuals of whom around thirty were clergy drawn from the Established, Free, United Presbyterian, Episcopal and Catholic Churches; the remainder were trades unionists, Labour activists, medical officers of health, academics, town councillors and MPs. Few of the clergy were socialist; the only one of note was John Glasse, minister of Old Greyfriars' Church in Edinburgh who was a devotee of Marx and Proudhon, an ILP sympathiser, and a friend of William Morris. For the remainder, a network of interlocking organisations provided an apparent ecclesiastical influence upon social-reform initiatives: organisations including the Scottish Council for Women's Trades, the Scottish Christian Social Union, and the Social Unions of Glasgow, Edinburgh and Dundee which were all active in the building of 'model' working-class housing, refuges and medical clinics between 1890 and 1914. The network of organisations created a unity amongst Christian socialist clergy, trades unionists and professional social reformers on a whole range of issues from the plight of women in 'sweat shops' to national insurance. It led ministers to conclude that 'if such things as Old Age Pensions, State intervention in Labour disputes, Labour Exchanges, and the Trades Boards Acts are Socialism, then Socialism is not a thing to be greatly dreaded'.[31]

This church-labour interaction was a process in which the churches passed the banner of social progress into the hands of others. The churches' own investigations spelled out a socialist message rather than a Christian one. The final report of the Established Church's Commission into the Religious Condition of the People stated that 'the Christian conscience has been aroused; and all persons, with some sense of justice as well as generosity, feel that the chasms between wealth-land and woe-land are a symptom of social unrighteousness'.[32] The churches started to acknowledge the need for unevangelical solutions to social problems. From 1892, congregations of the Established Church were handing out money to unemployed members in an effort 'to save all from want'. The dissenters clung on longer to traditional policies, avoiding handouts and social service in the 1890s as 'action that could not well be taken' by them. By 1904, the Established Church general assembly was persuaded by the Glasgow Christian socialists to abandon evangelisation in favour of social work in homes and 'labour colonies' for the elderly, disabled, inebriate, delinquent and unemployed, and the United Free Church followed suit after the depression of 1908–9 in which both denominations carried out systematic payments to unemployed adherents. In 1908 the Church of Scotland formed a Social Work

Committee; in 1910 the U.F. Church created its Social Problems Committee. A new social theology was in place in Scotland's two largest churches at the very time they were planning church union. 'A reunited Church of Scotland,' the moderator of the United Free Church general assembly said in 1914, 'should present itself in the eyes of their fellow countrymen as one concentrated force, bent, in Christ's name, on grappling with and ending the social sores from which our beloved land has suffered.'[33]

In effect, a remarkable reconciliation had occurred between the principal Protestant churches and the emerging labour movement. There had been a convergence in much of the social-policy agenda (though not all of it) and in joint work in social investigations and schemes to ameliorate social problems. The Scottish Catholic Church also joined the process. During the Victorian period the Catholic hierarchy and the Catholic press in Scotland had been very hostile to organised labour, in part because of ideological defensiveness by the priesthood and in part because of sectarianism. Not only were Catholics excluded from many skilled occupations by Protestant employers; Protestant workers excluded them from unions and some friendly societies. Despite increased unionisation amongst Catholics in the 1890s and 1900s, caused by recruitment to skilled jobs in mining for instance and by unionisation amongst the unskilled, the majority of Catholics did not align with Labour politics but continued to vote Liberal until 1918. The Catholic newspaper, the *Glasgow Observer*, stated in 1895 that 'the ILP is in effect the workman's wing of the Tory Party', whilst it described the Conservatives as 'hopelessly an anti-Catholic Party – the Party of ascendency and bigotry'.[34] But indications of a Catholic swing to Labour were evident by the early 1900s. Catholics in Coatbridge were starting to vote Labour by 1906, and in the next three years the Church's open hostility diminished markedly. A correspondence in the *Observer* in 1906–8 hotly debated Catholicism and socialism, and from it John Wheatley of the Catholic Socialist Society emerged as an acceptable leader of the laity. In the 1890s and 1900s, some Catholic clergy had been involved in social-investigation organisations, introducing them to both Christian socialists in the presbyterian churches and to leaders of the labour movement. In 1908 the archbishop of Glasgow made a turning-point speech which softened the Catholic hierarchy's attitude: 'What did capital risk? – Its money. What did labour risk? – Its life.'[35] Increasing access to skilled jobs over the next ten years, and especially during the war, infused Labour attitudes amongst Catholics, and the independence of Ireland and collapse of the Liberal Party released them from the early 1920s to vote Labour.

Between 1890 and 1914 there had been a substantive ecclesiastical compromise with the emerging labour movement. This was undoubtedly a wise strategy. To have directly opposed labour and adopted a coherently reactionary political stance would have intensified – or, as in Germany, completed – the alienation of the working classes from the churches.[36] However, the affirmation of a social gospel by the Scottish presbyterian churches rapidly came unstuck. The initial cause was the Great War of 1914–18 in which churchmen found difficulty in discerning moral and spiritual direction.[37] At the outset, the churches led the patriotic war effort by example; within months of war being declared, 200 parish ministers of the Church of Scotland offered themselves as military chaplains.[38] The outbreak of hostilities in 1914–15 initiated a surge in membership during a period of stagnancy; overall between 1913 and 1918, the number of members rose by 1.3 per cent in the Church of Scotland and by 3.3 per cent in the United Free Church. 'In this crisis,' one leading churchmen said at the outbreak of war, 'as so often in the past, the perils and uncertainties of war are leading us back to God.'[39] With churches filled, clergy discerned an opening for national unity and a rededication to God. The Church of Scotland and the United Free Church came closer together, and Protestant-Catholic relations improved. From the outset, the First World War turned into a jingoistic moral crusade in which the churches, with the connivance of the state, hijacked war culture and focused it on a puritanical campaign which associated morale with morals.

However, the church's self-confidence, as with the national mood, darkened as the trench warfare went on year after year. By 1917, hopes of a religious revival entertained by many ministers had vanished; church attendances and Sunday-school enrolments had fallen, and social problems and immoralities remained. As military chaplains, clergymen saw the working classes in a new light: 'Self-indulgence, riotous living, theft, obscenity, violence – these seem no longer wrong, and he who disclaims them seems unintelligible if not amusing.'[40] The soldiers saw the churches in the same old light; the men in a Highland regiment, according to one chaplain, considered the churches to be bastions of 'formality and class separateness' whilst avoiding 'social questions, moral reefage and wreckage, brotherhood and brotherliness'.[41] Evidence on the impact of the wars on combatants is confusing. One interdenominational study conducted in the later stages of the First World War and during demobilisation found that 20 per cent of troops in Scottish regiments had a 'vital relationship' with a church compared to 11.5 per cent in English regiments. However, higher figures were returned from largely middle-class Territorial regiments from Scotland, and a Church of

Scotland survey of one large troop base in France produced a figure of 40 per cent amongst Scottish soldiers (with all Catholics counted as 'vitally connected'). The lowest figures came from working-class battalions raised in industrial cities of both Scotland and England, and it was amongst these troops that the churches feared the greatest defection after the war.[42] The Home Front was no better; a Scottish officer on home leave noted: 'The lack of restraint and reserve since the war among women who were previously modest and respectable is an especially conspicuous and regrettable fact.'[43]

In the last two years of the war, the presbyterian churches appointed commissions to explore its moral and spiritual meaning, and a British interdenominational commission published detailed findings calling for 'social reconstruction' on a social-gospel agenda.[44] The Church of Scotland Commission on the War stated in its 1919 report: 'Our aim must be under God to make Scotland a Christian country in fact as well as name, to realise the vision of our fathers, and to build on Scottish fields a true city of God.'[45] This proved to be an elegy for the presbyterian social gospel, for the churches met all these reports and proposals with coolness. The Glasgow rents strikes and the emergence of 'Red Clydeside' between 1915 and 1918, set against the background of the Bolshevik Revolution in Russia, created a climate of hostility for Christian socialist ideas. Turning their backs on social reconstruction, the United Free Church and the Church of Scotland joined forces in December 1918 in calling a 'National Mission of Rededication'. It was a flop, regarded suspiciously by politicians and ignored even by church members.[46] The people seemed unresponsive to a national church revivalism, and the churches seemed unresponsive to the new political inclinations of the Scottish working classes.

The ideological divide between the suburban church of the middle classes created in the 1890s and 1900s and the intensely overcrowded inner-city working-class areas now came home to roost. In the context of economic slump in the 1920s and 1930s, a new generation of right-wing conservative clergy took control in both the Church of Scotland and the United Free Church, leading the churches towards reunion on a new agenda of social conservatism, anti-labourism and racism. Though the state had initiated a national programme of state housing in 1919, the government from 1921 retreated from social reconstruction and reverted to *laissez faire* capitalism. The Church of Scotland and the United Free Church followed suit, and by the mid 1920s the right-wing leadership of the Rev. John White in the Church of Scotland and the Rev. Alexander Martin of the United Free Church led both churches into confrontation with the working class during the General Strike of 1926. 'We are faced,' wrote Martin in *The Scotsman*, denouncing the strike, 'with the attempt of a self-constituted minority to impose its will upon the community by sheer weight of *force majeure*.'[47] After the general assemblies of both churches met miners' leaders with humiliating coolness, it was no surprise that the U.F. Church was forced to abandon an insensitive mission to Fife mining communities in the summer of 1926.

The right-wing stance of the churches during the General Strike was accompanied by growing antipathy towards the Irish Catholic community in Scotland. 'During the General Strike in the industrial areas', one churchmen informed the Scottish Office, 'nearly all the leaders were Irish. In the course of time instead of a Scottish proletariat there would be a body of people who had no regard for the United Kingdom and who were prone to revolutionary ideas.'[48] This merely confirmed, as far as many Protestants were concerned, that 'popery' and atheism went hand-in-hand. It was never accurate; the inter-war Scottish Labour leadership had a highly variegated religious composition: out of forty-two identified by William Knox, 31 per cent were members of the Church of Scotland, 26 per cent to the United Free Church, a further 17 per cent belonged to minor Protestant churches, and only 14 per cent were Catholic.[49] None the less, the growth of Catholic and labour influence was perceived by many presbyterians as connected, and this added an extra dimension to the negotiations which proceeded apace in the 1920s for the union of the Church of Scotland and the United Free Church. Union was set against a background of mounting anti-Irish sentiment within the churches and in the Protestant community in central Scotland. Special general assembly committees of both churches waged campaigns against 'Irish immigration', even though this was by then very low. In this context, church union was to be a restatement of the presbyterian nature of Scotland.

Though popular sectarianism was high in the 1930s, the campaign of the presbyterian churches did not instigate a mass Protestant revival. When the two churches united in 1929, a mission was started to the 'churchless million' in Scotland. This 'Forward Movement' of 1930–3 failed to catch the national interest, and, like a number of other schemes mooted by the right-wing Rev. John White, did little to instigate real enthusiasm. The presbyterian church sought to portray the union of 1929 as a great event in the nation's history, and it was attended by much pageantry. But it had been hitched to a socially-conservative, racist, anti-labour manifesto whilst the leaders of the Church washed their hands of the really big issue of the early 1930s – unemployment. In 1932, at the peak of the Slump, the Church and Nation Committee analysed the causes of unemployment, and concluded in the lamest of reports: 'The first cause is definitely religious.'[50] Apart from a small minority of socially-concerned clergy, the lessons of Christian socialism had been unlearnt, and the Church's stance and conduct during the 1920s and 1930s – certainly at national level – jeopardised its credibility with both civil authority and with the people.

CHURCH AND STATE

The church crisis had another vital dimension. In the second half of the nineteenth century, the presbyterian dissenters of the Free and United Presbyterian Churches had sought to undermine the traditional social-welfare monopoly of the Church of Scotland, and develop a system which did not terminate religious influence but perpetuated it. The parish was to be replaced by the burgh as the arena for evangelising by 'voting in' the kingdom of God. As church evangelisation started to falter, Scottish evangelicalism turned into an electoral mission, but it came to a humiliating end in the 1920s.

The state's take-over of traditional church functions in the Victorian period was actually nothing of the sort: it was a takeover by elected evangelical presbyterian dissenters. The withdrawal of poor-relief management from the Established Church in 1845, and the setting up of the state system of education in 1872, were major victories for religious and particularly evangelical interests. The creation of apparently 'secular' authorities was thus designed to preserve religious control of civil administration by making it elective and subject to interdenominational rivalry at the ballot box. Until the 1890s the churches were remarkably successful in their objectives. Between 1845 and 1894, poor relief was administered by parochial boards which were composed partly of elected members and partly of elders or heritors nominated by the local Established Church. In 1894 the boards were replaced by all elected parish councils which continued to be dominated by representatives of the churches and of the landowners. In Glasgow church nominees were still present in 1910, and even two of the three Labour members were dissenting ministers. In one rural parish near the Borders between 1894 and 1910, the parish council was invariably composed of the minister, one large farmer and three small ones, and it acted like a kirk session by stopping payments to claimants who were known to buy drink and by demanding that its medical officer – the local doctor – 'clear himself of the scandal' of adultery in a manner redolent of an eighteenth-century fornication case. [51] The intrusion of state control amounted to little more than the continuation of the *status quo*.

But in the 1910s and 1920s, though ministers and elders remained on parish councils, there was a secularisation of operations and rationale. In urban and industrial districts there was a great infusion of Christian socialists who agreed with new Labour representatives that the giving of relief should not be dependent on the appearance of evangelical virtues amongst the 'deserving poor'. Socially-concerned clergy recoiled at what one of them described in 1905 as the 'brutal and vicious' interrogation of applicants by a relief committee in Glasgow in which 'man after man walked up to the bar and had his life-record read out to him ... like judgement-day'.[52] But this system inaugurated the professionalisation of social service and the better regulation of statutory relief agencies. In the process, the role of churchmen, of evangelical attitudes and indeed of popular election diminished, and parish councils were abolished in 1929.

Much the same happened in the more significant area of education.[53] The establishment of elected school boards in every burgh and rural parish in 1873, coupled with the imposition of compulsory education, was widely welcomed by the presbyterian churches, though the Catholic Church refused to surrender its schools and continued to provide its own education. In most school boards, education settled down quickly into a pattern little changed since the days of church schools. Even in the largest school boards of Glasgow, Edinburgh and Govan, the contested elections regularly produced a denominationally balanced membership which instituted a solidly presbyterian form of religious education in the classroom. Catholic candidates, both clergy and laity, were elected to oppose the spending of ratepayers' money on presbyterian religious instruction, but they never gained more than a fifth of the seats on the city boards. School boards were thus able to sustain great continuity in the content and objectives of education. Despite a decline in the religious content of school books, caused by the government's insistence on 'timetabling' religion apart from other subjects, 'RI' was fixedly presbyterian and traditional, based on 'use and wont' when the schools were under church control. The Established, Free and United Presbyterian Churches were allowed by many boards to send in their own inspectors to check on the nature of religious education, and they came away completely satisfied – so satisfied that the Church of Scotland dismissed its Inspector in 1879.[54] The furtherance of literacy and evangelical virtues was safely in the hands of church nominees on school boards and teachers trained entirely at denominational training colleges.

But circumstances changed in the late 1880s and 1890s. Labour candidates started to stand and were progressively elected in urban areas, gaining about a fifth of the seats. They stood on the general 'ticket' of representing the working classes, but their policy of free education was a matter of great concern to evangelicals. In the evangelical design, popularised by Thomas Chalmers in the 1810s, parents should be charged fees for the education of their children because it encouraged self-reliance and especially thrift. During the 1870s and 1880s, only the very and 'deserving' poor were excused payments, and even when parliament ordered in 1889 that fees be abolished some boards like that of Glasgow maintained them because of pressure from middle-class parents fearing an influx of working-class children into the more expensive board schools. Not until 1893 did the Glasgow board abolish fees and thus reduce the social segregation between its schools. The evangelicals resisted until the last, one speaking 'decidedly about Dr Chalmers' scheme as the best', and when the board 'freed the schools' the evangelicals resigned from management posts. Henceforth, the Glasgow board was ruled by a loosely affiliated group of Christian socialists, Labour and Ladies representatives, with the occasional support of the Catholics. Thus there was no sudden removal of clergy from school-board management, but instead a fundamental shift in educational ideology. Issues of 'social justice', of providing free books, meals, spectacles and shoes, now symbolised the welfare function of education rather than its evangelical design.

The perception of fading evangelical, and indeed presbyterian, control of Scottish education was heightened by the government's decision in 1918 to make the country's Catholic schools the first in a predominantly non-Catholic nation to be incorporated within a state system. Historians of Scottish Catholicism and of sectarianism emphasise the importance of this aspect of the 1918 Education Act. For the Catholic community, it ended the discriminatory denial of full financial support from central government and local rates. Between 1873 and 1919, the Catholic Church was unable to meet the educational needs of the whole Catholic population: it had too few schools, too few properly qualified teachers, meagre post-primary provision, and in Lanarkshire at least gross overcrowding by 1918–19, with more than one-third of its schools enrolling more pupils than they had places. From 1900, the Church was keen to enter the state system on a basis that would protect its influence upon Catholic education, and many of the city school boards agreed. Negotiations were completed at the end of the war, and although the full absorption took ten years or more, the system of separate Catholic schools within the state system became an invaluable bulwark to the faith. The state now had to ensure that there were sufficient places for Catholic children, and Church funds were released for other vital purposes such as church-building.

Presbyterian hostility to the state take-over of Catholic schools was remarkably muted in 1918 as there were other aspects of the Education

Act which raised greater concern. But a Protestant outcry arose the following year after the elections for the new county education authorities. The system of proportional representation led in Glasgow to the return of large numbers of Catholic candidates and Labour representatives 'lifted in by the Roman Catholics who gave them their second vote'. At the next election in the city in 1922, fierce Protestant canvassing halved Catholic representation, but it rose again in 1925. Regarded by presbyterian ministers ever since as a burning issue and 'a tactical blunder', the Education Act became in the context of declining influence in civil administration in the 1920s a spark for Protestant reassertion.

The sense of insecurity within presbyterianism in the 1920s forced Protestantism on to the retreat. In one sense, this increased the urgency for reunion between the Established and United Free Churches, but in another sense it heightened presbyterian alarm. Union was preceded by the virtual disestablishment of the Church of Scotland – the breaking of its state connection – in order to satisfy the dissenting U.F. Church. This took various forms: new Articles for a refashioned Church of Scotland which were approved by both denominations in 1918–19 and by parliament in 1921; and a parliamentary Act of 1925, which commuted the teinds to a fixed payment of decreasing value, passed the ownership of churches from heritors, burgh councils and others to Church trustees, passed the ownership of churchyards to town and county councils, and deprived heritors of the right to own or allocate pews. The 1929 union of the two churches was welcomed by most members; only some 25,000 United Free Church adherents formally seceded during the next twenty years. But reunion also increased the presbyterian sense of crisis and retrenchment. For many Established churchmen, untying the knot with the state weakened the presbyterian character of Scotland, and the various measures enacted by parliament were carefully formulated to maintain the appearance of a church still protected by the state.

A final blow in the 1920s to evangelical presbyterianism's pretensions to govern Scottish society was the failure of 'the temperance reformation'. From the late 1880s, full-time missionaries campaigned strenuously for a parliamentary act to institute the local veto plebiscite by which communities could ban the sale of alcohol. At the same time, they used all means to attack the licensed trade. Evangelicals on town councils, school boards and parish councils did as much as they could to harrass the drinks trade and to promote the temperance cause: banning pubs near schools, banning licensed premises from municipal property (a ruling staying in force until the 1970s and accounting for the absence of public houses from council-housing schemes); banning barmaids since they enticed men to drink; making 'unreasonable' sanitary demands on publicans; and virtually quarantining public houses and their clients by insisting that passers-by be unable to see in, by banning 'family departments', and generally by making drinking appear as rough and uncivilised as possible. Burgh administrators became in effect agents of the temperance movement at the turn of the century. This was the *quid pro quo* of the civic gospel. As Bernard Aspinwall has said: 'In the generation before the first world war, Scottish identity was found not in the church, established or free, but in the town hall; in an ethical Christian community faith rather than "churchianity".'[55] So, a powerful, single-issue evangelical moral agenda survived side-by-side with the civic gospel of improvement.

However, teetotalism was actually failing amongst adults in the churches. In the 1890s only 14 per cent of the 34,000 registered abstainers in the United Presbyterian Church, and only 29 per cent of 48,000 abstainers and 'moderate drinkers' in the Established Church, were adults.[56] The movement was becoming dominated by youth pledge-takers and by women campaigners, and the failure amongst men drove militants to pursue ever more vigorously the imposition of prohibition. In 1913, parliament finally passed the Temperance (Scotland) Act which made it possible from June 1920 to hold local plebiscites on whether public houses should be banned or restricted in number. Evangelicals called plebiscites in over 500 local wards in Scotland in the first year, and city missionaries, Woman's Guilds, Bands of Hope and other church agencies were marshalled into a massive canvassing campaign, especially in the large cities. But the results were a grave disappointment, with few wards reached the necessary majority for going 'dry'. Those that did were in small fishing villages, middle-class suburbs of Glasgow like Kelvinside, Pollokshields, Cathcart, Camphill and Langside, some working-class districts like Whiteinch and Parkhead, and small mining and industrial communities like Kilsyth, Kirkintilloch, Stewarton, Cambuslang and Airdrie. In all, only around forty of the 584 Scottish wards polled went 'dry' in the early 1920s, and with re-polls organised by the licensed trade, and with Labour switching its allegiance from prohibition to a 'wet' policy, only seventeen wards remained without public houses by 1927. Evangelicals regarded this as a final rebuttal of their social programme. By 1926, the churches noted that the Bands of Hope were in decline, and the chairman of the Church of Scotland's temperance committee resigned in a mood of depression.[57]

So in the late 1920s, the electoral mission of the main presbyterian churches ground to a virtual halt. Since the 1870s, the presbyterian churches had revelled in electioneering and in promoting the idea that 'the vote is a sacred trust'.[58] Evangelicals and Christian socialists alike sought to found democratic 'cities of God' through participation in civic affairs permitted by the agreeable manner of state intervention. But the year 1929 concluded a period of profound change in the civil and secular significance of presbyterian religion. The union of the United Free Church and the Church of Scotland marked the end of dissenting evangelicalism and of the established state church; henceforth, the Church was 'National', recognised by the state and offered 'state protection', but in reality it was an independent entity relying on its own resources. Of equal significance, the *ad hoc* education and poor-relief authorities were abolished, depriving the presbyterian churches of the last means of major influence over their historic fields of interest. And although the local veto remained on the statute book until 1976, and a few places – most famously Kilsyth – remained 'dry', the prohibition cause and that of 'moral-force' puritanism generally died for most of Scotland in the 1920s. Evangelicalism was channelled in its decay into electioneering where it was rejected by the Scottish people.

POPULAR RELIGIOSITY

Fundamental to presbyterian churchmen's perception of the 'social question' was a crisis in working-class religion. Between 1890 and 1939, pessimistic churchmen shouted long and hard about the decline in religious habits and thinking, and about the blurring of the division between the sacred and the profane. For all that, as this section will show, little actually changed in terms of popular adherence to the churches. Indeed, new sources of evidence becoming available to historians are demonstrating that religion was extremely important in the lives of the common people.

The statistical data on religious adherence analysed in Chapter 3 showed that though church membership started to decline in 1905, this was a slow and discontinuous process throughout the inter-war years. Total church adherence continued to rise from a figure of 48 per cent of total population in 1890 to a peak of 50 per cent in 1905, and then fell to 49 per cent in 1914 – a level which resumed after the War in 1920 and remained unchanged until 1929. There seems to have been a loss of presbyterian communicants at the union of 1929, and after a slight recovery during 1931–33, slow decline resumed to a level of 44 per cent in 1939. These data indicate that despite the economic dislocation and high unemployment of both the 1920s and 1930s, adult Protestant church connection only fell very slightly overall. Indeed, there is considerable evidence that church connection grew during years of depression and declined in years of relative prosperity. Most interestingly, the largest single fall in presbyterian communion in the inter-war period occurred in 1926, the year of the coal strike and the General Strike.[59] Overall, the statistics thus show no sudden or significant breach of church connection between 1890 and 1939.

Other forms of evidence support this. Amongst a cross-section of Scots born between 1870 and 1914 and interviewed by historians in the 1970s, over half claimed that both of their parents were regular church-goers in the late Victorian and Edwardian periods – a figure higher than in any region of Britain except Wales.[60] In another oral-history project, of an occupationally-representative sample of fifty-five women born between 1894 and 1926 and interviewed in the Stirling area in 1988, 27 per cent stated that both parents attended church 'every Sunday', a further 40 per cent said they attended 'regularly', 11 per cent that their fathers only (9 per cent their mothers only) attended regularly or every Sunday, and a mere 13 per cent that neither parent attended church.[61] Even allowing for the shortcomings of memory, it is clear that Scottish adults at the turn of the century were, by all reasonable standards of comparison, a high church-going group.

This was a period when the associational ideal of the Victorian period was still very important. In a 1904 survey carried out by the Charity Organisation Society in Edinburgh, more of the working classes had affiliations with religious, church and temperance organisations (28 per cent of skilled workers and 22 per cent of semi- and unskilled) than with working men's clubs, sports clubs, political parties and hobby clubs (17 per cent of the skilled, 11 per cent of the semi- and unskilled).[62] Children's connections were even stronger. Of seventy-six Protestant women asked about their membership of youth organisations between the 1890s and 1939, 68 per cent had attended Sunday school, 36 per cent the Band of Hope (and a further 9 per cent other temperance organisations like the White Ribboners and the Good Templars), 13 per cent had belonged to the Brownies, Girl Guides, Girls' Guildry or Girls Association, and 14 per cent had been in church choirs. For boys, the Scouting movement and the Boys' Brigades were extremely important – and mostly congregational-based – organisations. Scottish membership of the Boys' Brigades rose from 12,796 in 1900 to 26,575 in 1910 and to 35,922 in 1934, with the greatest concentration in working-class areas of west-central Scotland, whilst the Cubs and Scouts had a more middle-class, suburban and east of Scotland image.[63] Whatever general crisis was afflicting the associational ideal for adults, it became stronger for Scottish children in the first half of the twentieth century.

However, even these figures do not do justice to the intensity of church connection that young people had during this period. In contrast to the impression given by contemporary churchmen, oral-history respondents interviewed during the 1980s and 1990s typically recall their early lives as 'all religion'. In interview after interview, the historian is faced with variations on the same theme. Mrs N.2(born 1906) was brought up in Glasgow, her father a tram conductor. Asked to recall how she spent Sundays as a child, she said:

> Sundays we were at church a lot. Church and the Sunday school. Then when I got older, the Bible class it was. But there was a lot of the church. And Monday was the Band of Hope (Laughs); I always remember that – the Band of Hope. Tuesday was the Girl Guides. You know it seemed to be all church things.[64]

In Larkhall in Lanarkshire in the 1920s, the same intense Protestant Sunday was apparent; Mrs W.2(1916) went to Sunday school during the day and 'at nights the Hebron Hall or any, you know, any meeting houses at night time.'[65] Mrs Q.2(1912) lived in a pit village in Stirlingshire where, during the week, she attended the Brownies, the Guides and the Rechabites for concerts and pantomimes, whilst on Sundays:

> You went to church and then you came home, had something to eat and you went to the Brethren in the afternoon – Sunday school, they let you go in there. You got these tickets, you know, verses on them and that, you know to learn, and maybe a cup of tea and a cake. I think it was the cake we went for [Laughs]. And then to the Evangelistic Meeting at night. That was really all we had, all our pastime you know ...[66]

With little variation, respondents tend to recall one church service and typically two Sunday-school sessions – frequently with different denominations. Many, like Mrs M.2(1915) from Bannockburn, recall morning and evening church services with Sunday-school in-between: 'we were never out of church on Sunday', she said.[67]

Sunday was still the Sabbath in Lowland as well as Highland Scotland in the first half of the twentieth century. Mrs O.2(1899) from Montrose remembered:

> Q So you could play in the [Sunday] afternoons? Were you allowed to?
> A No, no. All boots and shoes were cleaned the night before and of course the dishes and that were all washed ... every Sunday night she [mother] held a small service on her own, singing hymns and read out of the Bible and everything like that ... Just the family.[68]

On the Isle of Harris, Finlay J. MacDonald recalls in the 1930s how his grandparents would spend the Saturday night preparing for the Sabbath, including bringing buckets of water into the house to last the whole Sabbath; the declaration of war in 1939 was missed in his family because Neville Chamberlain's radio broadcast was on a Sunday.[69] In central

Scotland in the 1910s, Mrs R.2(1905) reflected: 'Sunday! You wouldnae dare lift a pair of scissors to cut your nails. My mother used to say that all the Sundays of the world would come down on you if you cut your nails on a Sunday.'[70] One of the few places in Scotland where shops and the streets were full was the Gorbals; but then it was quieter on the Jewish Sabbath – Saturday. Evelyn Cowan described how most Jewish women there had a non-Jewish friend who came in to light the fire or the gas on a Saturday; John Caldwell's little sisters earned a few pennies on a Saturday morning 'by waiting below the right tenement for a window to open and a Jewish housewife to call them up to light the gas'.[71]

The intensity of the religious environment heightened expectations. Mrs P.1(1913), who became a schoolteacher, reflected on religion:

> I suppose I understood more about it [as I grew older], but I've never been a person who had a wonderful transformation like the Damascus road or anything. I've never been like that. I mean any faith I have has just grown gradually from Sunday school days, Bible class days you know. Didn't join the Church 'til I was about twenty-one, which was old at the time because I was waiting for this wonderful experience which never came.[72]

Evangelical religion so dominated the organised recreational activity of Scots children, and was imparted so energetically by evangelists, that the gospel message could develop a literal interpretation. The evangelistic preaching at the teetotal Band of Hope so convinced Mrs V.2(1906) in the 1910s that she confessed in later life: 'I was so innocent, and I thought Jesus would come in the door that night! [Laughs] I really thought that, when they said "Jesus will come." I sat and watched that. [Laughs]'[73] It should not be inferred, however, that this was an overpowering and brutal propagandisation: 'we were encouraged, you know, to believe in God and things like that and to thank God for what we had received more or less. But it wasn't thumped into us, put it that way, it wasn't—no there was just a nice atmosphere.'[74]

Sunday was the pinnacle of the child's week, but respondents also recall religion in the 1920s and 1930s in terms of other days: 'Friday nights was always a night ... for this Band of Hope ... And I think the beginning of the [week] ... depended on what was on, but we used to go to the Salvation Army ... there was a Christian Endeavour and there was the Rechabites.'[75] The Band of Hope was a centre for technological demonstrations to children in the 1880s and 1890s: 'novelty' classes showing the workings of tramways, electricity and phonographs. It was in the Bands of Hope that most Scottish children first saw the 'cinematograph' between 1904 and 1910, but the ubiquitous medium for the teetotal message was the magic lantern. Mrs M.2(1915) recalled the Band of Hope conducted in Bannockburn by the daughter of the millowner:

we had lantern slides ... they were lovely. It was Miss Mitchell and Miss Wilson
who ran the Band of Hope and there were queues on a Monday night to get in to
the Band of Hope because there was no village cinema and that was the only
cinema we had in those days.[76]

And for many working-class lads, the main attraction of the Band of
Hope in the Glasgow area by the 1910s was its football competitions
with over seventy teams playing in the Band of Hope Union Cup.

Churchgoing and weekday-evening religious meetings played a central
part in the Scottish childhood before 1939. The fact that many of the
events were organised by non-mainstream churches is important, for the
independent evangelical sector was critical in the depressed conditions of
the period. This was especially true in mining and fishing communities.
Christopher Rush described how the fishing village of St Monans in Fife
has been regarded during this century as the 'Holy City' of the East
Neuk of Fife with a 'polyglot of sects': the Church of Scotland, Baptists,
Evangelists, Catholics, Congregationalists and four brands of 'fawnover-
coated and bowler-hatted' Brethren who 'hell-fired at you in the streets
and summoned you to judgement through your letter box'.[77] The offer
of food and 'treats' was a characteristic of the independent evangelical
sector in the recession years. In the mining village of Fallin in
Stirlingshire after the First World War, Mrs A.3(1913) went to the Band
of Hope 'and you took two pence – one for a collection, and one for as I
say your tinnie; you got hot peas and vinegar. That was on a Friday
night.'[78] Railwaymen opened a mission in Stirling to provide games for
children: 'they used to have wee meetings, and games; build things with
sand and, you know, just try and use your imagination, because there
were no picture houses then. And there were nothing for these children,
unless, in the street.'[79] Molly Weir recalls of inter-war Glasgow that as
well as 'the big Church, where we went to Sunday School and Bible
Class, and had our church parades of Girl Guides and the Boys' Brigade,
we had the excitement in summertime of tent missions coming to
Springburn to convert us'. She gives a strong impression of the way in
which Protestant working-class adults distributed their religious favours
amongst a variety of religious organisations (like the Salvation Army, the
Church of Scotland and evangelist meetings) for nothing but 'the sheer
enjoyment', and how some of the children went along indiscriminately to
religious meetings of Protestant, Catholic and Methodist churches 'just
because one gave tattie scones, the next sausage rolls and the other gave
pies'.[80] In this way, independent missions fitted into a very variegated
religious culture amongst the inter-war Protestant working class.

Tent missions, the Salvation Army and the like were sanctuaries to
many of the working classes during the depressed 1920s and 1930s. They

offered an open and effectual door to those suffering through unemployment and poverty, and made little financial demand upon followers who could in any event adopt an irregular connection with such organisations. The main presbyterian churches, because of their more rigid organisation and system of permanent membership, could make fewer concessions to fluctuating fortunes. During the slump of the early 1930s, working-class congregations of the Church of Scotland reported church attendance and recruitment of men fell sharply because those on the dole would not appear in church without suitable clothes and money for collection; in addition, seat-renting continued and the poor were often made to apply for suspension of payments or for use of free seats. It is perhaps no wonder that when revivalism burst out amongst striking miners and impoverished fishing communities in 1921–2, it was the independent missions which responded. At Inverallochy on the Moray Firth coast, evangelists like Jock Troup preached as work stopped, children knelt in prayer in the road, bonfires were started of cigarettes, playing cards, snakes-and-ladders boards and dancing shoes, and fishermen 'knelt down together on the shore and engaged in silent prayer, wringing their hands and swaying their bodies to and fro'.[81] The mainstream churches and the authorities could be disturbed by open-air prayer meetings; in the pit village of Plean 'the village constable deemed it his duty to order the meeting to disperse'.[82] Though the unemployed and the poor of the inter-war years kept their names on the communicants' rolls of the Church of Scotland or the U.F. Church, the stigma of the free seat drove many to the evangelistic missions.

The Catholic Church seems to have related better to its membership during the Slump, though it also had difficulties in pit villages. It seems that a disproportionate number of Communist Party recruits in Scotland were Catholic in the inter-war period, and fierce local contests built up between 'renegade' Catholics and priests during the General Strike and the Spanish civil war. In Fife during the coal strike of 1926 the scabs were identified as 'almost without exception composed of the religious fraternity', and when priests started anti-communist campaigning Party recruits 'vanished like snow off a dyke'.[83] Arguably, the Catholic Church was the best equipped denomination in tackling the adverse effects of economic depression, and does not seem to have suffered serious losses arising from recessionary periods. The Catholic faith is often seen as being invigorated by the combined effects of poverty and discrimination; priests tended to be drawn from the working classes and to relate well to economic hardship amongst their parishioners. Though Catholics moved increasingly during this period into skilled and white-collar jobs, the Catholic community retained a homogeneity which prevented a major social divide emerging between a practising Catholic bourgeoisie and a lapsed proletariat.

The experience of the Highlands and Hebrides was one of persistent economic depression. It also had the most committed churchgoers, overwhelmingly drawn from relatively poor crofting communities. In an area where state economic aid has been extensively used in trying to slow down the contraction of crofting, the disintegration of townships and out-migration of the young, southern commentators pointed to 'the tyranny of religion' of the puritanical Free Church, Free Presbyterian Church and even of the Church of Scotland in this region. The dissenting clergy disapproved of sport, secular Gaelic song and dance, and even of religious voluntary organisations. Amongst adherents to the Free and Free Presbyterian Churches, there was a fierce grip on the outward face of popular culture. Sabbatarianism was strict with Sunday activities centred on churchgoing and other tasks reduced to precisely catalogued acts of necessity (such as milking the cattle) and mercy; for Free Presbyterians, using public transport was forbidden as it gave 'a certain proportionate moral and material contribution towards the support of evil'.[84] In the Western Highlands and Hebrides, economic depression, the Gaelic language and the heritage of the Clearances combined to provided an environment in which puritanism was sustained.

Even with outbursts of revivalism still prevalent in inter-war Scotland, the face of presbyterianism was changing. Ministers started to be recruited proportionately more from the Lowlands than from the Highlands, and from the cities rather than rural areas, and this seems to have been instrumental in transforming the office of minister from the saving of souls to the organising of social and sporting events. Lavinia Derwent describes how the ageing incumbent of a Borders' parish had been in the 1920s 'awful holy and awful upright, ... awful strict, awful old, but not, I gathered, awful human', and how the new minister, her brother, brought a new style to church life. Whilst the 'auld meenister' 'kept his place, aloof from his parishioners', the new one 'appeared in plus fours and an open-necked shirt' and not only organised but joined in sporting events and Scout camps.[85] In the same vein, a 'bothy loon' – a young farm worker – in Kincardineshire was surprised in the early 1920s when the minister held a party at the manse for the Bible class and choir: 'The minister's wife hid romantic ideas, she hid the lads a' paired aff wi' lassies, bit she didna mak' a guid job o'd as far as it suited me ... Syne, they started tae play Postman's Knock, Pit the Cushions Doon and things like that. The minister and his wife wir ferr enjoyed'd, they wir takin' part in athing ...'[86] Many women respondents say that they met their husbands at the parish church. Mrs K.3(1906) recalled 'a superintendent in the primary who prided herself in getting young couples together, you know ... And I was the pianist, in the primary Sunday school, and she was a great one for making matches. And that was where I met my husband when we were seventeen.'[87] The ambience of the Lowland Church of Scotland was turning away from both puritanism and revivalism.

Taken together, the experiential and statistical evidence suggests that there was no major breach of the Scottish people from organised religion between 1890 and 1939. For the Catholic Church, its constituency almost doubled from 343,000 in 1892 to 614,469 in 1939; the period was one of institutional consolidation (especially by the state recognition of its schools after 1918), and of riding out the sectarian hostilities of the 1920s and 1930s. For the Protestant denominations, the suburban church had developed a major leisure function which, though challenged from the 1910s by commercial recreation for the middle classes, was still very active in the inter-war period. In working-class districts, despite the 'social question' and the right-wing shift amongst the presbyterian leadership after 1918, the growth of popularity of the independent evangelical sector was an addition, not an alternative, to attendance at the Church of Scotland or, before 1929, the United Free Church. However, problems loomed. Church union in 1929, the abandonment of Christian-socialist ideals and the widespread collapse of evangelical puritanism in the 1930s were to herald a difficult transition for the churches. In pre-industrial and industrial periods alike, Scottish society had been governed by a puritan creed; that creed had started to disintegrate, and it was far from clear at the eve of the Second World War how organised Christianity was going to adjust.

NOTES

1. Queen's Park Free Church, Glasgow, Mission District minutes, 1886-1901, GCA TD396/47.
2. See the books by McLeod, Wickham and Green in the Bibliography to chapter 1.
3. J. Begg, *Happy Homes for Working Men, and How to Get Them* (London and Edinburgh, 1866), p. iii.
4. Anon., *The Religious Doubts of Common Men: A Correspondence between Two Laymen* (Edinburgh, 1906), pp. 2–3.
5. A term developed in S. Yeo, *Religion and Voluntary Organisations in Crisis* (London, 1976), p. 296 and passim.
6. J. C. Gibson (ed.), *Diary of Sir Michael Connal, 1835 to 1893* (Glasgow, 1895), pp. 149, 334, 340.
7. I. Maclaren pseud. (Rev. J. Watson), *Church Folks* (London, 1901), pp. 41–2.
8. Quoted in W. Grant, *Edward Bayley: His Work Among Young Men and System of Guild Bible Classes* (Edinburgh, 1913), p. 30.

9. Renwick Free Church, Glasgow, Evangelistic Association minutes, 29 March and 3 May 1899, GCA TD396/33/1.
10. M. Kay, *Romance of the Martyrs' Christian Band* (Glasgow, 1939), p. 30.
11. G. Barron, *Our Lapsed Masses* (Edinburgh, 1884), p. 4.
12. D. Macleod, *Our Home Mission* (Edinburgh, 1893), pp. 12–13.
13. Ibid., p. 16.
14. D. Macleod, *Lines of Progress* (Edinburgh and London, 1895), pp. 21–2.
15. A. S. Matheson, *The Church and Social Problems* (Edinburgh and London, 1893), p. 4.
16. J. A. Campbell, *Elders in their Relation to Church Work* (Glasgow, 1884), p. 5.
17. M. MacCallum, *Religion as Social Justice* (Glasgow, 1915), p. 6.
18. D. Macleod, *Our Home Mission*, p. 16.
19. K. Hardie 'The church and the labour problem', *The Thinker*, vol. iii (1893), p. 108.
20. Glasgow United Trades Council, *Annual Report* (1882–3), p. 11.
21. Church of Scotland Presbytery of Glasgow minutes, 28 March 1888, SRO CH3/171/12.
22. A. S. Matheson, op. cit., p. 2.
23. A. S. Matheson, *The Gospel and Modern Substitutes* (Edinburgh, 1890), pp. 176–7.
24. D. Watson, *Social Problems and the Church's Duty* (London and Edinburgh, 1908), p. 5.
25. A. S. Matheson, *The Gospel and Modern Substitutes*, pp. 176–7, 184.
26. D. Watson, *Perfect Manhood* (London, 1905), p. vii.
27. W. S. Bruce, *Some Aspects of Christian Morality* (London, 1905), p. 237.
28. D . Watson, *Social Problems*, p. 109.
29. A. S. Matheson, *The City of Man* (London, 1910), pp. 196–9.
30. C. G. Brown, '"To be aglow with civic ardours": the "godly commonwealth" in Glasgow 1843–1914', *RSCHS*, vol. 16 (1996).
31. W. Muir, *Christianity and Labour* (London, 1910), p. 26.
32. *Reports of the Schemes of the Church of Scotland* (1896), pp. 806–7.
33. Rev. George Reith, quoted in S. J. Brown, 'The social vision of Scottish presbyterianism and the Union of 1929', *RSCHS*, xxiv (1990), p. 83.
34. Quoted in J. O'Malley, 'The drift towards socialism by the Irish Catholic community in Glasgow 1880–1910', unpub. BA diss., University of Strathclyde, 1976, p. 9.
35. Quoted in ibid., p. 25.
36. H. McLeod, 'Protestantism and the working class in Imperial Germany', *European Studies Review*, vol. 12 (1982).
37. The following six paragraphs rely heavily on the pioneering research of Professor Stewart J. Brown cited in the notes.
38. S. J. Brown, '"A solemn purification by fire": responses to the Great War in the Scottish presbyterian churches, 1914–19', *Journal of Ecclesiastical History*, vol. 45 (1994), p. 82.
39. Quoted in ibid., p. 87.
40. Quoted in ibid., p. 94.
41. Quoted in D. S. Cairns (ed.), *The Army and Religion* (London, 1919), p. 145.
42. Data in ibid, pp. 189–91.
43. Quoted in ibid, p. 223.
44. Commission on the War, *Reports on the Schemes of the Church of Scotland, 1918*, pp 624–25.
45. Quoted in S. J. Brown, '"A Victory for God": the Scottish presbyterian churches and the General Strike of 1926', *Journal of Ecclesiastical History*, vol. 42 (1991), pp. 598–99.

46. Commission on the War, *Reports of the Schemes of the Church of Scotland*, 1919, pp. 635–86.
47. Quoted in S. J. Brown, '"A Victory for God"', p. 604.
48. Quoted in ibid., p. 615.
49. W. Knox (ed.), *Scottish Labour Leaders, 1918–39: A Biographical Dictionary* (Edinburgh, 1984), pp. 30, 33.
50. Church and Nation Committee, *Reports to the General Assembly of the Church of Scotland*, 1932, p. 506.
51. J. Littlejohn, *Westrigg: The Sociology of a Cheviot Parish* (London, 1963), pp. 40–4.
52. D. Watson, *Perfect Manhood*, pp. 98–9.
53. The following paragraphs on school boards are based on C. G. Brown, 'Religion and the development of an urban society: Glasgow 1780–1914', unpub. PH.D. thesis, University of Glasgow, 1982, vol. 2, pp. 93–142.
54. Education Committee, *Reports on the Schemes of the Church of Scotland, 1879*, pp. 5–9, 83–4.
55. B. Aspinwall, 'The Scottish religious identity in the Atlantic world 1880–1914', in S. Mews (ed.), *Religion and National Identity* (Oxford, 1982), p. 505.
56. Figures calculated from data in Committee on Temperance, *Reports to the General Assembly of the Church of Scotland, 1897*, p. 917; and *Proceedings of the Synod of the U.P. Church*, 1891, p. 659.
57. Committee on Temperance, *Reports to the General Assembly of the Church of Scotland*, 1919–26; Committee on Temperance, *Reports to the General Assembly of the U.F. Church*, 1919.
58. D. Watson, *The Church at Work* (Edinburgh, 1926), p.125.
59. A fuller analysis of these and other data is given in C. G. Brown, 'Religion and secularisation' in A. Dickson and J. H. Treble (eds), *People and Society in Scotland, vol. III, 1914–1990* (Edinburgh, 1992), pp. 48–55.
60. H. McLeod, 'New perspectives on Victorian working-class religion: the oral evidence', *Oral History Journal*, vol. 14 (1986), p. 33.
61. C. G. Brown and J. D. Stephenson, '"Sprouting Wings?": women and religion in Scotland c.1890–1950', in E. Breitenbach and E. Gordon (eds), *Out of Bounds: Women in Scottish Society 1800–1945* (Edinburgh, 1992), p. 100.
62. R. Q. Gray, *The Labour Aristocracy in Victorian Edinburgh* (Oxford, 1976), p. 105.
63. J. Springhall, *Youth, Empire and Society: British Youth Movements, 1883–1940* (London, 1977), p. 31; and B. M. Fraser, 'The origins and development of the Boys' Brigade', unpub. PH.D. thesis, University of Strathclyde, 1980, pp. 350, 504.
64. SOHCA/006/Mrs N.2(1906), p. 6.
65. SOHCA/006/Mrs W.2(1916), p. 5.
66. SOHCA/006/Mrs Q.2(1912), p. 7.
67. SOHCA/006/Mrs M.2(1915), p. 3.
68. SOHCA/006/Mrs O.2(1899), p. 6.
69. F. J. MacDonald, *The Corncrake and the Lysander* (London, 1985), pp. 125, 158.
70. SOHCA/006/Mrs R.2(1905), p. 8.
71. E. Cowan, *Spring Remembered: A Scottish Jewish Childhood* (London, 1990), pp. 70–1; J. T. Caldwell, *Severely Dealt With: Growing up in Belfast and Glasgow* (Bradford, 1993), p. 119.
72. SOHCA/006/Mrs P.1(1913), p. 15.
73. SOHCA/006/Mrs V.2(1906), p. 7.
74. SOHCA/006/Mrs X.2(1920), p. 12.

75. Ibid., p. 14.
76. SOHCA/006/Mrs M.2(1915), p. 5.
77. C. Rush, *Peace Comes Dropping Slow* (Edinburgh, 1983), pp. 7, 131.
78. SOHCA/006/Mrs A.3(1913), p. 8.
79. SOHCA/006/Mrs T.2(1899), p. 2.
80. M. Weir, *Best Foot Forward* (London, 1972), pp. 69–71.
81. *Fraserburgh Herald,* quoted in P. Thompson et al., *Living the Fishing* (London, 1983), p. 205; J. A. Stewart, *Our Beloved Jock: Revival Days in Scotland and England* (Asheville, N.C., 1964), pp. 8–17.
82. *Stirling Observer,* 12 January 1922.
83. Quoted in I. MacDougall (ed.), *Militant Miners* (Edinburgh, 1981), p. 301.
84. Quoted in A. McPherson (ed.), *History of the Free Presbyterian Church of Scotland* (Inverness, c.1973), pp. 359–60.
85. L. Derwent, *Lady of the Manse* (London, 1985), pp. 65–6.
86. A. Smith, *Forty Years in Kincardineshire 1911–1951: A Bothy Loon's Life Story* (Forfar, 1990), p. 60.
87. SOHCA/006/Mrs K.3(1906), p. 16.

CHAPTER 7

THE HAEMORRHAGE OF FAITH 1939–97: THE CRISIS OF CHURCH CONNECTION

COUNTING THE UNGODLY?

The religious crisis which emerged during the second half of the twentieth century has been unprecedented. It is not a crisis that is peculiar to Scotland, but is indeed one that has been common to mainland Britain and is to be found developing in most of western society. It is a crisis of religious practice, a crisis of the people's connections with churches, and a crisis of even a diffusive Christianity.[1] In extremely large numbers, the people have stopped going to church, stopped becoming church members, and no longer recognise a substantive religious influence in their social lives. After adapting with success to industrial, urban and capitalist society in the eighteenth and nineteenth centuries, religion in the late twentieth century is losing its place in Scottish society.

Statistics provide a stark guide to Scottish secularisation. The data in Figure 5 (pp. 62–3) show that a minimum of 44 per cent of Scots had a formal church connection in 1939. After declining to 42 per cent in 1945, the figure climbed to almost 46 per cent in 1956 and then started to fall continuously and steeply to 27 per cent in 1994. The gradient of the decline in the 1990s is such that it shows no sign of 'bottoming-out', falling at a rate of more than half of one per cent per annum. If the annual rate of decline is sustained at the average between 1985 and 1994 (–1.69%), the proportion of Scots with a church connection will fall below a quarter in 1999, below a fifth in 2012 and below a tenth in 2053. However, things may be even more serious for organised religion.

Church membership figures show that nearly all Scottish churches have suffered a net decline since 1939 – the only exceptions being Islam, the Jehovah's Witnesses, the Mormons and a number of comparatively tiny 'new religions'. Most Protestant churches actually experienced growth in membership after 1939, and indeed attained post-war peaks or high points in the 1950s: the Church of Scotland and the Methodist Church in 1956, the United Free Church in 1955, the Scottish Episcopal

Church in 1955 (a minor revival after virtually continuous decline since its all-time high in 1921), whilst the Congregationalists and the Baptists had attained peaks earlier in 1934 and 1935 respectively. Despite this denominational variation, the late 1940s and first half of the 1950s was a period of fairly significant membership success for Protestantism in Scotland. The Catholic Church experienced a significantly later peak in the size of its community. Figures for estimated Catholic population show two peaks — one in 1966 (at 827,000) and the other in 1980 (at 828,000). Though this is not as useful an indicator of active religiosity, it is probably a fair reflection of how Catholic religious practise and adherence started its decline some two decades or so later than Protestantism. Only one denomination which experienced membership decline in Scotland has sustained a late-twentieth-century reversal – the Baptist Church. Baptist membership declined from the 1930s until 1976, and then started a modest but steady growth in the last quarter of the century. This is a distinctive pattern; there is some oral-history evidence that the Baptists have been recruiting amongst disaffected members of the Church of Scotland as well as from amongst English immigrants. The Baptist case may well be indicative of the ability of the smaller and more evangelical groups (which may include the Salvation Army and independent evangelical congregations) to attract and maintain worshippers by either remaining 'firm in the faith', or by modernising forms of worship and evangelical outreach to attract younger people.

Overall, the relatively high level of church adherence amongst the Scottish population after the Second World War was very significant. The proportion of Scots in formal connection to a church in 1956 was only five per cent lower than in 1905, the all-time high, and matched figures in the mid 1870s. However, the decline in church connection that commenced in the late 1950s, and which accelerated in the 1960s and 1970s, was unprecedented. Even by 1963, the level was the lowest this century, suggesting that in the space of seven years there had been a very dramatic change. However, things then got worse, notably after a watershed in the religiosity of Scots in the years 1963–5. In those three years, the proportion of marriages being religiously solemnised in Scotland took its first major peace-time drop in Scotland, from 80 to 77 per cent, and fell thereafter at more than one per cent per annum to reach 65 per cent in 1975 and 54 per cent in 1995. On top of this, an increasing proportion of marriages since the 1960s are re-marriages, and increasing numbers of young couples have since the 1970s opted for cohabitation without any form of marriage ceremony. In this respect, what started in the mid 1960s has become in the last quarter of the century the secularisation of family formation.

Other evidence reveals that the years 1963–6 were cataclysmic for the Protestant churches, both in terms of membership and Sunday-school enrolment. The Church of Scotland's success in recruiting from its own 'constituency', measured by the proportion of those baptised (mostly shortly after birth) who became communicants 18 years later, reveals major success between 1900 and 1956 with usually more than 75 per cent recruitment, peaking in 1955 with 126 per cent. But the rate then started to fall steeply, reaching 82 per cent in 1963, 60 per cent in 1965 and then a haemorrhaging rate of around 28 per cent between 1972 and 1990.[2] The number of baptisms in the Church has also fallen sharply from its all-time peak of 51,767 in 1961 to 17,164 in 1990 (the greatest single fall being of 13 per cent in the years 1963–5). This means that the 'constituency' of infants being inducted into the Church is dwindling away. With new communicants falling to just over 5,000 in 1996, the Church of Scotland in 2000 will be recruiting less than a tenth of the number it did in 1956. With an aging kirk population, this will translate into an even steeper decline in total membership.

One other factor is the collapse of Sunday schools. During the years 1941–56, there was a 41 per cent rise in Sunday-school enrolments in the Church of Scotland, but a plummet ensued from a peak of 325,200 in 1956 to 60,936 in 1994. Despite the fall in the birth rate, this represents a cataclysmic failure in the youth work of the Church. It seems certain that Sunday schools in the Church of Scotland will at least halve in size by 2004, and may well be close to disappearance by the end of that decade. Since the birth of the Sunday school in Scotland in 1787, the main presbyterian churches have come to rely on it for raising children in the faith; with no apparent adjustment to its disappearance in evidence, it is difficult to imagine how the Church is going to reach young people let alone recruit them.

Until the 1980s, it appeared that the Catholic Church in Scotland was less susceptible to these trends. The baptised Catholic 'constituency' in Scotland reached a high plateau of around 810,000 between 1963 and 1983 and then started to fall sharply to 743,000 by 1994. The first major discernible crisis occurred in the mid 1980s when a shortage of priests and of young men entering the priesthood was identified in Scotland.[3] In 1984 Catholics were the largest single group amongst Scottish church-goers: 43.4 per cent of all adult churchgoers went to the Catholic Church compared to 40.3 per cent going to the Church of Scotland.[4] Since then, evidence of a crisis in Catholic faith has been rising. The fall in the number of Catholic marriages has been very striking, from 7,099 in 1970 to 6,003 in 1975, 4,813 in 1985 and then 2,948 in 1995 – a level not seen since exactly one hundred years before. Its rate of decline is also accelerating, standing at 25 per cent in the period 1991–5 (compared to 15 per cent for the Church of Scotland). The conclusion from these data is that the decline of church connection has started late in the Scottish Catholic Church, but that it is turning into a much steeper crisis than that even of the Church of Scotland.

More than 82 per cent of church adherents and 84 per cent of churchgoers in Scotland are accounted for by the Church of Scotland and the Catholic Church. In 1965 there were 1,248,000 Church of Scotland communicants and 810,000 Catholics; in 1995 the figures were 698,000 and 743,000 respectively. Scots in the 1990s are forsaking their churches for worship, adherence, marriage, baptism and the religious education of their children. Secularisation as a widespread breach of popular church connection has developed in Scotland – as it has in England and Wales – in the space of little over thirty years. Accounting for this is the thorniest problem for the social historian of religion.

PROSPERITY AND SOCIAL CLASS

There has been a very varied social context for organised religion in Scotland since 1939. In general terms, the period has been much more prosperous for the Scottish people than the forty years that preceded it. Certainly, there has been agonising economic readjustment with the final collapse between the late 1960s and early 1980s of the country's heavy industrial base – shipbuilding, coalmining and heavy engineering – accompanied by high unemployment. Nonetheless, standards of living, housing and environmental amenity have risen much more dramatically than at any time in the country's history. Since church connection was relatively little affected by economic depression in the inter-war period, the issue arises whether prosperity has had a bearing upon secularisation.

The Second World War between 1939 and 1945 exacted a toll upon the Scottish churches, certainly in the short-term. Whilst the outbreak of hostilities in 1914–15 initiated a surge in membership during a period of stagnancy, the reverse happened in 1938–43 with a fall of 22 per cent in Church of Scotland members – in part the product of wartime dislocation of the civil population.[5] But more generally, the place of religion and religious culture was different in the Second World War compared to the First. Protestant churchmen, certainly the leadership of the Church of Scotland, entered the second war in a conservative and morally-defensive frame of mind, and became rapidly out of step with government policy and the temper of the times. In the first war, the equation of morale with morals had led to a puritan campaign against sport, frivolity and drink. In the second war, the government message was one of 'work hard, play hard'. The cinema, radio and light entertainment encouraged off-duty light relief from the exigencies of war, and puritanism became officially out of fashion. Almost immediately, this isolated churchmen. The Church of Scotland noted 'an extraordinary outburst of drunkenness in the first weeks of the war', and took it upon itself to attack 'the vulgarity of some BBC programmes' and their 'drink suggestiveness' – notably the 'ITMA' radio comedy programme series. The Church attacked the government for permitting beer consumption to rise and assisting the brewers in their efforts to 'capture the nation's youth'. The Temperance Committee reported in 1943 that 'the Church cannot accept as true and practicable the argument that alcohol is essential to maintain national morale'.[6] The militarisation of the north of Scotland challenged the remnants of puritan culture; the armed forces condoned drinking in 'dry' areas, and in the parish of Evie and Rendall in Orkney there was a clash with the locals over the hanging out of washing on the Sabbath.[7]

In these ways, the war accelerated the decline of puritanism in Scottish society. Its first perceptible effect was the post-war collapse of the temperance movement. Local-veto plebiscites in 1946–7 turned most of Scotland's remaining 'dry' areas 'wet' (including Wick, Lerwick, St Monans, Balfron and Fenwick), and 1947 legislation instituting state management of the drinks trade in the Scottish new towns then under construction was repealed in 1952. 'The outlook for temperance,' the Church of Scotland general assembly committee noted in 1946, 'is all the darker because of those war years.'[8] Servicemen from rural areas were found by ministers in the late 1940s to have lost their previous regard for religion, and they were widely attributed with initiating a sharp fall in churchgoing after demobilisation. This was noted even in towns. At Tayport it was reported: 'Adolescents and young folk who have been in the Forces seem particularly disinclined to attend.'[9] Similarly, at Auchterarder in Perthshire: 'War-time with its many calls on Sunday-time does not lead to observance of Sunday in peace-time.'[10]

Despite this reported fall in churchgoing in 1945, the end of the war brought a major return to presbyterianism with the number of communicants rising by 175,000 in 1946 – almost a quarter higher than in the last year of the war. However, the Church of Scotland did not regain its 1938 level of active communicants (those taking communion at least once a year) until 1959, indicating that the war had seriously retarded the already slow growth of the first half of the century. This creates something of a paradox, for – as we have already seen – the ten years between 1946 and 1956 saw remarkable growth in church connection, Sunday-school enrolment and new communicants. The evidence suggests that the strong interest in organised religion was amongst young people, perhaps especially those born just before and during the war years. It was this generation that experienced the last major exposure to the 'home mission'.

Between 1947 and 1956 there were a series of energetic evangelistic campaigns, dominated by the Church of Scotland. Campaigns with titles such as 'Christian Commandos', the 'Tell Scotland' movement, and the 'All Scotland Crusade', were led by teams of Protestant evangelists. One unprecedented feature that developed was the systematic co-operation of BBC radio in Scotland, which devoted considerable air-time to cover the evangelistic effort. The 'Radio Missions' of 1950-2 initiated team evangelism which led on to the controversial decision in 1955 to invite the American Southern Baptist preacher, Billy Graham, to lead the 'All Scotland Crusade'. His visit fostered widespread interest and mass audiences throughout the country. For six weeks around Easter 1955 nightly mass rallies of some 10,000 people packed the Kelvin Hall in Glasgow, and for two of those weeks others attended churches and halls around the country to participate in the services via relay television. The concluding Good Friday service at Hampden Park attracted just short of 100,000 people, and throughout the crusade both the BBC and especially the Scottish press were carefully and successfully manipulated by the interdenominational organising committees. There were meetings in factories, outside shipyard gates, and a return to house-to-house visitation on a scale probably not seen since before the First World War. The evangelists were well organised and became astute at promoting media coverage.[11]

The Billy Graham involvement split the Tell Scotland movement over the focus on personality and the 'crusade' style. A total attendance of over a million people was recorded in 1955 with 26,547 'enquiries' from those coming forward. An analysis of the principal rallies in Glasgow showed that only 20,000 (or under 3 per cent) of the 830,000 who attended came forward to 'make decisions for Christ'; of these 70 per cent were women, 73 per cent were under thirty years of age (11 per cent under twelve), and 62 per cent were already regular church attenders. These statistics confirm the impression that the Crusade does not deserve the term 'religious revival'. The occasions were visual spectacles, carefully orchestrated and designed, but not emotional outpourings. The audiences seem to have been composed overwhelmingly of the middle-aged and the elderly, mostly middle class, sitting stiffly erect and defensively muffled in sturdy overcoats with many of the women in their finest fur hats, coats and tippets. The 'enquirers' were the young, often the very young, and the lasting effects were slight. The bulk of the

Protestant clergy were faintly hostile to the Crusade and to the 'Tell Scotland' movement with which it was connected. Nearly 70 per cent of Church of Scotland ministers reported that all forms of evangelisation in 1954–6 had 'little or no effect' on their congregations. Certainly, critics made much of the fact that the Crusade was followed by the beginnings of rapid church decline.[12]

Why this surge in church connection turned quickly into decline awaits systematic enquiry, both in Scotland and in the international context. For Scotland, the re-housing of the people seems a critical and distinctive factor. Massive slum-clearance programmes and schemes of council-house and new-town construction started in earnest in the 1950s and came to an effective end in the early 1970s. The ecclesiastical response has been variable, and together with the grave problems of depersonalisation, isolation, high unemployment, vandalism and poor sense of community that afflicted many of the new sprawling 'schemes', this has created a different and difficult role for organised religion. The Catholic Church was the first off the mark; in the west of Scotland alone, it founded thirty-five new parishes in 1945–50, a further forty-one in 1951–60 and twenty-six in 1961–70 to cater for its adherents who were proportionately the most affected by rehousing in the post-war period. The Baptist and Episcopal Churches were also active, especially in the new towns, but the efforts of the Church of Scotland remained relatively sluggish. It was slower to initiate building than the Catholic Church immediately after the war, though between 1948 and 1959 it established 84 new parishes and erected 129 buildings – 108 of which were dual-role 'hall-churches'.[13] However, the surfeit of Victorian churches in wrong locations remained a millstone round the presbyterian church, and very quickly it would be turning to the problem of amalgamating parishes and closing churches.

The creation of housing schemes had two major consequences for the churches. Firstly, inner-city areas which were struck by slum-clearance in the 1950s and 1960s lost the communities which supported congregations, and secondly the new large peripheral housing schemes, such as Easterhouse and Drumchapel in Glasgow, and Craigmillar and Wester Hailes in Edinburgh, were rapidly perceived by many as 'problem' areas. There was a tendency in the early years to regard such schemes as places where clergy and Sunday-school teachers had to be 'sent in' in the manner of Victorian missions to the slums or Africa, and, though churches and congregational organisations did follow, the dislocation increased the fragility of popular church connection. Matters have not been helped by the leadership and the membership of the Church of Scotland becoming increasingly out of step with the political inclinations of both the Scottish people and the church's members. Whilst the Labour Party has consistently dominated Scottish politics since the 1950s, a survey in the mid 1960s found that three-quarters of elders attending the general assembly voted Conservative. In the mid 1980s, 45 per cent of Church of Scotland members voted Conservative with only 17 per cent voting Labour, less than for the centrist Liberals.[14] For the liberal and radical wing of Church of Scotland ministers, the issue of the church failing the poor has remained a live one.[15]

However, the social composition of church members has in fact changed little since the mid-nineteenth century. A major survey in the 1960s of Falkirk – taken to represent 'middle Scotland' – demonstrated that church affiliation was strongest amongst the small number of the professional classes (who were entirely Protestant), whilst the proportion of lower-middle (or 'intermediate') classes in both Protestant and Catholic churches was between two and three times higher than in the town's population as a whole. But as in Hillis's study of Victorian Glasgow, the bulk of church members came from the skilled working classes who made up just over half of the total population and of Church of Scotland members, 60 per cent of Catholic adherents, and two-thirds of the members of minority Protestant denominations. Though the partly skilled and unskilled were under-represented, making up a third of the inhabitants but only a fifth of Catholic adherents and 8 per cent of Church of Scotland members, the most active church members were in the lower social groups; 80 per cent of members amongst the partly skilled and unskilled claimed weekly church attendance compared with around 60 per cent for each of the higher social classifications.[16] A second study of the 1960s, of the Prestonfield district of Edinburgh, offered contrary evidence; it showed two-thirds of the working classes were non-attenders ('dormant') compared with 38 per cent of middle classes and 29 per cent of the lower-middle ('borderline') class.[17] But a third study offered corroboration to the Falkirk evidence. An examination of church membership in Alloa according to housing type demonstrated that 66 per cent of owner-occupiers were church members compared to 58 per cent of council tenants and 47 per cent of those in privately-rented property. The author concluded that church membership was very low amongst the unskilled working class, very high amongst the skilled workers, about average for the lower-middle and middle classes, and very low with the upper middle class.[18] The sustained religiosity of the Scottish working classes has unfortunately not always been recognised – even by one later Church of Scotland study.[19] With the adherence of the Catholic Church widely acknowledged to be predominantly working-class, the fact is that post-war church membership has drawn disproportionately heavily from the largest social group – the skilled working classes. Moreover, the religiosity of lower social groups is strong outwith the Lowlands; the most strongly churchgoing area of Britain (excluding Northern Ireland) in 1984 was the Western Isles and Lochalsh district of the West Highlands, where some 53 per cent of the predominantly crofter-fisher population attended church.[20]

The evidence of the sociological studies of the 1960s and early 1970s was taken at the very time when church decline was in its rapid early stages, and it showed no sudden reduction in the proletarian element in Scottish church life. The argument that secularisation was led or caused by the working classes in Scotland seems unsustainable – for any period. Indeed, there is a remarkable unanimity in all the evidence stretching back to the 1770s in Scotland as to the importance of the working classes in church life. Not only has the secularisation of the late twentieth century not been caused by a working-class evacuation of the churches, there is more compelling evidence that social class has very little to do with it. Rising standards of living and various cultural changes have reduced many of the sharper social divisions of Scottish society. For this reason, investigation of church decline has shifted since the early 1970s away from *class* analysis and towards *cultural* analysis. In particular, focus has increasingly fallen on the role of prosperity-induced cultural change in reducing the social significance of religion in people's lives.

CULTURE, LIFESTYLE AND THE DECLINE OF PURITANISM

One way of approaching this topic is to look at the very major changes to the built environment within which the people have reconstructed their popular culture since the 1950s. Pre-eminent amongst these has been new housing – mainly council housing between the 1950s and the mid 1970s, and new-build owner-occupied housing since then. The council house had a far more dramatic impact upon Scotland than England and Wales. By 1967, 52 per cent of Scottish housing was rent-subsidised state housing, compared to only 25 per cent in England and Wales, virtually all of it built since 1919; by 1981 at least 70 per cent of the housing stock in nearly two-thirds of Scottish local authority areas (including Glasgow and most west-of-Scotland towns) was council-owned.[21] Whilst council housing did not necessarily mean an age of luxury for the Scottish working classes, it helped to throw up new forms of leisure and culture which tended to undermine the received role of religion. For one thing, council housing dramatically increased the space available in the Scottish home. In 1901 about half the Scottish population lived in houses of one or two rooms (70 per cent in Glasgow, 72 per cent in Dundee and 48 per cent in Edinburgh); in 1931 the figures were little changed, but by 1951 the Scottish figure had fallen to 26 per cent. [22] Both working and middle classes in Scotland had become accustomed to small homes, and the distinctive 'single-end' and 'room-and-kitchen' homes of the Scottish tenement had made the working classes by far the worst housed in Europe. But during the 1930s, and especially in the 1950s and 1960s, many of the middle classes moved to villa and bungalow accommodation, and the remaining middle and working classes moved to council houses. The multi-roomed home made the space available for new forms of domestic leisure.

The Church of Scotland lost 20,000 communicants in 1940-1 as a result of council-house completions and war evacuation to places with few, if any, churches.[23] Even when churches were erected, the boom in domestic leisure was reported as having a severe impact upon church activities. From the mid 1930s clergymen identified the radio and, by the mid 1950s, the television as major causes of declining religious interest and churchgoing. The churches did not suffer in isolation. Rehousing badly affected all the principal forms of communal recreation. The rehousing to peripheral housing estates undoubtedly contributed to the decline of cinema audiences, football spectating, and dancing in the 1950s and 1960s. Cinema-going peaked in 1946, and the number of cinemas declined in the three decades that followed (from 104 in Glasgow in 1938 to 41 in 1965); Scottish football league spectators fell by 33.5 per cent between the 1948-9 and 1965-6 seasons, most of the fall occurring after 1959; and dance halls declined dramatically in number in the late 1950s and early 1960s.[24] All these forms of recreation suffered from the movement of people to outlying council schemes in which there was virtually no commercial leisure before the 1970s. In the shift from public house, cinema and dance hall, the churches and religious voluntary organisations also suffered.

With the expansion in the size and comfort of the Scottish home in the 1950s and 1960s came a higher public expectation of comfort which churches and church halls could rarely match. The bingo halls which exploded on the Scottish urban scene in 1958 and 1959 offered new excitements in palatial surroundings, attracting working-class women in very large numbers. The Church of Scotland reacted with alarm to the impact it had on churchgoing, asking the Scottish Office to license bingo clubs, and appealing to church members 'to refrain from participating in such activities'.[25] These developments were neatly summed-up by an elderly working-class widow from Whiteinch in Glasgow who in 1961 wrote to the Secretary of State for Scotland opposing the call of the

Church of Scotland and others to suppress bingo halls. With a parliamentary debate imminent, she wrote:

Dear Sir,

As a lonely widow of 60 years of age I hope you will be broadminded when this debate about Bingo come up July 20th.

I have led a lonely life since husbands death 10 yrs ago. A month ago a neighbour took me to Kelvin Arena Hall where I spent 3 happy hours in nice decent company. It was 2/- entrance fee and 13 games cost 1/-. For 3/- for that evening I had a happy night with music records & Bingo game.

Instead of going to the cinema young courting couples also married couples came workmen after a hard days work at the shipyards came & enjoyed a pleasant evening. No swearing, No fighting, everyone sociable & happy. When I think of the lonely nights I spent depressed & lonely & going to bed early Hoping for the next day to come. Why should these people want to spoil peoples' pleasure. You cant close pubs because [a] few foolish men get drunk. The *public* have *always* had *liberty* & There is *no* wrong in an evenings pleasure at Bingo. What do they want the people to do? Cinemas are closing fast & TV to a lot of people think most of the items poor. They will never fill the churches even if they did stop Bingo. The churches are far too draughty. Sermons are long & monotonous & the majority of ministers very very rarely visit the lonely widow. They couldnt care less & they blame Bingo for lack of attendance but then they blamed TV at the start. Do Sir please allow working class people to spend their 1/- on a little pleasure. Hundreds of lonely folk have found happiness and a new lease of life in the company of others in the evening & it is in sociable cheerful clean atmosphere.

St. Pauls chapel built lovely extension to their chapel with Bingo games twice a week. It does more good than harm. Sir I assure you[26]

The inability to maintain religious or church-based leisure in the weekly life of the people has been a major cause of the declining role of the church as a focus in urban community life. This change has been more slow and more uneven in rural districts, but all forms of voluntary organisation arrived quite late in country areas – mostly between 1880 and 1950 – and interacted with the transition to urban-style social divisions. The loss of local autonomy in the 1920s and 1930s, through the demise of parish councils, parish school boards and boards of heritors, ended the secular functions and symbolism of the minister, the schoolmaster and the parish church. The final ending of the practice of heritors reserving pews for tenants seems to have instigated a major breach in church connection amongst the rural middle ranks in the inter-war period; and with continuous advances in farming techniques, a falling workforce, and the wartime need for improved food supply, farmers were by the 1940s and 1950s pressing their employees to spend the Sabbath not for churchgoing but for the utilisation of expensive capital machinery in ploughing, harvesting and tending to livestock. The church union of 1929 also had an effect, with many lower social groups in the United Free Church being unable to countenance amalgamation with the traditional 'opposition' in the 'Auld Kirk'. Whilst a few rural parishes maintained very vigorous community religion – as in the village of Craigie in Angus where it was claimed in the late 1960s that every child was a member of the United Free Church Band of Hope – in general the arrival of improved bus services to nearby towns distracted the attention of the young from the local church, and with its decline the heart of many rural parishes was torn out. When urban commuters moved into the countryside between the 1970s and 1990s, rural *embourgoisement* did little to stem church decline.

The mechanism of church decline after 1956 seems to have centred on the young. Between the mid-1950s and 1980, the number of Church of Scotland Sunday-school pupils almost halved, and a spectacular fall in church baptisms followed: between 1967 and 1982, they fell by half in the Church of Scotland and by almost 40 per cent in the Catholic Church.[27] This rate of decline is higher than the fall in the birth rate, and would seem to indicate a considerable loss of church connection amongst young married couples. The origins of this alienation lay at a younger age. A Falkirk survey of over 200 schoolchildren in the 1960s found that 27 per cent stopped attending church before the age of ten, and that by the age of thirteen two-thirds had given up church connection. The crisis of the young reached its peak in the Church of Scotland between 1967 and 1974. The Church's preoccupations with promoting the temperance movement and opposing gambling virtually disappeared to make way for agonising over the revolution in youth culture during these years. In abandoning the temperance cause, the Church also tried to move with the times by seeking compromises with the hippy-inspired culture of love and opposition to war. There was much in the young's hostility to the Biafran and Vietnam wars, and in their humane and liberal outlook, with which the younger clergy could sympathise. The general assembly was clearly affected by the mood of the times, and was remarkably uncritical of the legalisation of abortion, the decriminalisation of homosexuality, and the liberalisation of divorce in the late 1960s and early 1970s. The 'moral metamorphosis' led the Committee on Moral Welfare to advise the assembly in 1970:

> Need the Church always deplore this new 'permissiveness' as an unalloyed disaster? If the sanctions of commandment and convention are gone, people are set free to respond to goodness for its own sake, under no compulsion, constrained and sustained by the love of Christ and not by the fear of a lost respectability.[28]

And the Church tried to envelop this conventionless morality of western youth within its pale. Energetic youth leaders started church dances and discos in 1966–9, but kirk sessions quickly became concerned with the frequency with which the police visited their premises late on Saturday nights to sort out minor gang fights and complaints from neighbours. The problem became, as one Angus church put it in 1970, to place youth activities on an 'acceptable footing'. It became clear by the early seventies that the Church could not pursue and court youth culture whilst retaining its traditional public standing. The Moral Welfare Committee changed its approach radically between 1970 and 1972. In the first year it found 'the spirit of the age with its new found freedom' providing a healthy challenge to Christians 'to re-think the implications of Christian morality', though in an arch piece of sexism it considered that 'it is the promiscuous girl who is the real problem'. But by 1972, the committee was quite exasperated with 'the turbulent continent of morality' and virtually ceased trying to construct responses to the unfolding 'promiscuous age'.[29] At congregational level, church dances and discos for young people – even for the prosperous youth of suburbia – were either abandoned or so heavily patrolled by elders that they became unappealing to young people of all social backgrounds. The church's status as a popular leisure centre for the young was crumbling.

It was also during the seventies that the Catholic Church first had to come to terms with a sizeable upwardly mobile and young middle class within its constituency which, in the suburbs of Glasgow and in new towns like East Kilbride, had pushed the Church towards a more bourgeois outlook. Catholics really only broke through in significant numbers into middle-class occupations after the Second World War, and mainly after the late 1960s, creating a growing section of prospering lapsed Catholics with which the Scottish Church has at times shown a lack of practise at dealing. The impact of youth culture upon the Catholic young was evident during the first papal visit to Scotland by Pope John Paul II in 1982. The visit bore some striking similarities in its impact on the Church to the visit of Billy Graham upon the Church of Scotland twenty-seven years before. There was an enormous show of enthusiasm, predominantly amongst the young – especially schoolchildren – at rallies in Edinburgh's Murrayfield Stadium and Glasgow's Bellahouston Park. It was significant that the vigorous and irrepressible children's chanting, which nearly overwhelmed John Paul's addresses, was not delivered in any available religious vocabulary but in the tunes and rhythms of the pop world and the football terracing. In terms of church connection, the papal visit does not seem to have stemmed the outflow which set in during the late 1970s in west central Scotland. From 1977 to 1983, the Catholic population of the country fell by just under 10,000 with the losses occurring entirely in the archdiocese of Glasgow and the dioceses of Motherwell and Paisley. As with Billy Graham's visit to Protestant Scotland, that of the Pope to Catholic Scotland came just as decline was setting in.

Explaining the reasons why prosperity appears to be contributing to rapid secularisation is more difficult than merely drawing the correlation. There has been no state-prosecuted frontal assault on religious habits or thinking, but there has still been change in regard to popular attitudes both to the churches and to the lexicon of precise 'beliefs', doctrines and practices they uphold. Trends in lifestyle – towards materialism, if you like – are important here, and notably amongst the younger generations of the upper working classes and the middle classes. A key factor is home ownership which has grown rapidly in Scotland since the late 1970s from a very low base, and which is effecting a marked distinction between the generations. Located in green-field sites of starter homes, a car-based lifestyle has been constructed around two incomes and smaller numbers of children. Pervasive and representative in the Lowlands is Sunday shopping which has advanced rapidly since 1970 in a part of Britain that was previously thought to be so Sabbatarian in its inclinations that prohibitive laws as in England and Wales were unnecessary. Using Sundays for shopping, work or DIY in the home and on the car are not, of course, denunciations of religious faith. But it does represent the failure of the acid test of Scotland's presbyterian culture.

Prosperity works against the churches in another way. With the advance of the state in social amelioration since the 1890s, the churches and religious charities have found a role in filling the social-work gaps in statutory provisions whilst at the same time pressing for legislation to eliminate those gaps. The churches themselves have become major providers of social services; the Church of Scotland by 1996 was the largest social work agency in the country, employing over 1,600 people in a wide range of residential and day-care centres – far more than its number of parish ministers. By generally excluding the laity, church members are decreasingly called upon to be the agents of Christian social action.

One area of Scotland has undergone remarkable cultural change in the second half of the twentieth century – the Highlands and Hebrides. Populated predominantly by crofter-fishers until the middle decades of this century, the Highlands and Hebrides were identified by some Lowland commentators as being under a 'tyranny of religion' which contributed to poor social life and out-migration by the young. The puritanism of the Free Church, Free Presbyterian Church and even the Church of Scotland in this region led to disapproval of sport, secular Gaelic song and dance, and even of religious voluntary organisations. Priests in the strongly Catholic southern Hebrides encourage such activities, contributing to a vibrant secular and Gaelic culture which co-exists happily within religious culture, leading one observer to suggest in the 1950s that a small Hebridean community 'would have a greater chance of survival if it were Catholic than if it followed one of the stricter sects of presbyterianism'.[30] Until the later 1970s, the strict Free and Free Presbyterian Churches held a fierce grip on the outward face of popular culture with Sabbatarianism a marked feature for holidaymakers from the south. At Inverasdale in Wester Ross even today, motorists are reminded by a large sign of the Lord's stricture in the Fourth Commandment. The summer communion season survives still in the Hebrides as an intensified and elongated Sabbath stretching from Thursday till Monday with fringe prayer groups as well as church services twice daily. The discourse on the 'ideal puritan' was until recently perpetuated in newspaper obituaries which invariably commented on the deceased's church record: 'She was a regular church attender and was interested in religious matters', and, of another: 'when at all possible, attended the means of grace'.[31] In church, the message of sermon and prayer in the Highlands is didactic, focusing on the sins and 'backsliding' of the flock. Denunciations of dancing, drinking and Sabbath breaches like watching television (including 'Songs of Praise') flow from the pulpit. Local government enforced a religious regime: in the mid 1930s, MacBrayne's ferry services to Lewis on Sundays were stopped, and since then virtually only Catholic islands are visited on the seventh day. In the 1950s BEA had to stop Sunday flights; in the 1960s the new NATO base became the object of presbyterian scrutiny; and in the 1970s oil-related industries had to give undertakings about Sabbath work.

However, the outwardly pious society of the Highlands has always been tempered by pragmatism and silent revolt (especially amongst men and the young); despite most of Lewis being 'dry' until the 1980s, illegal drinking in 'bochans' was prevalent. As one post-war observer remarked, the crofters were 'no more interested in the destiny of their souls than they were in the destiny of their poultry'.[32] And in the 1980s and 1990s, the culture of the presbyterian Highlands has undergone very dramatic change. Increasing in-migration by 'white settlers' from the Lowlands and England, economic diversification, improved road transport and expanded tourism (notably by year-round mountaineers and hill-walkers), has brought to the daily life of many communities a Lowland middle-class air. At the same time, the contraction of Gaelic-speaking has had its impact on religion. Both the language and the presbyterian puritanism have tended to fade simultaneously, first in much of the southern and central Highlands between the 1880s and 1940s, and since the 1970s in the northern and western Highlands. In Wester Ross in 1975, Gaelic morning worshippers outnumbered those at the evening

'English' service; by 1985 the popularity was reversed; and by 1995 Gaelic-language services had been virtually wiped out.

Matters in the Highland churches have not been helped by the startling scandals in the Free Presbyterian Church, the Free Church and the Catholic Church. In 1988–89, the F.P. Church was split after the conservative wing suspended its most celebrated member, Lord Mackay of Clashfern, the Lord Chancellor, for attending the Catholic requiem mass of a friend. Though Lord Clashfern did not instigate it, a liberal wing of the Church seceded to form the Associated Presbyterian Churches on the grounds that the F.P. majority had 'violated and ignored the Christian's right of private judgement'[33]. Seven years later, the Free Church was rocked by a criminal case against a professor at its Divinity College, the Rev. Donald Macleod, for alleged sexual harassment of female church members. The case was dismissed by the Sheriff who alleged that there was a campaign on the part of certain clergy and lay members of the church to have Macleod convicted and then removed from the church.[34] The Catholic Church was stunned in 1996 by the intense publicity when the Bishop of the Isles, Bishop Roddy Wright, fled his post in Oban with a woman. In the days that followed, it was revealed that he had had sexual relations with two women and had fathered a child.[35] All three cases – though especially the first two – may be seen as triggered by a crisis in Highland identity: the decay of puritanism and Gaelic cannot be divorced from current radical rethinking concerning land, livelihood and culture in the crofting counties.[36]

When the generation of Scots born in the first half of the century discusses why religion has been important in their lives, they characteristically give broken replies in which they resort to relating their own religious activity to that of their parents: 'I had always been used with — well, my father was an organist for a start', and 'Religion was well, my Dad was — They were very religious. I mean, it was a sort of routine we had been brought up to.'[37] When discussing their loss of religiosity, on the other hand, they tend to refer to their own children and cultural change. Mrs C.2(1912) from Edinburgh said:

I don't know when it [religion] ceased to be quite as important. I'll tell you what I think is wrong nowadays. You see so much about science on these [television] programmes that —. I remember when my son was taking medicine, not one of these students believed in anything. He did join Greyfriars Church initially but when he got further on and so steeped in science they would make you believe that you're just a chemical equation and that when you died it was just the chemical equation ceased working and that was it, you know. It used to depress me when I used to hear it because they could knock down every argument you had. And I'd say "but the Bible", and my son would say the Bible was written by a man — a man writes a book, he doesn't always stick to fact. And so what could you say to that because I suppose it was written by a man and then I started to listen to programmes on there, scientific programmes, and I really — am torn in two. I can't decide now whether —. I don't believe there's a hell, I think you make your own hell on earth ... I can't believe that there's a heaven where there's angels fluttering about and all that. I can't believe that nowadays, but I'd like to think there's another life ...[38]

This suggests that a generational change occurred in relation to Protestant religious practice between those born before about 1950 and those born after. What happened after 1956 was that, in some cases, the parents stopped going to church whilst still sending their children to Sunday school; in other cases, the children rebelled against or rejected the church-going habits of their parents. It is tempting to suggest that a similar pattern started for Scots Catholics in the late 1970s and 1980s. The consequence was an unprecedented breaking of a fundamental tradition which had previously passed unbroken from generation to generation: going to church, getting married in church, having children baptised in church. The mechanism of religious change is little understood, but ideological change of the 1890–1930 period, cultural change after 1940 and demographic shifts in the twentieth century as a whole may lie at the heart of Scottish (and indeed British) secularisation.[39] For those living through it, the impact of the cultural and then the lifestyle revolutions which started in the 1960s seem inescapably powerful for breaking religious sensibility and the ecclesiastical grip on everyday life. The result is that churchgoers are no longer the substantial minority of the eighteenth and nineteenth centuries, the custodians of social respectability and society's operating values. More profoundly, new research in the late 1990s is suggesting that an ultimate stage of secularisation may be now in progress in which the people – having shunned churchgoing, church membership and the religious rites of passage – are now losing their Christian faith; only just over 70 per cent of Scots in a 1997 opinion poll expressed a belief in God, a figure lower than those of ten and twenty years ago.[40] The stewardship of Scottish society is vested in generations which have become overwhelmingly 'secular' in their culture and thinking. The churches may not disappear, but Scotland is sharing with the rest of western Europe the rapid dissolution of Christian society.[41]

NOTES

1. A term developed by J. Cox, *English Churches in a Secular Society: Lambeth 1870–1930* (New York and Oxford, 1982), pp. 90–128.
2. A full discussion of these and other data appear in C. G. Brown, 'Religion and secularisation' in A. Dickson and J. H. Treble, *People and Society in Scotland, vol. III 1914–1990* (Edinburgh, 1992), p. 51.

3. *The Scotsman*, 28 February 1987.

4. Calculated from P. Brierley and F. Macdonald (eds), *Prospects for Scotland: Report of the 1984 Census of the Churches* (Edinburgh, 1984), p. 60.

5. A. Muir, *John White* (London, 1958), pp. 321–34.

6. Temperance Committee, *Reports to the General Assembly of the Church of Scotland*, 1940 p. 409; 1942 p. 307; 1943 p. 255.

7. R. Miller (ed.), *The Third Statistical Account of Scotland, The County of Orkney* (Edinburgh, 1985), p. 39.

8 Temperance Committee, op. cit., 1946 p. 256.

9. A. Smith (ed.), *The Third Statistical Account of Scotland, The County of Fife* (Edinburgh and London, 1952), pp. 793–4.

10. D. B. Taylor (ed.), *The Third Statistical Account of Scotland, County of Perth and Kinross* (Coupar Angus, 1979), p. 498.

11. D. P. Thomson, *Visitation Evangelism in Scotland 1946–1956* (n.p., 1956).

12. T. Allan (ed.), *Crusade in Scotland* (London, 1955), p. 108; J. Highet, *The Scottish Churches* (1960, London), pp. 70–123.

13. T. A. Fitzpatrick, *Catholic Secondary Education in South–west Scotland before 1972* (Aberdeen, 1986), pp. 156–70; J. Highet, op. cit., p. 132.

14. D. R. Robertson, "The Relationship between Church and Social Class in Scotland', unpub. PHD thesis, University of Edinburgh, 1966, pp. 364–6; *The Scotsman*, 15 May 1986.

15. See for instance J. Harvey, *Bridging the Gap: Has the Church failed the Poor?* (Edinburgh, 1987).

16. P. L. Sissons, *The Social Significance of Church Membership in the Burgh of Falkirk* (Edinburgh, 1973), pp. 60, 71.

17. D. R. Robertson, op. cit., p. 48.

18. K. J. Panton, 'The church in the community: a study of patterns of religious adherence in a Scottish burgh', in M. Hill (ed.), *A Sociological Yearbook of Religion in Britain, vol. 6* (London, 1973).

19. J. N. Wolfe and M. Pickard, *The Church of Scotland: An Economic Survey* (London, 1980), p. 73.

20. Calculated from P. Brierley and F. Macdonald (eds), op. cit., p. 102.

21. Figures for 1967 calculated from data in Tables 10.10 and 10.11 in C. Rollett, 'Housing', in A. H. Halsey (ed.), *Trends in British Society since 1900* (London, 1972), p. 303; data for 1981 is from R. Rodger, 'Urbanisation in twentieth-century Scotland', in T. M. Devine and R. Finlay (eds), *Scotland in the Twentieth Century* (Edinburgh, 1996), p. 146.

22. J. Butt, 'Working class housing in the Scottish cities 1900–1950', in G. Gordon and B. Dicks (eds), *Scottish Urban History* (Aberdeen, 1983), pp. 234, 248, 260.

23. A. Muir, op. cit., pp. 321–34.

24. J. Wilson, 'The history of the cinema, 1915–1965, with special reference to Glasgow', unpub. BA diss., Dept. of History, Univ. of Strathclyde, pp. 36–7; C. G. Brown, 'The Scottish Office and sport, 1899 1972', *Scottish Centre Research Papers in Sport, Leisure and Society*, vol. 2 (1997); H. Tomney, 'Dancing Daft: Glasgow's dance halls c.1920–c.1960,' unpub. BA diss., Dept. of History, Univ. of Strathclyde, 1994.

25. SRO HH43/194, Betting and Lotteries, Tombola, 1960–63; Temperance and Morals Committee, *Reports to the General Assembly of the Church of Scotland*, 1962 p. 445, 1963 p. 399.

26. Letter to Secretary of State for Scotland, 8 July 1961, SRO HH 43/194.

27. Figures calculated from *Church of Scotland Yearbook* and *The Catholic Directory for Scotland*.
28. *Reports to the General Assembly of the Church of Scotland*, 1970, p. 399.
29. Ibid., 1970 pp. 407, 410; 1972 p. 448.
30. F. Fraser Darling (ed.), *West Highland Survey* (London, 1955) pp. 315–16.
31. These examples taken from *Stornoway Gazette*, 2 August 1986.
32. L. Beckwith, *The Sea for Breakfast* (London, 1968), p. 104.
33. Deed of Separation [of the A.P. Churches from the F.P. Church], 27 May 1989.
34. J. Macleod, *No Great Mischief if You Fall: The Highland Experience* (Edinburgh and London, 1993), pp. 90–154; *The Herald*, 5 August and 8 October 1996.
35. *The Herald*, 8 October 1996.
36. See for instance J. Macleod, op. cit., passim; and J. Hunter, *On the Other Side of Sorrow: Nature and People in the Scottish Highlands* (Edinburgh and London, 1995).
37. SOHCA/006/Mrs G.3(1925) and Mrs I.2(1907). I am grateful to my BA Hons. student, Sarah Smith, for this observation.
38. SOHCA/006/Mrs C.2(1912), pp. 22–3.
39. C. G. Brown, 'The mechanism of religious growth in urban societies: British cities since the eighteenth century', in H. McLeod (ed.), *European Religion in the Age of Great Cities 1830–1930* (London and New York, 1995).
40. *Scotland on Sunday*, 11 May 1997; S. Bruce 'Religion in Britain at the close of the 20th century: a challenge to the silver lining perspective', *Journal of Contemporary Religion*, vol. 11 (1996), pp. 269–70.
41. H. McLeod and W. Ustorf (eds), *The Decline of Christendom in Western Europe 1750–2000* (Orbis, forthcoming).

CHAPTER 8

RELIGION AND IDENTITIES
SINCE 1707

Religion has shaped modern societies in a variety of ways. It has influenced both the public and private worlds of the people. On the one hand, the construction of communal worship and leisure, the religious impact on social welfare, and the formal and informal systems for regulating public morality, have shaped the public domain. On the other hand, religion has shaped the private world – in the family, in personal faith and prayer, and the ordering of values for the conduct of the individual's life. If nothing else, the preceding chapters have shown how the people could identify very strongly with and through religion – with the churches, with religious organisations, with values of personal conduct derived from religion. Religion could demand incredible commitment; we have noted how evangelicalism drove both men and women to extensive endeavour in the home-mission field, and how values like thrift and sobriety and self-improvement could operate within a *mentalité* of religious respectability. This chapter seeks to explore the issue further, deconstructing religious identities and their contributions to other identities – national identities, sectarian identities and gender identities.

RELIGION AND SCOTTISH IDENTITY:
PROTESTANTISM AND CIVIL SOCIETY

Historians and commentators on Scottish civil life have been of recent years increasingly asserting the role of religion in Scottish identity. In the midst of campaigns for constitutional change in late twentieth-century Scotland, many historians have identified the religious heritage of Scotland as significant to national identity under the Union, and as crucially different from the religious tradition of England. There are two main strands to the issue of religion and national identities in Scotland. The first and longest standing concerns the role of religion, specifically presbyterianism, in moulding a distinctive civil society and civil consciousness in Scotland. The second strand, developed since the late

1980s, is that Scottish identity after 1707 was emasculated or absorbed by the development of a British identity based on Protestant anti-Catholicism. The latter will be discussed in the next section, but here we focus on the argument (or rather series of arguments) that the presbyterian kirk sustained Scottish national identity within the British nationstate.

Historians take three main approaches to this: doctrinal distinctiveness fostering national character, the kirk institutionally substituting for a national legislature, and ecclesiastical affairs acting as a focus for nationalist revolt.

Religious doctrine and nation. In 1963 the Marxist historian Edward Thompson excluded Scotland from his study of *The Making of the English Working Class* because: 'the Scottish story is different. Calvinism was not the same thing as Methodism, although it is difficult to say which, in the early nineteenth century, was worse.'[1] A Scottish Marxist historian, Allan MacLaren, took this as a cue to argue that Calvinism was, if anything, 'worse', spreading through most of the Scottish Protestant churches, but reaching its height in the Free Church of 1843. For him, the Free Church sought 'to regulate society on Calvinist principles', with the bourgeois 'elect' using evangelisation as an attack on the working-class 'non-elect'.[2] This essentially negative vision of Calvinist Scotland has been widespread amongst commentators on Scottish character, especially where the object is to criticise puritanism or to seek the origins of Scots' sense of inferiority.

But there have been more positive interpretations of the Calvinist heritage. Max Weber referred only briefly to Scotland in his *The Protestant Ethic and the Spirit of Capitalism* published early this century, but many Scottish historians in the 1970s and 1980s argued that Calvinism's 'this worldly asceticism' was a vital ingredient in Scotland's economic progress. Gordon Marshall argued that between 1560 and 1707 Calvinist theology played an instrumental role in the evolution of the secular ethic of modern Scottish capitalism and identified the doctrine of predestination as crucial to the inculcation of entrepreneurial attitudes: because salvation is already decided yet is unknown for certain, the individual strives in life for the assurance of redemption which comes from worldly success.[3] In looking at the Industrial Revolution, Roy Campbell attributes to presbyterian theology the encouraging of social action by the individual in partnership with God which produced 'the utter self-confidence and assurance of his actions ... necessary for a successful entrepreneur'.[4] Calvinism, according to Sydney and Olive Checkland, provided Scots with their 'sense of absolute rightness, the accompaniment of their steadfastness', 'together with a system of values appropriate to economic success.'[5] Many Marxist historians argue similarly, though with different stresses. Keith Burgess has seen Calvinism as 'an ideology ready-made for a comparatively backward society embarking on a course of capitalist development', and argues that predestination 'tended to justify social mobility and personal wealth as proof of being one of the "elect".'[6] However, the role of Calvinism – as distinct from Protestantism generally – in Scottish entrepreneurial identity is uneasily suited to verification. The most business-history research seems to be able to indicate is the extent of 'religious preferences' amongst the leaders of commerce and industry – which in most cases shows no substantive difference in extent between Scotland and the rest of Britain, and seems unable to show how denominational or doctrinal affiliations influenced entrepreneurship or the conduct of business.[7]

On an associated aspect of economic change, several historians including R. H. Campbell and T. C. Smout have attributed to Calvinism the suppressing of Scottish plebeian revolt against the injustices of capitalist advance; Smout argued that since for Calvinists reward came in the afterlife, 'How could there conceivably be any point in protest or revolt?'[8] Here historians are identifying Calvinism as an 'internal social control', suppressing impulses to revolt. One major problem with this is that by far the most widespread and common forms of social protest in Scotland between the 1710s and the 1840s were disputes in the Kirk – notably over patronage. As has been suggested in earlier chapters, this made the kirk the principal venue for the emergence of class identity and class segregation within both rural and urban popular culture.[9]

Even more fundamental to discussion of Calvinism in Scottish identity are the problems of whether Scotland was in any meaningful sense Calvinist at all, and whether such Calvinism as there was can be said to be distinctive of Scotland. Part of this thesis rests on the identification by some ecclesiastical historians of heresy trials in the presbyterian churches – trials which they use as evidence of a sustained attachment to Calvinist precepts. Such trials took place in the Established Church in the 1820s and 1830s, in the Secession Church in the 1840s, in the Free Church in the 1870s, and in the United Free Church at the start of this century. The issues here are twofold: firstly, was Scotland more Calvinist than England, and secondly were these heresy trials really indicative that presbyterianism remained doctrinally Calvinist?

Attributing a distinctive Calvinism to Scots Protestants compared – as most historians do – to English Protestants ignores the extremely influential role of Calvinism south of the border within many Christian denominations, including Methodism. Indeed, as theological historians point out, there was a shared doctrinal spring from which all British churchmen drank after 1700,[10] and denominations such as the Calvinistic Methodists (now the Presbyterian Church of Wales) and the United Reformed Church (England's largest Nonconformist church) have very profound presbyterian roots. Secondly, the recent trend in theological scholarship has been to identify the confluence of, as well as the contradictions between, Arminianism and Calvinism – as embodied especially within evangelicalism, a disparate yet powerful tradition that embraced much of the Christian church throughout Britain from the eighteenth century.

Calvinist theology in the Scottish churches – including the most ostensibly 'fundamentalist' of them – was under challenge from at least the 1750s from Arminianism and an open evangelicalism of a Methodist variety, all tending to confound attempts to ascribe easy doctrinal epithets to distinguish Scotland from England or any other Protestant country. It is this last problem upon which the attempt to make modern Scotland distinctively 'Calvinist' founders. The emphasis of Scottish presbyterianism from the 1790s at the latest was on religious opportunity. In the context of an expanding economy generated in large measure by entrepreneurial zeal and skill, evangelicalism became readily associated with the holistic advance of the individual. In this way, evangelicalism complemented economic individualism. Between 1780 and 1850, the stress of presbyterian preaching and policy was on what Ian Muirhead described as the 'individualism of conversion',[11] on rebirth through education, reading the Bible, private prayer and contemplation. This focus strengthened in the nineteenth century, and after 1850 gave way to a widespread acceptance, including amongst the middle classes, of revivalism as the route to salvation. In 1874 this trend reached its zenith during the visit of the American evangelists Dwight Moody and Ira Sankey. First in Edinburgh and then in Glasgow, they preached to hundreds of meetings, notably lunchtime assemblies in the business quarters and in the evenings in suburban middle-class churches. The visit culminated in April at the Kibble Palace in Glasgow's Botanic Gardens where 7,000 of the city's well-dressed and well-heeled crowded in for the final meeting leaving thousands more outside. They marvelled at Sankey's joyous singing and his playing of the 'Kist o' Whistles' (or harmonium), and listened with mounting anticipation to Moody's short sermon calling forth people to the new life. Clearly, by then, the Scotland of the covenanters and Calvinism was much transformed.

The doctrinal decline of Calvinism started even earlier. Initially in the eighteenth century, the dilution of presbyterian doctrinal standards was most marked in the Moderate faction in the Established Church. Thus, it is possible to regard the dissenters of the Secession and Reformed

Presbyterian Churches as reacting to this liberalising tendency amongst the effete landed classes. In the late 1780s the synod of the Antiburgher Church complained that 'Arminianism is become the too fashionable doctrine of the day',[12] and predestination theology was certainly still taught to dissenting divinity students until the middle decades of the nineteenth century. But the dissenters were from the start in the mid eighteenth century torn apart by internal conflict over predestination versus Arminianism – that is, over the extent of the Atonement given by Christ on the cross. Preachers in the extremely puritanical and Calvinist sect of Scotch Baptists, which was popular in parts of Fife in the second half of the eighteenth century, held to the doctrine of predestination, 'yet they think it dangerous to comfort people by those considerations when they are in a backsliding state'.[13] The desire of the dissenters to offer the gospel, to win recruits and to maintain allegiance amongst a shifting population, created great anxiety that people should be motivated to search for the Scriptural message; Calvinist doctrine was an impediment to that, and was being downgraded.

As a result, the preaching of predestination and of the Elect was relegated to the background. In many cases, it was entirely substituted by an Arminian offer of Christ. In this way dissenting clergy got into trouble with hard-liners in their denominations. Nearly half of the Reformed Presbyterian Church, the direct and most Calvinistic descendant of the covenanters, adopted universal salvation in 1749–53 and were forced to leave to found the separate Reformed Presbytery of Edinburgh.[14] Many ministers in the Burgher and Antiburgher Churches were preaching Arminianism from the 1790s and remarkably few were brought to book for it. Church leaders were aware of the divisions amongst clergy and members, and chose wherever possible to ignore the demands for heresy trials emanating from predominantly rural ministers. Every major decree of the Secession Church on doctrinal issues involved accommodation between predestination and Arminianism. An Act of that Church in 1742 stated: 'For the record of God being such a thing as warrants *all* to believe in the son of God, it is evident that it can be no such warrant to tell men that God hath given eternal life to the elect', and added that 'our faith and good works ... are the cause of our *eternal salvation*'.[15] In 1828 the Church issued a 'balancing formula' which decreed that whilst 'Christ died for the elect', yet 'His death has also a relation to mankind sinners, being suitable to all and sufficient to the salvation of all'.[16] Even the puritanical presbyterians in the Highlands were in the eighteenth century avoiding predestination. Lachlan Mackenzie of Lochcarron preached a typical evangelical gospel: 'The rock gave water not for one or two only, but for all the congregation';

'And if a man wait on the means of grace, shall his labour be in vain? God forbid.'[17] The offer of salvation, if it was to be attractive in a rapidly changing society, had to be wide and achievable within a reasonably short time.

Differences of emphasis were infinite, and it could be observed in any case that the preaching of an evangelical predestinarian might not be so different from that of a salvationist. The issue only surfaced when a minister under examination by a church court openly avowed the doctrine of universal salvation. James Morison did this in the Secession Church in the early 1840s, and his ejection from it is often cited as evidence of the Calvinistic leanings of the Seceders. But his going fomented a vigorous debate which concluded in 1845 with a formula which conceded to the rampant anti-Calvinists 'a full, sincere, and consistent offer of the Gospel to all mankind'.[18] There was obfuscation of the issue, but the trend was clear. Whilst the doctrine of predestination was rarely denied formally, it was equally rarely preached in the main presbyterian churches of the nineteenth century. Even in the eighteenth century, as one church historian has noted, evangelical Calvinists were reaching beyond predestinarian theology 'in their offer of the gospel and their anxiety that their hearers should "close with Christ"'.[19] The novelist Tobias Smollett reflected general understanding of the Seceders in 1771 when he wrote of them that 'they maintain methodist doctrines of the new birth, the new light, the efficacy of grace, the insufficiency of works, and the operations of the spirit.'[20] Amongst all of the published output of Thomas Chalmers, the most popular minister of modern times, his pamphlets on the doctrine of salvation by grace alone sold very poorly.[21] One Free Church leader had to defend himself in 1844 against what he claimed was public misinterpretation of his fading Calvinism, caused by his failure to proof-read a speech.[22] The Free Church, as with the other presbyterian dissenters, was extremely sensitive to any public acknowledgement of the decay of Calvinist doctrine; there was deprecation of what one Calvinist hard-liner in the Free Church called 'a doctrine, which has of late years become unhappily fashionable, even in Scotland'. Challenging Calvinist doctrine disturbed sensibilities, but it did not conceal the essential anti-Calvinist influence of rampant evangelicalism. 'Bare old Calvinism', as Thomas Carlyle observed in 1844, was 'under sentence of death'.[23] From the middle of the eighteenth to the end of the nineteenth centuries, Calvinism was the ghost at the banquet of Scottish presbyterianism. It was a heritage that the main Scottish churches rarely denied till the 1890s, but it was constantly dividing them, leading to the formation of new denominations, and was being largely ignored in the bulk of evangelical preaching. Much of what is regarded as distinctive in Scottish presbyterianism of the industrial period was in fact a product of evangelicalism of the style and doctrine which took a hold amongst the English Methodists and other nonconformists.

The supposed contributions of Calvinism to national character do not end there. In a recent textbook on the sociology of Scotland, David McCrone writes:

> Presbyterianism was clearly a more democratic form of church government than Catholicism or Episcopalianism, and the doctrine of predestination, the essence of Calvinism, helped confirm the equality of this elect. Its association with national identity helped it retain its hold for longer than elsewhere.[24]

The doctrinal impact of Calvinism is thus extended from merely national character to 'democracy' based on national intellect – to ways of thinking and to ways of organising social institutions (from schools to universities and on to notions of social justice). In the 1960s George Davie popularised the notion that Scotland's presbyterian heritage lay at the root of what he called 'the democratic intellect' which distinguished Scotland from England.[25] This intellect favoured a breadth of learning in distinction to English specialisation, and fed into a real democratic access to learning and opportunity (in parish schools and in universities) less apparent south of the Tweed. The 'lad o' pairts', the gifted boy (though not the girl), had been able, no matter the economic circumstances of his parents, to gain within the parish school of the presbyterian system the advanced schooling necessary for admission to one of Scotland's four also 'democratic' universities. Despite the evidence of much empirical research that the Scottish educational system (including its church-controlled elements) was far from 'democratic' in its accessibility to all social classes and both sexes,[26] the 'egalitarian myth' has gained a strong foothold amongst Scottish intellectuals.

In particular, it has helped foster a notion prevalent under the post-1979 Conservative government that Scottish religion – especially its ostensibly 'democratic' presbyterianism – is the foundation for a distinctively-Scottish welfarist social policy which conflicted with Thatcherite social policy and economics in 1979–97. The conflict of ideas was symbolised for many Scots in their hostile reaction to Margaret Thatcher's 'Sermon on the Mound' of 1988 when she expounded to the General Assembly of the Church of Scotland her belief in the Scriptural foundations for her government's disengagement from state intervention. Democratic social policy, deriving from a presbyterian democracy, is thus seen as an element in Scottish national identity in the late twentieth century. This association of a national political ideology of democracy raises problems – certainly in the eighteenth and nineteenth centuries, when the presbyterian churches in Scotland were if anything more quick than Anglican clergy to welcome and praise the advent of industrial capitalism and the free market system. The pages of the *Old Statistical Account* of the 1790s are replete with ministers craving for 'the coming of industry' to their parish to reform the idle and indolent 'lower classes'. 'Social justice' was not the hallmark of men like Thomas Chalmers, the popular advocate of abandoning poor relief because of its tendency to undermine self-reliance.

Scottish Calvinism and the 'democratic intellect' have developed into discourses of distinction for many Scottish historians and nationalist writers in contemporary Scotland. They are deployed in the historical narrative as emblems of Scotland's identity and of her 'distinctive' civil and ecclesiastical society within Britain. But they must remain discourses in need of much deconstruction. When Calvinism in particular is traced as a doctrinal influence within the churches, the challenge to it from the 1740s onwards reduces its potential as a distinguishing feature of Scottish identity.

Institutional religion and identity. If we move from intellectual to institutional issues, there appears greater validity to the proposition that the kirk played a significant role in Scottish national identity after 1707. It has been suggested that the ostensibly democratic nature of presbyterian church government permitted the supreme court of the Established Church of Scotland, the general assembly, to become a surrogate Scots parliament after 1707. Its wide-ranging debates on social policy – especially in the Victorian period – are seen as the venue for the formation of public policy (especially by local authorities) in a wide range of spheres from education to model housing for the working classes. Certainly the debates were not confined to ecclesiastical matters but extended in some depth into issues such as housing, education and social welfare, and they attracted wide public attention through the publication of reports and the verbatim reporting of assembly speeches in Scottish newspapers. Church discussions could be extremely influential in many areas of Scottish social controversy – for example, the state of rural and urban housing, the drinks laws and education.

The main flaw in this case, though, is that there was not one general assembly in the nineteenth century but several: the Free Church, the U.P. Church Synod, not to mention the minor presbyterian churches. The Established Church assembly represented less than a third of the churchgoing Scots, and less than a sixth of the population at large. Indeed, until the 1980s, the religious divisiveness of Scotland was a problem for nationalist writers in search of a 'national identity' which overrode party and petty concerns. Christopher Harvie wrote in 1977 that 'religion had frustrated nationalism' at many turns in recent Scottish history.[27] But the creation of the Free Church in 1843 has recently been subjected to a very radical reassessment, and the 1842 *Claim of Right* which gave rise to it was used in 1988 as the title for the Scottish Constitutional Convention's public petition demanding home rule for Scotland. At the same time, the formation of the Free Church has come under close scrutiny from historians, with some asserting that the Disruption was little short of a nationalist revolt. This amounts to something of a turnabout in appraisal. Two ecclesiastical historians of the early 1970s saw 1843 as a disaster for the country: 'Before the Disruption Scotland had a national history; afterwards she had not.'[28] Harvie commented that it 'destroyed the possibility of any Scottish consensus and placed the initiative in legislation securely in the hands of Westminster politicians who ... simply did not care about Scottish affairs.'[29] But in 1982 one historian suggested tentatively that the Disruption was 'partly fuelled by something very close to nationalism',[30] and in 1992 a television documentary interpreted the whole Disruption, including the Ten Years Conflict which preceded it, as close to a nationalist uprising. William Storrar, a Church of Scotland minister, argued in a book that the essence of Scottish national identity was a vision of the Godly Commonwealth that was lost at the Disruption. Not mincing his words, Storrar spoke of there being a 'godly vision of Scottish nationhood' until 1843, quoting another historian, Monica Clough, who had written of the events of 1843 that 'what might have developed into a declaration of independence, had there been leaders more concerned with the underlying political implications than with religious ones, merely turned into the Disruption of the Kirk, and not the rupture of the state'.[31]

That view must be considered extreme, if not implausible. A more considered interpretation comes from Stewart J. Brown who stated : 'The Disruption undermined the Presbyterian nationalism that had shaped early modern Scotland, with its ideal of the democratic intellect preserved in its parish schools, kirk sessions and presbyteries.'[32] This is very much a Chalmerian view. The man whose charisma inspired and effectively commanded the Disruption sought to restrain the grassroots pressure for radical action. In the context of the 'hungry forties' of Chartist revolt and potato famine, the man who had a lifelong fear of the 'brawny mass' of the people feared that he might have inadvertently unleashed it in 1843. For this reason, he took pains to assure MPs in 1847 that there was no violence intended by him or the Free Church towards landowners and the establishment he controversially dubbed 'a moral nuisance'.[33] For him, the event was one of great sadness, and he 'went out' reluctantly. But this did not apply to the vast bulk of his followers. The notion that the Disruption was a venting of nationalist sentiment, even if it destroyed a consensual presbyterian national identity, undervalues the tremendous exaltation amongst Free church people (and other dissenters) at the Disruption and in the sixty years following. A Christian-configured civil society was the dream of those who created the home-mission industry and the electioneering evangelicalism of the second half of the nineteenth century. The civic gospel of Victorian Scotland was the new 'godly commonwealth', modernised for implementation through town councils, school boards, parochial boards and – it was hoped – the local veto plebiscites for creating prohibition. In reality, the Disruption unleashed the evangelical social vision for its finest hour between 1843 and 1914.

Others acknowledge the problems of identifying a nationalist revolt in the Disruption. Lindsay Paterson, a Scottish nationalist, recognises that the English did not cause the Disruption and that the United Kingdom parliament was 'dragged into the disputes by Scottish invitation.'[34] More fundamentally, the Disruption if viewed from 'below' – from the divisions at parish and community level in Scotland – takes on a very different hue. As we saw in Chapter 5, much of the detailed research that has taken place into the event has emphasised the grassroots origins and the class dimensions of it. In short, the main research issue at stake is how the Disruption took shape as a result of social forces in a fracturing Scottish society. Anyone reading in Scottish Victorian journals, books and commentaries can have no doubt that those who left the Church of Scotland in 1843 went with great gusto, enthusiasm and commitment, and built from scratch the most dynamic and successful denomination that modern Scotland ever saw or is likely to see again.

Victorian commentators regarded the formation of the Free Church not as undermining but enhancing the sense of institutional democracy in Scotland. The Free Church and Established Church general assemblies met simultaneously every May in Edinburgh, and speakers referred to the meeting 'over the way' in a manner consciously redolent of the Houses of Lords and Commons in London. Robert Louis Stevenson observed that 'the Parliaments of the Established and Free Churches ... can hear each other singing psalms across the street'.[35] But the issues they discussed were social issues, and ones which were not automatically agreed to by Parliament. Indeed, it was often English Nonconformist MPs, the ones most ecclesiastically close to Scots presbyterians, who blocked the wishes of Scottish evangelicals; a national education system, backed by the Scottish electorate in the 1850s, did not materialise until 1872. More importantly, the assemblies were loyal British institutions, not given – as they could have been – to encouraging disaffection from rule from Westminister; they did not choose to become a focus for political nationalism in nineteenth-century Scotland, and in the twentieth century, as we saw in Chapter 7, their leaders were Conservatives with little inclination to promote a nationalist agenda. For these reasons, the notion of a single surrogate parliament, representing and uniting Scots' sense of identity, becomes – at the very least – muddled.

Some international scholars of religion and national identity have long held that Scotland was one of a number of regions within European countries where the secularisation of religion had been held in check by the association of religion with a thwarted political nationalism.[36] This used to be based on the assumption that religious observance and church adherence were significantly higher in Scotland (as well as in Northern Ireland and Wales) than in England, representative of a distinctive 'Celtic fringe' of religion. The evidence for this is thin. In the religious census of 1851, Sunday attendances at church represented 60.7 per cent of Scottish population and 58.1 per cent of English and Welsh population which, by the standards of enumeration at the time, is a negligible difference. In the Bible Society censuses of 1979–84, adult church attenders as a proportion of population was estimated at 11 per cent for England, 13 per cent for Wales and 17 per cent for Scotland, with the major factor accounting for the difference being the high level of churchgoing by west of Scotland Catholics.[37] Much more important is the fact that churchgoing and church membership data over the period from 1840 to the present indicates that Scotland fits closely to a common British pattern of church growth and decay.[38]

The emphasis of many historians has been on the 'religious peculiarities of Scotland' and their divergence from 'a British norm'.[39] Scottish religion still seems to many to be the one remaining 'national' characteristic capable of explaining difference from England: the Welsh have their language; the Scots, with few Gaelic speakers, have their 'National' Church. It has been too easy for commentators to say that 'God was securely in his heaven, perceived in a distinctively Scottish way'[40] without analysing the empirical evidence and deconstructing terms like the 'Calvinist Scot'. Equally vital, the historians must explore the contribution of Scottish presbyterianism to British integration.

RELIGION AND BRITISH IDENTITY

After the Union of Parliaments in 1707 the economic development of Scotland fell rapidly in step with that of England, and Scotland encountered the same social consequences of rapid economic change:

dramatic population growth, urbanisation, factory production and the social divisions it created, and the problems of poverty, health, housing and sanitation. The political system of Britain was integrated, and popular movements, ranging from trade unionism to the feminist movement, developed in tandem. In the process of integration and construction of British identity, religion played its part.

Though the 1707 Union preserved presbyterianism in the Established Church of Scotland (in contrast to the episcopalian established churches of England, Wales and Ireland), Parliament effectively granted religious toleration in Scotland five years later. This permitted the pluralisation of religion on a common basis within Britain, and allowed evangelicalism in particular to integrate British Protestantism. George Whitefield's visit to the Cambuslang revival in 1742 heralded sustained pulpit exchange, joint missionary endeavour and pressure-group campaigning from the 1790s. The evangelical interchange between England and Scotland developed from those beginnings to be a major feature of British ecclesiastical life in the nineteenth and early twentieth centuries. Thomas Chalmers became a well-known figure south of the Border, and English preachers like Brownlow North became celebrated guests of the Free Church. In the Victorian period, the self-stylisation 'evangelical' came to be an avowal of Protestant orthodoxy, uniting the vast majority of Nonconformists and Methodists in the south and presbyterians and Protestant dissenters in Scotland. Evangelical campaigns and innovations were freely and energetically exchanged within mainland Britain, and evangelical home missions were the cement of British religious identity from the 1790s until the 1910s. With the decline of evangelicalism, the trend towards unity within British Protestantism increased. Throughout the twentieth century, religious responses to the rise of the labour movement, to world wars and economic depression became increasingly matters of British interdenominational concern. Joint committees, conferences and reports proliferated, doctrinal and political issues generated much inter-church debate, and ecumenical initiatives were instituted from the 1950s to explore possibilities of denominational union amongst Scottish and English churches in various permutations. Though few church unions have been achieved (the United Reformed Church of 1970 being the major exception), the ecclesiastical atmosphere became charged with issues thrown up overwhelmingly in a British context: abortion, homosexuality, nuclear weapons and unemployment.

These developments did not eradicate the distinctiveness of the Scottish presbyterian tradition, but they did tend to erode the differences within British Christianity and to make it possible for ecumenical exchange and union to be explored. Down to 1929, ecumenicism was interpreted in Scotland as presbyterian reunion, but within three years of the final and major reunion in that year, the first of three major series of 'conversations' to explore ecumenical possibilities commenced between the Church of Scotland and the Scottish Episcopal Church and have continued through to the 1990s. There have been hostile reactions from some presbyterians to the major suggestions of these conversations – notably in 1934, 1957 and in the 1980s – for the Church of Scotland to adopt or recognise bishops.[41] Though union between episcopacy and presbyterianism seems unlikely, the closing of ranks by churches in the face of decline is indicative of how presbyterianism is dwindling as a feature of Scottish identity.

As well as the trend towards the erosion of presbyterian tradition and the integration of British Protestantism, Protestantism itself was important to the integration of Britain. Linda Colley has argued in an influential recent study that British identity was forged between 1707 and 1837 through a common Protestant identity, coupled with an antagonism towards Roman Catholicism. She quotes with approval the words of David Bebbington: 'Outside England popular Protestantism was emphatically British in flavour rather than Welsh or Scottish, for Britain as a whole seemed a Protestant bastion against Roman ambitions.'[42] Colley's convincing core thesis is that during this period the identity of Britain was forged (much of it by Scots) in the context of a shared Protestant culture and hostility to Catholicism at home and abroad:

> Protestantism ... gave the majority of men and women a sense of their place in history and a sense of worth. It allowed them to feel pride in such advantages as they genuinely did enjoy, and helped them endure when hardship and danger threatened. It gave them identity. There were other powerful identities at work, of course. A sense of Protestant unity did not always override social class, anymore than it overwhelmed the profound cultural and historical divisions between the English, the Scottish and the Welsh ... Great Britain might be made up of three separate nations, but under God it could also be one, united nation. And as long as a sense of mission and providential destiny could be kept alive, by means of maintaining prosperity at home, by means of recurrent wars with Catholic states of Europe, and by means of a frenetic and for a long time highly successful pursuit of empire, the Union flourished, sustained not just by convenience and profit but by belief as well. Protestantism was the foundation that made the invention of Great Britain possible.[43]

However, according to Colley this Protestant core to British identity broke down with the emancipation of Catholics in 1829.[44] Irish Catholics were by then part of Britain's industrial proletariat, and Catholicism was no longer a 'common enemy'. A new focus for British identity evolved, and especially for Scots: the Empire. In the second half of the nineteenth and early twentieth centuries, Scots located their destiny in the idea and reality of Empire; in Scottish heavy industry (especially in the Glasgow conurbation) which relied on producing products for imperial trade, in Scots' role in the imperial civil service, and most importantly – so it is argued – in the missionary work of the Scottish presbyterian churches. Foreign missions re-cemented a sense of Britishness in the face of other cultures, and bound Scots for another century or so to a British identity.

Here Colley has aroused disagreement concerning her emphasis that 'Britishness' was essentially the same in every part of Britain. Graham Walker and others have argued that Scotland's imperial mission had distinctive features. He wrote that 'the Scottish Protestant imperial impulse was part of the attempt to infuse arenas of Empire ... with Scottish ethics and aspects of Scottish civil society.'[45] Scots at home, Walker proposes, had a distinctive view of Empire which celebrated Scottish missionaries such as David Livingstone: 'The Scots felt that they took the task of spreading Christianity more seriously than the English, and that Scottish Presbyterianism in general was more morally serious and less corruptible.'[46] As a result, Walker goes on, there was not at that time 'any real sense of Scottish destiny, whether economic, cultural or political, not being bound up firmly with Britain and the Empire.'[47] This development of the Colley thesis deserves attention, but also caution. The lack of comparative research into the importance of foreign missions makes it difficult to say with certainty that they were more important in Scotland than in England or Wales. Moreover, there are difficulties in ascribing to Scotland a distinctive missionary enterprise when Scottish churches and Scottish missionaries, as well as undertaking their own foreign missions, also operated through London-based organisations like the London Missionary Society.

Thus, Scottish identity is being perceived by some scholars as being 'locked into' a larger British identity by a common anti-Catholic Protestantism down to the 1830s, and by an imperial identity from then until the early and mid-twentieth century. Subsequently, it is being argued, Scottish identity has been undergoing 'release' from British bondage in the twentieth century: by the decline of empire between the 1920s and the 1960s (which caused the decline of Scottish heavy industry and the decline of foreign missions) and by the decline of religion at home from the 1950s. In the vacuum, Scottish national identity re-emerged between the 1960s and 1990s as a new self-confident belief in political and cultural destiny. As Colley says, 'Protestantism, that once vital cement, has now a limited influence on British culture, as indeed has Christianity itself ... God has ceased to be British, and Providence no longer smiles.'[48] The very symmetry of this evolving historical narrative on Scottish identity since the Union – and religion's role within it – should foster caution. So much turns on the key role of religion in first uniting Protestant Scots in a sense of Britishness and then fading to release them to develop a self-standing Scottish identity. It leaves many thorny problems. One is the schismatic effect of religious dissent within presbyterianism, let alone Protestantism as a whole, which rendered religious identities highly fragmented. A second difficulty is that Protestant anti-Catholicism has shown a remarkable resilience in Scottish culture from the eighteenth to the twentieth centuries. It continued to unite and agitate Scots Protestants long after Catholic emancipation in 1829 – arguably increasingly – and reaching a peak in the 1920s and 1930s when anti-Catholicism formed the basis of a distinctly racist Scottish national identity.

SECTARIAN IDENTITIES

Protestant-Catholic antagonism in Scotland stretches back to the Reformation, but it was enlivened in the nineteenth century by the immigration of both Protestants and Catholics from Ireland. Anti-Catholic ideology stems from the anti-papist theology and political philosophy of the early-modern period, the strains of which were resilient both in the presbyterian churches and in the civil state in Scotland until well into the twentieth century. In presbyterian political theology, Catholicism is an undemocratic tyranny which represses civil rights and individual conscience. From Rome, the 'anti-Christ' (the Pope) usurps the Protestant constitutions of other countries by employing unbiblical rites and practices (such as the mass) to destroy rationality. Thus, religious worship has political implications. In 1778, the Glasgow synod of the Church of Scotland warned against giving freedom to the Catholic Church because people 'are seduced into that detestable superstition whose peculiar worship is idolatry ... which, the more it advances, the more powerfully it operates in pulling up the foundations of the Protestant state'.[49] The notion that popery diminishes liberty is central to the ideology of anti-Catholicism, giving rise to the Protestant march which in Scotland since the 1870s has been taken as the acid test of 'freedom': if the police and civil authorities prevent Orange marchers from going where they please – in practice through Catholic districts – then the Protestant state is crumbling. The level of violence attending such occasions increased from the 1870s to the 1920s, and though it has diminished in the second half of the century, trouble seems to rise in periods of economic recession, including the early and mid 1980s.[50]

Until the nineteenth century, anti-popery was orchestrated by the presbyterian churches with the overt assistance of the political establishment. But from the 1790s, there began a protracted ecclesiastical disengagement from sectarianism as ministers found the 'roughness' of popular bigotry distasteful. Yet though ministers like Thomas Chalmers supported the Catholic Emancipation Act of 1829, the immigration of Irish Protestants spread the Orange Lodges amongst their skilled working class and some ministers, particularly from the Calvinist wing of the Free Church, developed links with artisan Protestant defence organisations. The range of Protestant attitudes was apparent during the celebrations in 1860 for the tercentenary of the Scottish Reformation when most church courts declined to participate. The principal event was a four-day conference in Edinburgh which awkwardly combined academic historical lectures by divinity professors with rousing anti-Catholic speeches by vociferous anti-papists. The organisers invited every Protestant clergyman in Scotland, but were disappointed when only 150 turned up, outnumbered by ministers from Ireland and overseas. But in August 1860, just when the presbyterian churches were playing down what one newspaper called 'the hackneyed subject of Popery', disturbances erupted on successive Sundays in the Catholic Briggate district of central Glasgow in response to anti-Catholic preaching by a Free Church minister from an elevated external pulpit attached to a mission church built for the religious revival of the time. The scheme 'to harangue the multitude on Sundays' was described by a Catholic newspaper as 'an audacious impertinence', but the local Protestant press regarded the unrest and the eventual police instruction to desist preaching as 'a plot ... of the Romish authorities matured in cold blood, for the purpose of putting down the right to proclaim the Gospel'. Sixteen hundred Orangemen, ready to fight, congregated at the end of the month to disperse 'groups of navvies, mechanics, and masculine-looking women, of unmistakeable Hibernian aspect, [who] might be seen laying their heads together in a low earnest manner, that meant mischief'.[51] The sectarian appeal to the Protestant working class, and attempts to convert Catholics, were significant ingredients in Victorian evangelisation. But they lacked the enthusiastic sanction of the presbyterian churches as a whole, and with the decay of church missions after 1890 the leadership of the Protestant crusade visibly passed to mostly independent and proletarian missions.

But anti-Catholicism was revived with a vengeance in the presbyterian churches in the 1920s and 1930s. As we saw in Chapter 6, the crisis in presbyterianism brought a Conservative, anti-labour and anti-Irish group of men to the leadership of the Church of Scotland and the U.F. Church. Electoral campaigning at parish-council, education-authority and temper-ance-plebiscite elections was accompanied by frenzied verbal attacks on

Catholics. A high-powered report of the Church of Scotland general assembly of 1923 urged the government to stem Irish immigration (although it was fairly low by then), stating of Irish Catholics:

> They cannot be assimilated and absorbed into the Scottish race. They remain a people by themselves, segregated by reason of their race, their customs, their traditions, and above all, by their loyalty to their Church, and gradually and inevitably dividing Scotland, racially, socially, and ecclesiastically.

The Irish, the report went on, were undermining Scots' thriftiness, independence and reverence for the Sabbath; and having already destroyed 'the unity and homogeneity of the Scottish people', what was next in prospect was 'the loss of the Scottish race to civilisation'. [52] Many presbyterian ministers promulgated this racist discourse about the 'Irish' Catholics living in Scotland. The Rev. Duncan Cameron of Kilsyth was quoted as saying in a lecture in Glasgow in 1927:

> The development he saw was in the direction of internal racial antagonism and bitter rivalry, accompanied by constant emigration of the Scot from Scotland until eventually in the industrial areas the majority of the working classes would be Irish Roman Catholics; and it is not difficult to realise what would be the consequence of their assumption of municipal and parliamentary power.[53]

Virulent sectarianism was being enriched with racist eugenics. Such posturing by presbyterian leaders must have contributed to Parliament's abolition in 1929 of the education authorities and the parish councils on which clergy had dominated for so long. With the Church of Scotland unable to rally the Protestant popular vote at *ad hoc* elections any more, political movements of Protestant extremists emerged as a significant electoral force in the early 1930s: the Scottish Protestant League in Glasgow and Protestant Action in Edinburgh, each of which gained as much as a third of municipal votes in the early thirties. Interestingly, they attracted little church support, and their ideology lacked theological underpinning. Their popularity hinged on Protestant unemployment during the slump, and was all but lost with economic recovery in the later 1930s. Nonetheless, they marked an important stage in the separation of the churches from Protestant extremism.

Scottish Catholics had many reasons to perceive Scottish (and British) society as discriminatory. Penal laws were slow to be repealed between 1793 and 1926, and the British state still discriminates against a Catholic assuming the Crown. The Catholic Church encouraged something of a 'fortress' mentality amongst its adherents as the best defence of both faith and community in such a hostile Protestant society. In the nineteenth and early twentieth centuries, the Church sought to provide all the recreational, charitable and welfare organisations for Catholics, and with the recognition of Catholic schools within the state system of education after 1918, the maintenance of the faith became linked to an institutional separateness. Discrimination in employment has been the longest-standing grievance of the Catholic community. Entry to skilled occupations was restricted both by employers and Protestant unions; during the slump of the 1930s signs saying 'No Catholics need apply' appeared at factory gates. Catholic entry to higher education was restricted until the 1960s and 1970s by poverty, cultural division and perhaps by discrimination. With increased employment by local authorities and international companies, such discrimination markedly fell in the last half of the century, but occasional allegations of 'Orange' foremen blocking Catholic advancement – especially in engineering companies – allows the perception of discrimination to persist even in the 1990s.

The most significant change in modern sectarianism has been its shift from the arena of work to the arena of leisure. From the 1890s, Rangers and Celtic football clubs developed as focuses of Protestant and Catholic loyalties respectively, and the 'Old Firm' matches between them became the occasions for significant sectarian rivalry, often ending in violence. After 1945, with political sectarian parties virtually extinct, and with the beginnings of decline in church adherence, these two clubs came to represent the secularised nature of modern sectarianism. Inspiration has emanated less and less from the religious tradition of the Scottish covenanters, for whose seventeenth-century battles there has been dwindling anniversary attendances, and more and more from the Protestant loyalists of Northern Ireland. The images and slogans which attract the Orange Order's 80,000 Scottish members are the Red Hand of Ulster and 'No Surrender', and splinter groups have a small but energetic following who find the main Order too passive in its anti-Catholic stance. The same images and slogans and their Catholic equivalents relating to Irish republicanism are to be found in and around Rangers and Celtic football grounds and represent the best-known feature of religious bigotry in modern Scotland. Though ethnic identification at other Scottish clubs has dwindled or been extinguished, the two Glasgow clubs have developed a strong national following. Irrespective of club policy, the two clubs have remained focuses of sectarian identity symbolised in the different flags (the Irish Tricolour and the Union Jack) which fly above their stands, and manifested in the violence which has punctuated the history of the 'Old Firm' fixtures.

For some historians,[54] Rangers-Celtic rivalry is the last vestige of the post-war decline in sectarianism. Evidence for its diminishing relevance includes the general decay of religious affiliation, the secularisation of society at large, the reduced extent of religious discrimination in employment, and the 'de-ghettoisation' of Catholics and Protestants through slum clearance and council-house building. The Glasgow sectarian street gangs of the 'Norman Conks' (Catholics) and the 'Billy Boys' (Protestants) – the latter reputedly 800-strong in its heyday in the early 1930s – have disappeared, and by comparison with religious conflicts in other parts of the world (including Ulster) institutions like the Orange Order seem more like social clubs than manifestations of serious civil schism. But a sanguine view based on studies of organised sectarianism may underestimate the vibrancy of the popular culture of bigotry. Sectarianism is still a factor in the day-to-day lives of many working-class Scots, to be seen in popular graffiti which are almost entirely sectarian – 'FTP', 'FTQ' and 'FKB' (short-hand expletives addressed at the Pope, the Queen and King Billy). Whilst religious ghettoisation has been much reduced in Glasgow, in surrounding towns it is still significant – even perhaps heightened by council-house letting policy in towns like Greenock, Port Glasgow, Airdrie and Coatbridge. Flute and pipe bands of both religions train every year to lead marches in Scotland, Northern Ireland or the Irish Republic, accounting for a significant part of youth voluntary activity in west-of-Scotland towns. The 1990s have undoubtedly seen a reduction in the intensity of sectarian bitterness; this has arisen in football partly as a result of the anti-bigotry policies of Rangers and Celtic football clubs, and partly as a result of modernised all-seater stadiums and expensive ticket prices. But incidents still occur. In 1986, the leader of Midlothian District Council was forced to resign after describing Catholics as 'the enemy' at an Orange rally, and a sheriff-court judge in Kilmarnock was disciplined for demanding that the defendant in an assault case sing the sectarian Protestant tune 'The Sash' and, when the latter refused, for singing two versions of it himself from the bench.[55] Protestant extremist marches are still to be seen virtually every Saturday morning in the east end of Glasgow, and bitterness can run deep in decaying industrial communities (such as in Ayrshire). In 1994, the communities of predominantly Protestant Airdrie and predominantly-Catholic Coatbridge were riven by accusations that a Catholic Labour Party group on the local council favoured Coatbridge with infrastructure and other developments; this had a major impact on a parliamentary by-election in the constituency in which the Protestant and Catholic votes were strikingly divided between the SNP and Labour Party candidates respectively. In this way, sectarianism still has the potential for political division.

Scottish national identity has never fully integrated Catholic and Protestant. In the late twentieth century, there is still evidence of religious-based ethnic division which confounds a common identity. Predominantly-Protestant Rangers football supporters, for instance, tend to identify with Britain and its symbols (like the Union flag) as an act of solidarity with Northern Ireland Loyalists; predominantly-Catholic supporters of Celtic, on the other hand, associate poorly with both British and Scottish symbols of identity, and relate strongly with the Irish Republic.[56] As support for these two clubs has expanded from the Glasgow hinterland to many parts of Lowland Scotland (and even into the Highlands as well as into Ulster), the two clubs sustain an influential Irish agenda in Scottish society which seems to compromise the wider formation of a single sense of Scottish identity.

On 31 May 1982, when Pope John Paul II entered the precincts of the Church of Scotland divinity college and general assembly building in Edinburgh, and shook hands with the moderator beneath the statue of the Scottish reformer, John Knox, only one hundred demonstrators, led by the Rev. Ian Paisley from Northern Ireland, bothered to turn up to protest at the admission of the Pope – the Protestants' 'Anti-Christ' – to the palace of world presbyterianism. Yet two years earlier, at the start of the 1980s' recession, there had occurred a major riot at Hampden Park in Glasgow at the end of the Scottish Cup Final when Protestant-Catholic hatred fired Rangers and Celtic supporters to running skirmishes on the pitch with mounted police attempting to restore order by repeated cavalry charges. For Protestants the Church of Scotland in the late twentieth century has failed to arouse enough interest or passion to 'defend' it against perceived threats. Yet, if secularisation has undermined popular presbyterianism, it has thus far not destroyed sectarian identities in Scotland.

PIETY AND FEMININITY

Sectarianism, at least in its public manifestations, is mainly men's work. It is a public sphere predominantly characterised by machismo and male aggression. The institutions of sectarian identity, from the Orange Order to football support, form an overwhelmingly male domain for the expression of masculinity. This is not the only way in which religion has a gendered form, for it is clear that men's and women's expressions of religiosity are manifested in different ways. Moreover, discourses on religiosity have been highly gendered. The 'home heathen' popularised by Thomas Chalmers in the nineteenth century was – in most representations – a man; a woman, on the other hand, was 'an angel' in need of training.

In Falkirk in the mid-1960s, only 37 per cent of boys who attended church expressed a belief in God compared to 47 per cent amongst non-attenders; in contrast, the situation was reversed amongst girls with figures of 75 per cent for churchgoers and 40 per cent for non-churchgoers.[57] In a national survey in 1984–6, 85 per cent of Scottish women said they believed in God compared to 73 per cent of men, and 40 per cent of women claimed to pray every day compared to 24 per cent of men. Women emerge from such surveys as substantially more committed to church; they read the Bible more, and are firmer in their beliefs in God and in life after death.[58] Many have observed since the 1960s that women outnumber men in religious worship in the order of two to one, with the imbalance rising to well over 70 per cent in a significant number of Church of Scotland congregations. In many countries since the eighteenth century, the religiosity of women is widely acknowledged to have been greater than that of men.

Religion, especially Protestantism, came to play different roles in women's and men's identities in modern society. Studies of England and North America in the eighteenth century have suggested that there was a complex feminisation of religion.[59] Men became resistant to Calvinism because it denigrated human abilities and the worth of their own efforts in improving their status, and they found in Arminian evangelicalism greater sympathy for the male role in dynamic commercial and industrial society. But even within evangelicalism, the increasing tendency to emotionalism alienated men. It has been suggested that a more widespread resistance to Protestant religion developed in the nineteenth century, with men perceiving in the evangelical conversion a much less emotional and intimate relationship with God than was felt by women.[60] Evangelicalism focused religious discourse with increasing intensity upon the home and family, and upon the inculcation of religious and moral values in the next generation through the piety of mothers.[61] The way in which religion – specifically Protestantism – operated within personal identities, and the way in which men and women associated with the churches, diverged.

In the late eighteenth century the rise of evangelicalism and moderatism in Scotland gave rise to discussion on the nature of piety. John Dwyer has described how eighteenth-century Englightenment writers in Scotland discussed the peculiar virtues and the ideals of women. Moralist writers, including Moderate clergy, moving in the fashionable literary and religious circles of Edinburgh, explored the female role in the 'virtuous discourse' they were developing. The expatriot Rev. James Fordyce wrote about this in the *Scots Magazine* in the 1760s and 1770s, and notably in his *Sermon to Young Women* where he attacked upper-class female schools in which young girls learned 'nothing that is domestic or rational', but instead received an education which perpetuated 'the effeminate, trifling, and dissolute character of the age'.[62] For practical moralists like Fordyce, Christ was to be a model for the innate qualities of meekness and gentle sensibility of women – qualities that were essential for the creation of a harmonious home, the upbringing of children, and the reformation of society at large. Though the *milieu* in which this discourse on female virtue developed was socially exclusive, it laid the basis for the more pervasive and influential evangelical focus on feminine piety that was to follow.

The evangelical revival has been seen as emblematic of the way in which the evangelical conversion was feminised.[63] At the Cambuslang revival of 1742, 68 per cent of those classified as converts were women, of whom 75 per cent were unmarried and the vast majority in their teens and twenties; in 1955 during Billy Graham's 'All Scotland Crusade', there were 19,835 who made 'decisions for Christ' in the Glasgow meetings of whom 71 per cent were women and 73 per cent were under thirty years of age.[64] Young women and girls were especially attracted to evangelical events. The theatricality of the revivalist preacher, and of the call to the saved to come forward, appears frequently in the oral testimony and autobiographies of women from the late nineteenth century onwards. Molly Weir speaks of the attraction of Jock Troup's tent preaching in Springburn between the wars; he was such 'great value' that he could 'make the flames of hell so real, we felt them licking round our feet, and the prospect of heaven so alluring we often stood up to be saved several times during the week'; once home, she re-enacted the service to her Grannie.[65] In Chapter 6 it was noted how girls were strongly attracted to religious services in the early twentieth century, and they place their recollections within a context of aesthetic sensibility. At the teetotal meetings of the Band of Hope in the 1910s, Mrs R.2(1905) recalled:

> We would meet in the Band of Hope. There was an old Church stood in the middle of the Brae and it was a lovely, *beautiful* Church and the velvet where the — preacher stood was just – oh, it wasnae much broader than that cabinet and it was red velvet, I can mind. And we had cantatas and things like that ... Peggy and I used to sing – oh what was it? 'Count your blessings', and we'd stand as proud as be. And we had white frocks and because I thought I was the king – the Queen of everything. Mine was lacy and Peggy's was plain. Oh, we used to rival in good fun.[66]

Religious worship was a vital venue for young working-class girls to express their femininity. Their testimony comes alive when discussing the 'Sunday best' dresses. Mrs V.1(1914) recalled:

> Well, Sunday was my day because Sunday I was up and I was born, I mean brought up a Protestant, but on a Sunday morning I got dressed – you had a Sunday outfit you see, you only wore it on a Sunday, no other day except a Sunday. Well I went to my two pals, they went to the Catholic Church, so I went

with them to mass on a Sunday morning so's I'd have my Sunday clothes on. When I came home I'd go to the [Protestant] church with my mother and then when I came home from that I kept on my clothes because I was going to the Sunday school, and then we went to Bible class at night. And the reason I went to all that was because I got wearing my Sunday clothes. As soon as I was finished from the Bible class you'd to take them off, hang them up and put on your ordinary clothes. You weren't allowed to wear your Sunday best for playing with. So the one [day] I looked forward to is a Sunday just for that – to keep my Sunday clothes on.[67]

It was the same for young Catholic girls. 'Sunday-best' dresses were bought annually, usually in Spring, as Mrs F.3(1910) recalled:

First Sunday in May, that's when you got your summer clothes bought ... And all you did was, she did was, to go down to the village shop; they were Baptist folk, and very nice people ... Mrs Bingham would get the order and she would go to the Glasgow warehouse, and just exactly, she just took a tape and measured us, and she brought back the beautifulest clothes. It was the talk of the village 'I wonder what the [Smith] girls will have this May?' Sometimes be shepherd's tartan with velvet; another time it would be green velvet ...[68]

The dresses are remembered with great clarity: the parade to church in 'our button boots and our parasols ... black button boots we had on, and eh a black dress. It was awfy fancy made with frills, puff sleeves and everything.'[69] Mrs E.2(1905) remembers being taken for a new Sunday best outfit, but after making a scene in the draper's shop she was threatened with the punishment of *not* going to church:

And I remember this day; I always wanted green, I was terrible for green when I was young, and ... I remember mother got the thing and the woman brought this brown – the coat and, you know, the wee muff for your hands and a hat and a wee muff with the white and black tails on the wee fur and your muff was the same. And eh, that's what I got for, for going to the Sunday school and the Church ... mother was fair taken on with this brown rig out, you know, and it was green I wanted and I kicked up terrible. Oh my mother was fair ashamed; I stamped my feet ... 'I don't want that brown, I don't like it!' ... I didn't win, mind you ... I had to take the brown ... Oh my, the lecture I got when I got home (laugh). No church for me on Sunday, I wouldn't get it. But I got the church.[70]

Evangelical Protestantism expected much of women, and many employers ensured their religious training. Around a third of all Scottish women in the late nineteenth and twentieth century undertook domestic service in their teens and early twenties, and they were almost uniformly required by their middle- and upper-class employers to attend church on the alternate Sundays they had 'off'. The experience of Mrs T.1(1906), a table maid in a large house at Killearn, is typical:

We were encouraged of course to go to church, we were allowed to go to church, maybe every second Sunday. We wouldn't be allowed to go every Sunday but every second Sunday anyway and I remember when I was quite young we were encouraged to join the church then. I was about sixteen when I joined the church you know where the minister took a class of us. Several of us would go at an appointed time to the minister, to the manse and we got instruction on joining the church and we had set things to learn. We learned the Creed. We had to repeat the Creed to him and there was several bits from the Scripture that we had to learn and then that was us a member of the church for life.[71]

Domestic service encapsulated the characteristics which evangelicalism expected of working-class women. The vast religious press of the nineteenth century – journals, magazines, tracts and books, much of it distributed as Sunday-school prizes – developed in Scotland from the 1840s a discourse on the role of women in family life. In stories and vignettes, historical biographies and in straight exhortation, a pious femininity was portrayed as the basis of national greatness. The Scottish revivalist magazine *The Day-Star* stated in 1856:

> WOMEN AND RELIGION.– It has been eloquently and truly said, that if Christianity were compelled to flee from the nations of the great, the academies of philosophers, the halls of legislators, or the throngs of busy men, we should find her last retreat with woman at the fireside. Her last audience would be the children gathering round the knee of a mother; the last sacrifice, the secret prayer, escaping in silence from her lips, and heard perhaps only at the throne of God.[72]

Women were the moral heart of the family, battling with dissipated and drunken husbands: 'The all-engrossing occupations of a wife and a mother seemed soon to absorb her whole being; – only one theme occupied her, – the training of her children; ... the midnight hours, which she past in watching and labouring for him and his children, were spent by her husband in scenes of folly and of vice.'[73] Articles on 'Good Wives' and 'Good Mothers' abounded, using examples from 'real life', from Scripture, or idealised models. 'The best qualities to look for in a wife,' advised *The Day-Star* in 1855, 'are industry, humility, neatness, gentleness, benevolence, and piety.' It went on: 'When you hear a lady say, "I shall attend church, and wear my old bonnet and every-day gown, for I fear we shall have a rain-storm," depend upon it she will make a good wife.'[74] Woman was the moral linchpin of society:

> The character of the young men of a community depends much on that of the young women. If the latter are cultivated, intelligent, accomplished, the young men will feel the requirement that they themselves should be upright, and gentlemanly, and refined; but if their female friends are frivolous and silly, the young men will be found dissipated and worthless. But remember, always, that a sister is but the guardian of a brother's integrity. She is the surest inculcator of faith in female purity and worth.[75]

The evangelical movement had many examples of upper-class women to deploy as role models for wider female involvement in evangelical work: in Scotland women like Lady Glenorchy and the 'Ladies of the

Covenant'.[76] The Free Church, a denomination which recruited women to the home mission in large numbers (as Sunday-school teachers, Band of Hope leaders, Bible women and district visitors), laid down specific guidelines for women's 'rational and purposeful role' in society. The *Free Church Magazine* in 1844 published an article on 'Female Methods of Usefulness' in which women were described as 'benevolent from natural sensibility, active from constitutional inclination, amiable from temper'. Yet, such 'respectable, and in many ways highly useful persons' could not be thought of as automatically 'renewed characters'; women had to be called forth in Christian action with a 'becoming spirit':

> Zeal and activity are, in their own places, excellent and essential qualities; but Christian women require to be very cautious, lest, even in the midst of praiseworthy exertions, they sacrifice those meek and lowly tempers which are so calculated to adorn and promote the cause they love and advocate. Female influence should shed its rays on every circle, but these ought to be felt, rather in their softening effects, than seen by their brilliancy. There are certain duties which sometimes call Christian women out of their quiet domestic circle, where both taste and feeling conspire to make them love to linger; such duties will, we humbly think, be best performed by those who enter this enlarged field, not from any desire of a more public sphere, but because, in obedience to the precepts of their divine Lord, the hungry are to be fed, the sick comforted, the prisoners visited.[77]

The organising and campaigning role of women in evangelical and temperance work in the second half of the nineteenth century took the evangelical message from the private world of personal conduct into the public world. In campaigns to rescue and reform prostitutes and wayward girls, women social reformers took a step out of women's traditional role into the public sphere. 'If every woman in the country' wrote one Scottish female campaigner in 1911, 'would take one family and look after them and bring them and themselves to Christ's feet, we should have a better and happier world.'[78] Evangelical social action, as Epstein argues, thus constituted a 'proto-feminism', combining protest against female subordination with a commitment to puritanical morality, which presaged a wider and secular feminism in the twentieth century.[79]

The evangelical message was to liberate women by perfecting, not eroding, their role in the domestic sphere:

> Mother! young mother! you have the little immortal creatures yet around your path; care you not what they shall be, and where they shall dwell for ever? Will you not begin now to teach the young heart to pray, and lead the little feet towards the heavenly home? All you are doing now will give shape and colour to your child's future character, impressing the lineaments of a pious family, or leaving the stamp of a prayerless, a godless mother![80]

Women, and especially mothers, had a special role in combating the evils of drink:

If then, O mothers of Britain, you will only sweep your own hearthstones, and each one cleanse their own from this insidious foe, and firmly resolve it shall never cross your threshold more, the homes of Britain will blossom as the rose. The mother and child will sing songs of joy and gladness. The father will go forth in the morning strong, well fed, and well clad to his daily toil, and will return in the evening with pleasure and gratitude, to his now happy home.[81]

The Band of Hope's magic lantern stories of female victims of male drink are widely recalled in first-hand testimony:

... they had lantern slides and they were absolutely beautiful and it was usually always the ones that I can remember, with them being coloured – [they] remind me now of what I think of stained glass windows. You would see the mother would probably be in bed, and she'd either just had an addition to her family or she was ill with tuberculosis. And you usually saw the father who had been drunk, and it was always perhaps the eldest sister was looking after, you know, a big family. And this was brought home to you about, you know, drink, you know, how it was the downfall of your eh — So, with the result that when you would go to these things, you know, you'd sometimes come away with your face all tear-stained ...[82]

In the evangelical and temperance movements, women were the moral guardians of their families – of fathers, brothers, husbands and sons. The British Women's Temperance Association, the 'White Ribboners', was active from the 1880s in Scottish industrial communities, seeking to provide moral and spiritual protection for working-class women in vulnerable occupations (notably mill-work) by confronting male drunkenness and vice. The White Ribboners parade placed the daughters of drunken fathers, dressed in white, at the head of parades through their communities.[83] Virtue and piety were on parade, and they were female.

Just as women were seen in the evangelical discourse as vital to national piety, they were also blamed for religious decline. Throughout the Edwardian period, the leading evangelical magazine of the Scottish publishers John Menzies, *The Morning Watch*, carried a running cartoon series on 'Reasons for not going to Church', and in virtually every one of these women were to blame because of the failings of their innate character: taking slight at a minister's remarks, because they feared getting their dresses wet on the way to church, or because they did not wish to get a crick in the neck from watching the minister in the pulpit. One caption beneath a sketch of a fashionably-dressed young woman read: 'This lady has changed her mind, and is not going to church to-day, because her sister, who has just returned from London, tells her than in that dress she is "a perfect fright, a regular frump – the skirt is not HALF tight enough to be in the fashion!" *(I think her sister envied her!)*' By the early 1960s, when church membership was in severe decline, women's susceptibility to the new craze of Bingo was identified by the churches as a key factor. The Scottish Churches' Council spoke of 'the Bingo crisis' – 'part of an unhappy trend in the life of the nation at the present time' – and petitioned the Secretary of State for Scotland to outlaw commercial bingo. It was reported that 'Bingo is a social menace; that it causes women to neglect their children and homes and to spend money that ought to go to the welfare of their families.'[84] Women were morally vulnerable – none more so than in 1972 when the Church of Scotland Moral Welfare Committee stated of the sexual revolution: 'it is the promiscuous girl who is the real problem'.

The evangelical discourse on female piety and 'respectability' did not in itself empower women or limit their subordination in society at large. It was an acknowledgement that the church had gendered functions. For women, despite work as Sunday-school teachers and district visitors, going to church and to religious organisations was to embrace a male-dominated institution, with male clergy and male church elders. In so doing, religion was absorbed by women into their private sphere, defining them by their piety and morality, and giving them the guidelines for their domestic role, in household and child-rearing. Even though women's evangelical work was a stage in the development of a female public sphere, it was an extension of the private sphere – from their own family to that of other dysfunctional families or to 'fallen' women. For men, on the other hand, religion was part of their public sphere, especially within presbyterianism. Church and Sunday school, home mission and charity, were adjuncts to business, realms where they brought skills as entrepreneurs, accountants, doctors or teachers to the work of ecclesiastical social policy, and to the operation of the church as a business. The church conferred worldly status, offering them routes to social respect and public function as philanthropists, Sunday-school superintendants (who were invariably men, not women), and members of 'the vice-presidential class' of religious patrons. Above all, presby-terianism conferred the status of the eldership which, as MacLaren and Hillis have both shown, was frequently a reward for success in business.[85]

Of course changes to this gendering of religion occurred within Protestantism. In the late nineteenth and early twentieth century, the presbyterian churches were starting to allocate salaried roles to women as deaconesses and evangelising 'Bible women', and pressure built up to admit women to the eldership and the ministry. The first to do so in the 1930s were the Congregationalists and the very liberal remnant of the United Free Church; though the issue was under discussion in the Church of Scotland in the same decade, it was not until the late 1960s that it followed suit. By 1986 women accounted for around 10 per cent of the clergy in the Kirk, and by 1996 15 per cent.[86] Most Scottish denominations now admit women to the clergy, and the rise of debates on 'the Motherhood of God' have introduced a new feminisation of religion which may be transforming female piety into a public sphere. But this is occurring in the context of a profound secularisation. Indeed, there is an emerging school of thought that the basis of not just Scottish but western dechristianisation in the last forty years of the twentieth century has been the product of a 'de-pietisation of femininity', combined with a 'de-feminisation of piety'. From the 1960s, women's liberation involved a discarding of the traditional discourse on 'the angel in the house', with all the female virues with which it was associated, and its displacement by a sexual, occupational and cultural freedom which denied traditional 'feminine' religiosity a place. Being religious could no longer be founded on 'old' female virtues, and being feminine could no longer be founded on religious ones. With this death of an essentially evangelical discourse on female piety, a vacuum has been left in the popular acceptance of what being 'religious' means. Secularisation has been the ongoing accompaniment, and the outcome at the end of the second millenium is the rapid dechristianisation of Scottish society.[87]

NOTES

1. E. P. Thompson, *The Making of the English Working Class* (Harmondsworth, 1968), p. 14.
2. A. A. MacLaren, *Religion and Social Class: The Disruption Years in Aberdeen* (London and Boston, 1974), p. 28. See also A. A. MacLaren (ed.), *Social Class in Scotland: Past and Present* (Edinburgh, n.d.), pp. 3–5, 36–54.
3. G. Marshall, *Presbyteries and Profits: Calvinism and the Development of Capitalism in Scotland, 1560–1707* (Oxford, 1980).
4. R. H. Campbell, *The Rise and Fall of Scottish Industry, 1707–1939* (Edinburgh, 1980), p. 28.
5. S. and O. Checkland, *Industry and Ethos: Scotland 1830–1914* (London, 1984), pp. 7, 12.
6. Keith Burgess, in T. Dickson (ed.), *Scottish Capitalism: Class, State and Nation from Before the Union to the Present* (London, 1980), pp. 114, 214.
7. David Jeremy, *Capitalists and Christians: Business Leaders and the Churches in Britain 1900–1960* (Oxford, 1990), pp. 368–88.
8. T. C. Smout, *A History of the Scottish People 1560–1830* (Glasgow, 1972), pp. 308–9.
9. See also C. G. Brown, 'Protest in the pews: interpreting presbyterianism and society in fracture during the Scottish economic revolution', in T. M. Devine (ed.), *Conflict and Stability in Scottish Society 1700–1850* (Edinburgh, 1990).
10. The most thorough examination of the shared evangelicalism of the British churches in this period is in D. Bebbington, *Evangelicalism in Modern Britain: A History from the 1730s to the 1980s* (London, 1989).
11. I. A. Muirhead, 'The revival as a dimension of Scottish church history', *RSCHS*, vol. xx (1980), 191.
12. Quoted in J. McKerrow, *History of the Secession Church* (Glasgow, 1841), p. 371.

13. Quoted in D. B. Murray, 'The social and religious origins of Scottish non-presbyterian Protestant dissent from 1730–1800', unpub. PhD thesis, University of St Andrews, 1977, p. 111.

14. M. Hutchison, *The Reformed Presbyterian Church in Scotland* (Paisley, 1893), pp. 194–201.

15. Quoted in McKerrow, op. cit., p. 180.

16. Quoted in J. R. Fleming, *A History of the Church of Scotland 1843–1874* (Edinburgh, 1927), p. 10.

17. Quoted in J. Macinnes, *The Evangelical Movement in the Highlands of Scotland 1688 to 1800* (Aberdeen, 1951), pp. 184–5.

18. Quoted in Fleming, op. cit., pp. 45–7.

19. D. B. Murray, op. cit., p. 16.

20. T. Smollett, *Humphry Clinker* (Harmondsworth, orig. 1771, 1967), p. 262.

21. S. J. Brown, *Thomas Chalmers and the Godly Commonwealth in Scotland* (Oxford, 1982), p. 145.

22. Robert Candlish, in *Free Church Magazine*, November 1844, pp. 369–72.

23. *Free Church Magazine*, September 1847, p. 292; Quoted in W. Ferguson, *Scotland 1689 to the Present* (Edinburgh and London, 1968), p. 336.

24. David McCrone, *Understanding Scotland: The Sociology of a Stateless Nation* (London, 1992), pp. 36, 99.

25. G. Davie, *The Democratic Intellect: Scotland and her Universities in the Nineteenth Century* (Edinburgh, 1961).

26. See R. D. Anderson, 'In search of the "lad of parts": the mythical history of Scottish education', *History Workshop*, vol. 19 (1985); idem, *Education and Opportunity in Victorian Scotland* (Edinburgh, 1983), esp. pp 24–6, 343–4; H. Corr, 'An exploration into Scottish education', in W. H. Fraser and R. J. Morris (eds), *People and Society in Scotland, vol. ii, 1830–1914* (Edinburgh, 1990).

27. C. Harvie, *Scotland and Nationalism: Scottish Society and Politics 1707–1977* (London, 1977), p. 115.

28. A. L. Drummond and J. Bulloch, *The Church in Victorian Scotland 1843–1874* (Edinburgh, 1975), p. 4.

29. C. Harvie, op. cit., p. 86.

30. H. R. Sefton, 'The Church of Scotland and Scottish nationhood', in S. Mews (ed.), *Religion and National Identity* (Oxford, 1982), p. 549.

31. W. Storrar, *Scottish Identity: A Scottish Vision* (Edinburgh, 1990), pp. 36, 51.

32. S. J. Brown, 'The Ten Years' Conflict and the Disruption of 1843', in S. J. Brown and M. Fry (eds), *Scotland in the Age of the Disruption* (Edinburgh, 1993), p. 2.

33. *Free Church Magazine*, August 1847, pp. 245–57.

34. L. Paterson, *The Autonomy of Modern Scotland* (Edinburgh, 1994), p. 57. See also M. Fry, 'The Disruption and the Union', in Brown and Fry (eds), ibid., pp. 31–2.

35. R. L. Stevenson. *Edinburgh: Picturesque Notes* (London, 1879), p. 16.

36. D. Martin, *A General Theory of Secularization* (Oxford, 1978), pp. 55, 77, 80, 142.

37. For a geographical analysis of the 1851 and 1979–84 censuses, see C. G. Brown, 'Religion', in R. Pope (ed.), *Atlas of British Social and Economic History since c.1700* (London, 1989), pp. 211–23.

38. C. G. Brown, 'A revisionist approach to religious change', in S. Bruce (ed.), *Religion and Modernization: Sociologists and Historians Debate the Secularization Thesis* (Oxford, 1992), pp. 32–58; M. Hechter, *Internal Colonialism: The Celtic Fringe in British National Development 1536–1966* (London and Henley, 1975), pp. 172–6.

39. Ibid., pp. 167–76.
40. S. and O. Checkland, *Industry and Ethos: Scotland 1832–1914* (London, 1984), p. 10.
41. *Christian Unity – Now is the Time: The Multilateral Church Conversation in Scotland Report* (Edinburgh, 1985), p. 7.
42. Quoted in L. Colley, *Britons: Forging the Nation 1707–1837* (London, 1996), p. 24.
43. Ibid., pp. 57–8.
44. Ibid., p. 382.
45. G. Walker, *Intimate Strangers: Political and Cultural Interaction between Scotland and Ulster in Modern Times* (Edinburgh, 1995), p. 20.
46. Ibid., p. 20.
47. Ibid., p. 23.
48. Colley, op. cit., p. 395.
49. Quoted in Senex (pseud.) *Glasgow Past and Present, Vol. II* (Glasgow, 1884), p. 265.
50. For a sample of incidents in 1986–7 alone, see *The Scotsman*, 16 January and 30 May 1987; *The Guardian*, 16 and 24 February 1987; *Stirling Observer*, 4, 9 and 11 April 1986, 17 April 1987; *Falkirk Herald*, 28 November 1986; *Sunday Post*, 6 April 1986.
51. *Glasgow Free Press*, 25 August 1860; *Scottish Guardian*, 28 August 1860; *North British Daily Mail*, 27 August 1860.
52. *Reports on the Schemes of the Church of Scotland, 1923*, pp. 750–61.
53. *Stirling Observer*, 13 December 1927.
54. Such as Steve Bruce and Tom Gallagher; see bibliography.
55. *The Scotsman*, 14 March, 3 and 5 July 1986.
56. See J. M. Bradley, *Ethnic and Religious Identity in Modern Scotland: Culture, Politics and Football* (Aldershot, 1995); J. M. Bradley, 'Football in Scotland: A History of Political and Ethnic Identity', *International Journal of the History of Sport*, vol. 12 (1995). See also C. G. Brown, 'Religion and national identity in Scotland since the Union of 1707', in I. Brohed (ed.), *Church and People in Britain and Scandinavia* (Lund, 1996).
57. P. L. Sissons, *The Social Significance of Church Membership in the Burgh of Falkirk* (Edinburgh, 1973), p. 325.
58. (A. Robertson), *Lifestyle Survey* (Edinburgh, 1987), pp. 80–6.
59. P. Crawford, *Women and Religion in England 1500–1720* (London, 1993), pp. 204–8; A. Fletcher, *Gender, Sex and Subordination in England 1500–1800* (New Haven and London, 1995), pp. 347–63; S. Gill, *Women and the Church of England from the Eighteenth Century to the Present* (London, 1994), pp. 83–98; H. McLeod, *Religion and Society in England 1850–1914* (Basingstoke, 1996), pp. 156–68.
60. B. L. Epstein, *The Politics of Domesticity: Women, Evangelism and Temperance in Nineteenth-century America* (Middletown, Connecticut, 1981), pp. 45–66.
61. J. Rendall, *The Origins of Modern Feminism: Women in Britain, France and the United States 1780–1860* (London, 1985), pp. 73–107.
62. Quoted in J. Dwyer, *Virtuous Discourse: Sensibility and Community in Late Eighteenth Century Scotland* (Edinburgh, 1987), p. 120.
63. Epstein, op. cit., pp. 11–66; Rendall, op. cit., pp. 77–101.
64. T. C. Smout, 'Born again at Cambuslang: new evidence on popular religion and literacy in eighteenth-century Scotland', *Past and Present*, 97 (1982), p. 116; T. Allan (ed.), *Crusade in Scotland* (London, 1955), p. 108.
65. M. Weir, *Best Foot Forward* (London, 1972), p. 69.
66. SOHCA/006/Mrs R.2(1905), p. 4.
67. SOHCA/006/Mrs V.1(1914), p. 8.

68. SOHCA/006/Mrs F.3(1910), p. 13.
69. SOHCA/006/Mrs U.1(1898), p. 8.
70. SOHCA/006/Mrs E.2(1905), p. 5.
71. SOHCA/006/Mrs T.1(1906), p. 13.
72. *The Day-Star*, vol. 12 (1856), p. 97.
73. *The Edinburgh Christian Magazine*, vol. 3 (1851), p. 203.
74. *The Day-Star*, vol. 11 (1855), p. 266.
75. *The Day-Star*, vol. 10 (1854), p. 112.
76. J. Anderson, *The Ladies of the Covenant: Memoirs of Distinguished Scottish Female Characters* (Glasgow, 1851). On English exemplars, see G. Malmgreen (ed.), *Religion in the Lives of English Women 1760–1930* (London, 1986).
77. *Free Church Magazine*, vol. 6 (1844), p. 171.
78. Griselda Cheape, quoted in L. Mahood, 'Family ties: lady child-savers and girls of the street 1850–1925', in E. Breitenbach and E. Gordon (eds), *Out of Bounds: Women in Scottish Society 1800–1945* (Edinburgh, 1992), p. 42.
79. B. L. Epstein, op. cit., passim.
80. *The Day-Star*, vol. 12 (1856), p. 196.
81. Ibid., p. 13.
82. SOHCA/006/Mrs X.2(1920), p. 11.
83. For an example of how this experience affected one young girl, see. C. G. Brown and J. D. Stephenson (eds), '"Sprouting wings"? Women and religion in Scotland 1890–1950', in E. Breitenbach and E. Gordon (eds), op. cit., pp. 105–6, 115–6.
84. S.R.O., HH43/194, Betting and Lotteries; Tombola, 1960–3.
85. See Chapter 5.
86. Figures calculated from *The Church of Scotland Yearbook* 1986 and 1996.
87. C. G. Brown, 'The secularisation decade: the haemorrhage of the British churches in the 1960s' in H. McLeod and W. Ustorf (eds), *The Decline of Christendom in Western Europe 1750–2000* (London, Orbis Books, forthcoming).

BIBLIOGRAPHY

This bibliography provides a guide to further reading, concentrating on accessible secondary sources. Fuller bibliographies are to be found in:

C. G. Brown, *Protest in the Pews: Religion and Society in Scotland since 1780* (Economic and Social History Society of Scotland, 1993)

J. F. McCaffrey, 'Scottish Church history in the nineteenth century: a select critical bibliography', *RSCHS*, vol. 23 (1989)

G. White, 'Scottish overseas missions: a select critical bibliography', *RSCHS*, vol. 20 (1980)

CHAPTER I
RELIGIOUS CHANGE AND SECULARISATION

C. G. Brown, 'Did urbanisation secularise Britain?', *Urban History Yearbook* 1988

S. Bruce (ed.), *Religion and Modernization: Sociologists and Historians Debate the Secularization Thesis* (Oxford, 1992)

A. D. Gilbert, *Religion and Society in Industrial England: Church, Chapel and Social Change 1740–1914* (London, 1976)

S. J. D. Green, *Religion in the Age of Decline: Organisation and Experience in Industrial Yorkshire 1870–1920* (Cambridge, 1996)

K. S. Inglis, *Churches and the Working Classes in Victorian England* (London, 1963)

J. Morris, *Religion and Urban Change: Croydon, 1840–1914* (Woodbridge, 1992)

H. McLeod, 'New perspectives on Victorian working-class religion: the oral evidence', *Oral History Journal*, vol. 14 (1986)

H. McLeod (ed.), *European Religion in the Age of Great Cities 1830–1930* (London and New York, 1995); M. Smith, *Religion in Industrial Society: Oldham and Saddleworth 1740–1865* (Oxford, 1994)

E. R. Wickham, *Church and People in an Industrial City* (London, 1969 ed.)

S. Williams, 'The language of belief: an alternative agenda for the study of Victorian working-class religion', *Journal of Victorian Culture*, vol. 1 (1996)

CHAPTER 2

D. W. Bebbington (ed.), *The Baptists in Scotland: A History* (Glasgow, 1988)

S. J. Brown and M. Fry (eds), *Scotland in the Age of the Disruption* (Edinburgh, 1993)

A. C. Cheyne, *The Transforming of the Kirk: Victorian Scotland's Religious Revolution* (Edinburgh, 1983)

T. M. Devine (ed.), *Irish Immigrants and Scottish Society in the Nineteenth and Twentieth Centuries* (Edinburgh, 1991)

A. L. Drummond and J. Bulloch, *The Scottish Church 1688–1843: The Age of the Moderates* (Edinburgh, 1973)

A. L. Drummond and J. Bulloch, *The Church in Victorian Scotland 1843–1874* (Edinburgh, 1975)

A. L. Drummond and J. Bulloch, *The Church in Late Victorian Scotland 1874–1900* (Edinburgh, 1978).

J. E. Handley, *The Irish in Scotland 1798–1845* (Cork, 1945)

J. E. Handley, *The Irish in Modern Scotland* (Cork, 1947)

C. Johnson, *Developments in the Roman Catholic Church in Scotland 1789–1829* (Edinburgh, 1983)

D. McRoberts (ed.), *Modern Scottish Catholicism 1878–1978* (Glasgow, 1979)

D. J. Withrington, 'The Disruption: a century and a half of historical interpretation', *RSCHS*, vol. 25 (1993)

CHAPTER 3

C. G. Brown, 'Religion' in R. Pope (ed.), *Atlas of British Social and Economic History* (London, 1989)

R. Currie, A. Gilbert and L. Horsley, *Churches and Churchgoers: Patterns of Church Growth in the British Isles since 1700* (Oxford, 1977)

J. Darragh, 'The Catholic population of Scotland since 1680', *Innes Review*, vol. iv (1953)

J. Darragh, 'The Catholic population of Scotland, 1878–1977', in D. McRoberts (ed.), *Modern Scottish Catholicism* (Glasgow, 1979)

J. Highet, *The Churches in Scotland Today* (Glasgow, 1950)

J. Highet, *The Scottish Churches: A Review of Their State 400 Years after the Reformation* (London, 1960)

D. J. Withrington, 'The 1851 census of religious worship and education: with a note on church accommodation in mid-nineteenth century Scotland', *RSCHS*, vol. xviii (1974)

CHAPTER 4

THE PRE-INDUSTRIAL FORM OF RELIGION

A. A. Cormack, *Teinds and Agriculture* (London, 1930)

A. Edgar, *Old Church Life in Scotland* (Paisley and London, 1885)

J. H. Gillespire, *Dundonald: A Contribution to Parochial History*, vol. 2 (Glasgow, 1939)

T. Hamilton, *Poor Relief in Ayrshire 1700–1845* (Edinburgh, 1942)

R. Mitchison and L. Leneman, *Sexuality and Social Control: Scotland 1660–1780* (Oxford, 1989)

THE IMPACT OF ECONOMIC AND SOCIAL CHANGE IN THE LOWLANDS

I. Carter, *Farmlife in Northeast Scotland 1840–1914: The Poor Man's Country* (Edinburgh, 1979)

R. Sher and A. Murdoch, 'Patronage and party in the Church of Scotland, 1750–1800', in N. MacDougall (ed.), *Church, Politics and Society: Scotland 1408–1929* (Edinburgh, 1983)

R. B. Sher, 'Moderates, managers and popular politics in mid-eighteenth-century Edinburgh: the Drysdale "Bustle" of the 1760s', in J. Dwyer et al. (eds), *New Perspectives on the Politics and Culture of Early Modern Scotland* (Edinburgh, n.d.)

T. C. Smout, 'Born again at Cambuslang: new evidence on popular religion and literacy in eighteenth-century Scotland', *Past and Present*, 97 (1982)

E. Vincent, 'The responses of Scottish churchmen to the French Revolution 1789–1802', *SHR*, vol. lxxiii (1994)

D. J. Withrington, 'Non-churchgoing, c.1750–c.1850: a preliminary study', *RSCHS* vol. xvii (1970)

THE HIGHLANDS, HEBRIDES AND NORTHERN ISLES

D. B. A. Ansdell, 'The 1843 Disruption of the Church of Scotland in the Isle of Lewis', *RSCHS*, vol. 24 (1991)

S. Bruce, 'Social change and collective behaviour: the revival in eighteenth-century Ross-shire', *British Journal of Sociology*, vol. 34 (1983)

J. Hunter, 'The emergence of the crofting community: the religious contribution 1798–1843', *Scottish Studies*, vol. 18 (1974)

J. Hunter, *The Making of the Crofting Community* (Edinburgh, 1976)

J. Macinnes, *The Evangelical Movement on the Highlands of Scotland 1688 to 1800* (Aberdeen, 1951)

C. W. J. Withers, *Gaelic in Scotland 1698–1981* (Edinburgh, 1984)

CHAPTER 5

CIVIC ADMINISTRATION AND RELIGION

B. Aspinwall, *Portable Utopia: Glasgow and the United States 1820–1920* (Aberdeen, 1984)

B. Aspinwall, 'The Scottish religious identity in the Atlantic world 1880–1914', in S. Mews (ed.), *Religion and National Identity* (Oxford, 1982)

C. G. Brown, '"To be aglow with civic ardours": the "godly commonwealth" in Glasgow 1843–1914', *RSCHS*, vol. 26 (1996)

S. J. Brown, *Thomas Chalmers and the Godly Commonwealth in Scotland* (Oxford, 1982)

R. Cage and O. Checkland, 'Thomas Chalmers and urban poverty: the St. John's Parish experiment in Glasgow 1819–1837', *Philosophical Journal*, vol. 13 (1976)

EVANGELICALISM AND THE RISE OF THE MIDDLE CLASSES

C. G. Brown, 'The Sunday-school movement in Scotland, 1780–1914', *RSCHS*, vol. 21 (1981)

S. J. Brown, 'The Disruption and urban poverty: Thomas Chalmers and the West Port operation in Edinburgh, 1844–47', *RSCHS*, vol. 20 (1978)

O. Checkland, *Philanthropy in Victorian Scotland* (Edinburgh, 1980)

N. D. Denny, 'Temperance and the Scottish churches 1870–1914', *RSCHS*, vol. 23 (1988)

P. Hillis, 'Education and evangelisation: presbyterian missions in mid-nineteenth century Glasgow', *SHR*, vol. 66 (1988)

J. L. Duthie, 'Philanthropy and evangelism among Aberdeen seamen 1814–1924', *SHR*, vol. 63 (1984)

A. A. MacLaren, *Religion and Social Class: The Disruption Years in Aberdeen* (London and Boston, 1974)

A. A. MacLaren, 'Class formation and class fraction: the Aberdeen bourgeoisie 1830–1850', in G. Gordon and B. Dicks (eds), *Scottish Urban History* (Aberdeen, 1983)

S. Mechie, *The Church and Scottish Social Development 1780–1870* (Oxford, 1960)

RELIGION AND THE MAKING OF THE SCOTTISH WORKING CLASSES

C. G. Brown, 'The costs of pew-renting: church management, churchgoing and social class in nineteenth-century Glasgow', *Journal of Ecclesiastical History*, vol. 38 (1987)

R. Q. Gray, *The Labour Aristocracy in Victorian Edinburgh* (Oxford, 1976)

P. Hillis, 'Presbyterianism and social class in mid-nineteenth-century Glasgow: a study of nine churches', *Journal of Ecclesiastical History*, vol. 32 (1981)

A. A. MacLaren, 'Presbyterianism and the working class in a mid-nineteenth-century city', *SHR*, vol. 46 (1967)

H. McLeod, *Religion and the Working Class in Nineteenth-Century Britain* (London, 1984)

W. M. Walker, 'Irish immigrants in Scotland: their priests, politics and parochial life', *Historical Journal*, vol. 15 (1972)

C. W. J. Withers, 'Kirk, club and culture change: Gaelic chapels, Highland societies and the urban Gaelic subculture in eighteenth-century Scotland', *Social History*, vol. 10 (1985)

CHAPTER 6

THE DECAY OF EVANGELICALISM

R. Q. Gray, 'Religion, culture and social class in late nineteenth and early twentieth century Edinburgh' in G. Crosssick (ed.), *The Lower Middle Class in Britain* (London, 1977)

D. J. Withrington, 'Non-church-going, church organisation and "crisis in the church" c.1880–c.1920', *RSCHS*, vol. 24 (1991)

W. M. Walker, *Juteopolis: Dundee and its Textile Workers 1885–1923* (Edinburgh, 1979)

THE CHALLENGE OF LABOUR AND THE LOSS OF 'SOCIAL PROPHECY'

S. Gilley, 'Catholics and socialists in Glasgow 1906–1912', in K. Lunn (ed.), *Hosts, Immigrants and Minorities* (Folkestone, 1980)

D. S. Smith, *Passive Obedience and Prophetic Protest: Social Criticism in the Scottish Church 1830–1945* (New York, 1987)

D. J. Withrington, 'The churches in Scotland c. 1870–c.1900: towards a new social conscience?', *RSCHS*, vol. 19 (1977)

I. Wood, 'Drink, temperance and the labour movement', *Journal of the Scottish Labour History Society*, vol. 5 (1973)

CHURCH AND STATE

S. J. Brown, 'The social vision of Scottish presbyterianism and the Union of 1929', *RSCHS*, vol. 24 (1990)

S. J. Brown, '"Outside the Covenant": the Scottish presbyterian churches and Irish immigration 1922–38', *Innes Review*, vol. xlii (1991)

S. J. Brown, '"A Victory for God": the Scottish presbyterian churches and the General Strike of 1926', *Journal of Ecclesiastical History*, vol. 42 (1991)

S. J. Brown, '"A Solemn Purification by Fire": reponses to the Great War in the Scottish presbyterian churches 1914–19', *Journal of Ecclesiastical History*, vol. 45 (1994)

F. Lyall, *Of Presbyters and Kings: Church and State in the Law of Scotland* (Aberdeen, 1980)

POPULAR RELIGIOSITY

C. G. Brown, 'Religion and secularisation' in T. Dickson and J. H. Treble (eds), *People and Society in Scotland, vol. 2 1830–1914* (Edinburgh)

H. McLeod, 'New perspectives on Victorian working-class religion: the oral evidence', *Oral History Journal*, vol. 14 (1986)

CHAPTER 7

C. G. Brown, 'Religion and secularisation', in T. Dickson and J. H. Treble (eds), *People and Society in Scotland, vol. 2 1830–1914* (Edinburgh)

S. Bruce, 'Out of the Ghetto: the ironies of acceptance', *Innes Review*, vol. xliii (1992)

J. Highet, *The Scottish Churches: A Review of their State 400 Years after the Reformation* (London, 1960)

P. L. Sissons, *The Social Significance of Religion in the Burgh of Falkirk* (Edinburgh, 1973)

D. R. Robertson, 'The relationship of church and class in Scotland' in D. Martin (ed.), *A Sociological Yearbook of Religion in Britain* (London, 1968)

T. M. Owen, 'The communion season and presbyterianism in a Hebridean community', *Gwerin*, vol. 1 (1956)

CHAPTER 8

RELIGION AND SCOTTISH IDENTITY; RELIGION AND BRITISH IDENTITY; SECTARIAN IDENTITY

C. G. Brown, 'Religion and national identity in Scotland since the Union of 1707', in I. Brohed (ed.), *Church and People in Britain and Scandanavia* (Lund, 1997)

S. Bruce, *No Pope of Rome: Anti-Catholicism in Modern Scotland* (Edinburgh, 1985)

L. Colley, *Britons: Forging the Nation 1707–1837* (London, 1992)

R. K. Donovan, 'Voices of distrust: the expression of anti-Catholic feeling in Scotland 1778–1781', *Innes Review*, vol. 30 (1979)

R. Finlay, 'Nationalism, race, religion and the Irish question in inter-war Scotland', *Innes Review*, vol. 42 (1991)

T. Gallagher, 'Protestant extremism in urban Scotland 1930–1939: its growth and contraction', *SHR*, vol. lxix (1985)

T. Gallagher, *Glasgow: The Uneasy Peace: Religious Tension in Modern Scotland* (Manchester, 1987)

T. Gallagher, *Edinburgh Divided: John Cormack and No Popery in the 1930s* (Edinburgh, 1987)

B. Murray, *The Old Firm: Sectarianism, Sport and Society in Scotland* (Edinburgh, 1984)

G. Walker and T. Gallagher (eds), *Sermons and Battle Hymns: Protestant Popular Culture in Modern Scotland* (Edinburgh, 1990)

G. Walker, *Intimate Strangers: Political and Cultural Interaction Between Scotland and Ulster in Modern Times* (Edinburgh, 1995)

PIETY AND FEMININITY

K. M. Boyd, *Scottish Church Attitudes to Sex, Marriage and the Family 1850–1914* (Edinburgh, 1980)

C. G. Brown and J. D. Stephenson, '"Sprouting wings"? Women and religion in Scotland 1890–1950', in E. Breitenbach and E. Gordon (eds), *Out of Bounds: Women in Scotland in the Nineteenth and Twentieth Centuries* (Edinburgh, 1992)

K. Carmichael, 'Protestantism and gender' in G. Walker and T. Gallagher (eds), *Sermons and Battle Hymns* (Edinburgh, 1990)

N. Dickson, 'Modern prophetesses: women preachers in the nineteenth-century Scottish Brethren', *RSCHS*, vol. 25 (1993)

E. Ewan, 'Women's history in Scotland: towards an agenda', *Innes Review*, vol. xlvi (1995)

L. Leneman, 'The Scottish churches and "Votes for Women"', *RSCHS*, vol. 24 (1991)

R. Mitchison and L. Leneman, *Sexuality and Social Control: Scotland 1660–1780* (Oxford, 1989)

INDEX